CONTENTS

	PAGE
TOO TRUE TO BE GOOD: A POLITICAL EXTRAVAGANZA	**1**
Preface—Money and Happiness	3
The Vampire and the Calf	4
The Old Soldier and the Public House	6
The Unloading Millionaires	7
Delusions of Poverty	8
Trying it for an Hour	9
Consolations of the Landed Gentry	11
Miseries of the Vagrant Rootless Rich	12
The Redemption from Property	14
Fundamental Natural Conditions of Human Society	16
The Catholic Solution	18
Need for a Common Faith	19
Russia Rediscovers the Church System	20
Why the Christian System Failed	22
Government by Everybody	24
Failure All Round	25
Obsolete Vows	27
Supernatural Pretensions	28
Eclectic Democracy	29
VILLAGE WOOING: A COMEDIETTINA FOR TWO VOICES	**137**
First Conversation	139
Second Conversation	149
Third Conversation	161
ON THE ROCKS: A POLITICAL COMEDY	**175**
Preface—Extermination	177
Killing as a Political Function	177

v

PAGE

The Sacredness of Human Life 178
Present Exterminations 179
Previous Attempts Miss the Point 180
King Charles's Head 182
Right to Exterminate Conferred by Private
  Property 183
Disguises Under Which Private Extermination
  Operates 184
Private Powers of Life and Death . . . 185
Cruelty's Excuses 188
Leading Case of Jesus Christ 189
"Crosstianity" 191
Christianity and the Seventh Commandment . 193
The Russian Experiment 194
Inadequacy of Penal Codes 195
Limited Liability in Morals 196
Natural Limit to Extermination 198
Incompatibility of Peasantry with Modern Civ-
  ilization 200
A Peasant Victory is a Victory for Private
  Property 201
Preventive Extermination: its Difficulties . . 202
Temperamental Difficulties 204
Importance of Laziness for Fallowing . . 205
Standard Religion Indispensable 206
Eclectic Religions 207
Importance of Free Thought 209
Toleration Mostly Illusory 210
Leading Cases: Socrates and Jesus . . . 212
The Case of Galileo 213
Figment of the Selfregarding Action . . . 214
Incompleteness of the Great Trials . . . 216
A Modern Passion Play Impossible . . . 217
Difference Between Reader and Spectator . 218
The Sacredness of Criticism 229

TOO TRUE TO BE GOOD

A POLITICAL EXTRAVAGANZA

1931

PREFACE

Money and Happiness

Somehow my play, Too True To Be Good, has in per-
formance excited an animosity and an enthusiasm which
will hardly be accounted for by the printed text. Some
of the spectators felt that they had had a divine revelation, and overlooked the fact that the eloquent gentleman through whose extremely active mouth they had
received it was the most hopeless sort of scoundrel: that
is, one whose scoundrelism consists in the absence of conscience rather than in any positive vices, and is masked
by good looks and agreeable manners. The less intellectual journalist critics sulked as they always do when
their poverty but not their will consents to their witness-
ing a play of mine; but over and above the resultant
querulousness to which I have long been accustomed I
thought I detected an unusual intensity of resentment, as
if I had hit them in some new and unbearably sore spot.

Where, then, was the offence that so exceedingly dis-
gruntled these unhappy persons? I think it must have
been the main gist and moral of the play, which is not,
as usual, that our social system is unjust to the poor, but
that it is cruel to the rich. Our revolutionary writers have
dwelt on the horrors of poverty. Our conventional and
romantic writers have ignored those horrors, dwelling
pleasantly on the elegances of an existence free from
pecuniary care. The poor have been pitied for miseries
which do not, unfortunately, make them unbearably miserable. But who has pitied the idle rich or really believed

3

that they have a worse time of it than those who have to live on ten shillings a day or less, and earn it? My play is a story of three reckless young people who come into possession of, for the moment, unlimited riches, and set out to have a thoroughly good time with all the modern machinery of pleasure to aid them. The result is that they get nothing for their money but a multitude of worries and a maddening dissatisfaction.

THE VAMPIRE AND THE CALF

I doubt whether this state of things is ever intentionally produced. We see a man apparently slaving to place his children in the position of my three adventurers; but on closer investigation we generally find that he does not care twopence for his children, and is wholly wrapped up in the fascinating game of making money. Like other games it is enjoyable only by people with an irresistible and virtually exclusive fancy for it, and enough arithmetical ability and flair for market values to play it well; but with these qualifications the poorest men can make the most astounding fortunes. They accumulate nothing but powers of extracting money every six months from their less acquisitive neighbors; and their children accumulate nothing but obligations to spend it. As between these two processes of bleeding and being bled, bleeding is the better fun. The vampire has a better time than the calf hung up by the heels with its throat cut. The money-getter spends less on his food, clothes, and amusements than his clerks do, and is happy. His wife and sons and daughters, spending fabulous sums on themselves, are no happier than their housemaids, if so happy; for the routine of fashion is virtually as compulsory as the routine of a housemaid, its dressing is as much dictated as her uniform, its snubbings are as humiliating, and its monotony is more tedious because more senseless and useless, not to mention that it must be pleasanter to be tipped than to tip. And, as I surmise, the housemaid's day off or evening off is really off: in those hard earned hours she ceases to be a housemaid and can be herself; but the lady of fashion never has a moment off: she has to be fashionable even in her little leisure, and dies without ever having had any self at all. Here and there you find rich ladies taking up occupations and interests which keep them so busy doing profesional or public work that they might as well have five hundred a year as fifty thousand "for all the good it does them" as the poor say in their amazement when they see people who could afford to be fashionable and extravagant working hard and dressing rather plainly. But that requires a personal endowment of tastes and talents quite out of the common run.

I remember a soldier of the old never-do-well type drifting into a little Socialist Society which I happened to be addressing more than fifty years ago. As he had evidently blundered into the wrong shop and was half drunk, some of the comrades began to chaff him, and finally held me up to him as an example of the advantages of teetotalism. With the most complete conviction he denounced me as a hypocrite and a liar, affirming it to be a well-known and inexorable law of nature that no man with money in his pocket could pass a public house without going in for a drink.

THE OLD SOLDIER AND THE PUBLIC HOUSE

I have never forgotten that soldier, because his delusion, in less crude forms, and his conception of happiness, seem to afflict everybody in England more or less. When I say less crude forms I do not mean truer forms; for the soldier, being half drunk, was probably happier than he would have been if quite sober, whereas the plutocrat who has spent a hundred pounds in a day in the search for pleasure is not happier than if he had spent only five shillings. For it must be admitted that a private soldier, outside that surprising centre of culture, the Red Army of Russia, has so little to be happy about when sober that his case is hardly a fair one. But it serves to illustrate the moral of my play, which is, that our capitalistic system, with its golden exceptions of idle richery and its leaden rule of anxious poverty, is as desperate a failure from the point of view of the rich as of the poor. We are all amazed and incredulous, like the soldier, when we hear of the multimillionaire passing the public house without going in and drinking himself silly; and we envy his sons and daughters who do go in and drink themselves silly. The vulgar pub may be in fact a Palace Hotel, and the pints of beer or glasses of whisky an elaborate dinner with many courses and wines culminating in cigars and liqueurs; but the illusion and the results are cognate.

I therefore plead for a science of happiness to cure us of the miserable delusion that we can achieve it by becoming richer than our neighbors. Modern colossal fortunes have demonstrated its vanity. When country parsons were "passing rich with forty pounds a year" there was some excuse for believing that to be rich was to be happy, as the conception of riches did not venture beyond enough to pay for the necessities of a cultivated life. A hundred years ago Samuel Warren wrote a famous novel about a man who became enormously rich. The title of the novel was Ten Thousand a Year; and this, to any resident Irish family in my boyhood, represented an opulence beyond which only Lords Lieutenant and their like could aspire. The scale has changed since then. I have just seen in the papers a picture of the funeral of a shipping magnate whose income, if the capital value of the property left by him be correctly stated, must have been over four thousand pounds a day or a million and a half a year. If happiness is to be measured by riches he must have been fourteen thousand times as happy as the laborer lucky enough to be earning two pounds a week. Those who believe that riches are the reward of virtue are bound to conclude that he was also fourteen thousand times as sober, honest, and industrious, which would lead to the quaint conclusion that if he drank a bottle of wine a day the laborer must have drunk fourteen thousand.

The Unloading Millionaires

This is so obviously monstrous that it may now be dismissed as an illusion of the poor who know nothing of the lives of the rich. Poverty, when it involves continual privation and anxiety, is, like toothache, so painful that the victim can desire nothing happier than the cessation of the pain. But it takes no very extraordinary supply of money to enable a humble person to say "I want for nothing"; and when that modest point is reached the power of money to produce happiness vanishes, and the trouble which an excess of it brings begins to assert itself, and finally reaches a point at which the multimillionaires are seen frantically unloading on charitable, educational, scientific, religious, and even (though rarely) artistic and political "causes" of all kinds, mostly without stopping to examine whether the causes produce any effects, and if so what effects. And far from suffering a loss of happiness every time they give away a thousand pounds, they find themselves rather in the enviable state of mind of the reveller in The Pilgrim's Progress with his riddle "There was a man, though some did think him mad, the more he gave away the more he had."

DELUSIONS OF POVERTY

The notion that the rich must be happy is complemented by the delusion that the poor must be miserable. Our society is so constituted that most people remain all their lives in the condition in which they were born, and have to depend on their imagination for their notions of what it is like to be in the opposite condition. The upstarts and the downstarts, though we hear a great deal about them either as popular celebrities or criminals, are exceptional. The rich, it is said, do not know how the poor live; but nobody insists on the more mischievous fact that the poor do not know how the rich live. The rich are a minority; and they are not consumed with envy of the poor. But the poor are a huge majority and they are so demoralized by the notion that they would be happy if only they were rich, that they make themselves poorer, if hopefuller, by backing horses and buying sweepstake tickets on the chance of realizing their daydreams of unearned fortunes. Our penny newspapers

now depend for their circulation, and consequently for
their existence, on the sale of what are virtually lottery
coupons. The real opposition to Socialism comes from
the fear (well founded) that it would cut off the possi-
bilities of becoming rich beyond those dreams of avarice
which our capitalist system encourages. The odds against
a poor person becoming a millionaire are of astronomical
magnitude; but they are sufficient to establish and maintain the Totalisator as a national institution, and to
produce unlimited daydreams of bequests from imaginary long lost uncles in Australia or a lucky ticket in the
Calcutta or Irish Sweeps.

Trying it for an Hour

Besides, even quite poor people save up for holidays
during which they can be idle and rich, if not for life,
at least for an hour, an afternoon, or even a week. And
for the poor these moments derive such a charm from
the change from the monotony of daily toil and servitude, that the most intolerable hardships and discom-
forts and fatigues in excursion trains and overcrowded
lodgings seem delightful, and leave the reveller with a
completely false notion of what a lifetime of such
revelry would be.

I maintain that nobody with a sane sense of values can
feel that the sole prize which our villainous capitalist
system has to offer, the prize of admission to the ranks
of the idle rich, can possibly confer either happiness or
health or freedom on its winner. No one can convict me
of crying sour grapes; for during the last thirty-five
years I have been under no compulsion to work, nor had
any material privation or social ostracism to fear as a

consequence of not working. But, like all the intelligent rich people of my acquaintance, I have worked as hard, ate and drunk no more, and dressed no better than when I had to work or starve. When my pockets were empty I did not buy any of the luxuries in the London shops because I had no money to buy them with. When, later on, I had enough to buy anything that London could tempt me with, the result was the same: I returned home day after day without having made a single purchase. And I am no ascetic: no man alive is freer than I from the fancy that selfmortification will propitiate a spiteful deity or increase my balance in a salvation bank in a world beyond the grave. I would and could live the life of the idle rich if I liked it; and my sole reason for not living it is that I dont like it. I have every opportunity of observing it both in its daily practice and its remoter results; and I know that a year of it would make me more unhappy than anything else of an accepted kind that I can imagine. For, just as the beanfeaster can live like a lord for an afternoon, and the Lancashire factory operative have a gorgeous week at Blackpool when the wakes are on, so I have had my afternoons as an idle rich man, and know only too well what it is like. It makes me feel suicidal.

You may say that I am an exceptional man. So I am, in respect of being able to write plays and books; but as everybody is exceptional in respect of being able to do something that most other people cannot do, there is nothing in that. Where I am really a little exceptional is in respect of my having experienced both poverty and riches, servitude and selfgovernment, and also having for some reason or other (possibly when I was assured in my infancy that some nasty medicine was delicious) made up my mind early in life never to let myself be persuaded that I am enjoying myself gloriously when I am, as a matter of fact, being bored and pestered and plundered and worried and tired. You cannot humbug me on this point: I understand perfectly why Florence Nightingale fled from fashionable society in London to the horrors of the Crimean hospitals rather than behave like a lady, and why my neighbor Mr Apsley Cherry-Garrard, the sole survivor of what he calls with good reason "the worst journey in the world" through the Antarctic winter, was no poor sailorman driven by his need for daily bread to make a hard living before the mast, but a country gentleman opulent enough to choose the best that London society could offer him if he chose. Better the wards of the most terrible of field hospitals than a drawingroom in Mayfair: better the South Pole at its blackest six months winter night and its most murderous extremities of cold than Sunday by the Serpentine in the height of the season.

CONSOLATIONS OF THE LANDED GENTRY

To some extent this misery of riches is a new thing. Anyone who has the run of our country houses, with their great parks and gardens, their staffs of retainers, indoor and outdoor, and the local public work that is always available for the resident landed gentry, will at once challenge the unqualified assertion that the rich, in a lump, are miserable. Clearly they are nothing of the sort, any more than the poor in a lump. But then they are neither idle nor free. A lady with a big house to manage, and the rearing of a family to supervise, has a reasonably busy time of it even without counting her share in the routine of sport and entertainment and occasional travel which to people brought up to it is a necessary and important part of a well ordered life. The landed gentry have enough exercise and occupation and sense of social importance and utility to keep them on very good terms with themselves and their neighbors. If you suddenly asked them whether they really enjoyed their routine and whether they would not rather be Communists in Russia they would be more sincerely scandalized than if you had turned to them in church and asked them whether they really believed every clause in the Apostles' Creed. When one of their ugly ducklings becomes a revolutionist it is not because countryhouse life is idle, but because its activities are uncongenial and because the duckling has tastes or talents which it thwarts, or a faculty for social criticism which discovers that the great country house is not built on the eternal rock but on the sandy shore of an ocean of poverty which may at any moment pass from calm to tempest. On the whole, there is no reason why a territorial lady should not be as happy as her dairymaid, or her husband be as happy as his gamekeeper. The riches of the county families are attached to property; and the only miserable county people are those who will not work at their job.

Miseries of The Vagrant Rootless Rich

But the new thing is riches detached from real property: that is, detached from work, from responsibility, from tradition, and from every sort of prescribed routine, even from the routine of going to the village church every Sunday, paying and receiving calls, and having every month set apart for the killing of some particular bird or animal. It means being a tramp without the daily recurrent obligation to beg or steal your dinner and the price of your bed. Instead, you have the daily question "What shall I do? Where shall I go?" and the daily answer "Do what you please: go where you like: it doesnt matter what you do or where you go." In short, the perfect liberty of which slaves dream because they have no experience of its horrors. Of course the answer of outraged Nature is drowned for a time by the luxury merchants shouting "Come and shop, whether you need anything or not. Come to our palace hotels. Come round the world in our liners. Come and wallow in our swimming pools. Come and see our latest model automobile: we have changed the inventor's design for-better-for-worse solely to give you an excuse for buying a new one and selling your old one at scrap iron prices. Come and buy our latest fashions in dress: you cannot possibly be seen in last season's garments." And so on and so forth. But the old questions come home to the rich tourists in the palace hotels and luxury liners just as they do to the tramps on the highroad. They come up when you have the latest car and the latest wardrobe and all the rest of it. The only want that money can satisfy without satiating for more than a few hours is the need for food and drink and sleep. So from one serious meal a day and two very minor ones you go on to three serious meals a day and two minor ones. Then you work another minor one between breakfast and lunch "to sustain you"; and you soon find that you cannot tackle any meal without a cocktail, and that you cannot sleep. That obliges you to resort to the latest soporific drug, guaranteed in the advertisements to have none of the ruinous effects of its equally guaranteed forerunner. Then comes the doctor, with his tonics, which are simply additional cocktails, and his sure knowledge that if he tells you the truth about yourself and refuses to prescribe the tonics and the drugs, his children will starve. If you indulge in such a luxury as a clerical spiritual adviser it is his duty to tell you that what is the matter with you is that you are an idle useless glutton and drunkard and that you are going to hell; but alas! he, like the doctor, cannot afford this, as he may have to ask you for a subscription tomorrow to keep his church going. And that is "Liberty: thou choicest treasure."

This sort of life has been made possible, and indeed inevitable, by what William Cobbett, who had a sturdy sense of vital values, denounced as The Funding System. It was a product of war, which obliged belligerent governments to obtain enormous sums from all and sundry by giving them in exchange the right to live for nothing on the future income of the country until their money was returned: a system now so popular among people with any money to spare that they can be induced to part with it only on condition that the Government promises not to repay it before a certain more or less remote day. When joint stock companies were formed to run big industrial concerns with money raised on the still more tempting terms that the money is never to be repaid, the system became so extensive that the idle upstart rich became a definitely mischievous and miserable class quite different in character from the old feudal rich.

THE REDEMPTION FROM PROPERTY

When I propose the abolition of our capitalistic system to redeem mankind from the double curse of poverty and riches, loud wailings arise. The most articulate sounds in the hubbub are to the effect that the wretched slaves of the curse will lose their liberty if they are forced to earn their living honorably. The retort that they have nothing to lose but their chains, with the addition that the gold chains are as bad as the iron ones, cannot silence them, because they think they are free, and have been brought up to believe that unless the country remains the private property of irresponsible owners maintaining a parliament to make any change impossible, with churches schools and universities to inculcate the sacredness of private property and party government disguised as religion education and democracy, civilization must perish. I am accused of every sort of reactionary extravagance by the people who think themselves advanced, and of every sort of destructive madness by people who thank God they are no wiser than their fathers.

Now I cannot profitably discuss politics religion and economics with terrified ignoramuses who understand neither what they are defending nor what they are attacking. But it happens that Mr Gilbert Chesterton, who is not an ignoramus and not in the least terrified, and whose very interesting conversion to Roman Catholicism has obliged him to face the problem of social organization fundamentally, discarding the Protestant impostures on English history which inspired the vigorous Liberalism of his salad days, has lately taken me to task for the entirely imaginary offence of advocating government by a committee of celebrities. To clear up the matter I have replied to Mr Chesterton very fully and in Catholic terms. Those who have read my reply in the magazines in which it appeared need read no further, unless they wish, as I should advise, to read it twice. For the benefit of the rest, and to put it on permanent record, here it is.

FUNDAMENTAL NATURAL CONDITIONS OF HUMAN SOCIETY

1. Government is necessary wherever two or three are gathered together—or two or three billions—for keeps.

2. Government is neither automatic nor abstract: it must be performed by human rulers and agents as best they can.

3. The business of the rulers is to check disastrously selfish or unexpected behavior on the part of individuals in social affairs.

4. This business can be done only by devizing and enforcing rules of social conduct codifying the greatest common measure of agreement as to the necessary sacrifice of individual liberty to the good of the community.

5. The paradox of government is that as the good of the community involves a maximum of individual liberty for all its members the rulers have at the same time to enslave everyone ruthlessly and to secure for everyone the utmost possible freedom.

6. In primitive communities people feed and lodge themselves without bothering the Government. In big civilizations this is impossible; so the first business of the Government is to provide for the production and distribution of wealth from day to day and the just sharing of the labor and leisure involved. Thus the individual citizen has to be compelled not only to behave himself properly, but to work productively.

7. The moral slavery of the compulsion to behave properly is a whole-time compulsion admitting of no liberty; but the personal slavery of the compulsion to work lasts only as many hours daily as suffice to discharge the economic duties of the citizen, the remaining hours (over and above those needed for feeding, sleeping, locomotion, etc.) being his leisure.

8. Leisure is the sphere of individual liberty: labor is the sphere of slavery.

9. People who think they can be honestly free all the time are idiots: people who seek whole-time freedom by putting their share of productive work on others are thieves.

10. The use of the word slavery to denote subjection to public government has grown up among the idiots and thieves, and is resorted to here only because it is expedient to explain things to fools according to their folly.

So much for the fundamental natural conditions of social organization. They are as completely beyond argument as the precession of the equinoxes; but they present different problems to different people. To the thief, for instance, the problem is how to evade his share in the labor of production, to increase his share in the distribution of the product, and to corrupt the Government so that it may protect and glorify his chicaneries instead of liquidating him. To Mr Chesterton the Distributist (or Extreme Left Communist) and Catholic (or Equalitarian Internationalist) it is how to select rulers who will govern righteously and impartially in accordance with the fundamental natural conditions.

The history of civilization is the history of the conflict

between these rival views of the situation. The Pirate King, the Robber Baron, and the Manchester Man produced between them a government which they called the Empire, the State, the Realm, the Republic, or any other imposing name that did not give away its central purpose. The Chestertonians produced a government which they called The Church; and in due time the Last of the Chestertons joined this Catholic Church, like a very large ship entering a very small harbor, to the great peril of its many rickety old piers and wharves, and the swamping of all the small craft in its neighborhood. So let us see what the Catholic Church made of its governmental problem.

The Catholic Solution

To begin with, the Church, being catholic, was necessarily democratic to the extent that its aim was to save the souls of all persons without regard to their age, sex, nationality, class or color. The nobleman who felt that God would not lightly damn a man of his quality received no countenance from the Church in that conviction. Within its fold all souls were equal before God.

But the Church did not draw the ridiculous conclusion that all men and women are equally qualified or equally desirous to legislate, to govern, to administer, to make decisions, to manage public affairs or even their own private affairs. It faced the fact that only about five per cent. of the population are capable of exercising these powers, and are certain to be corrupted by them unless they have an irresistible religious vocation for public work and a faith in its beneficence which will induce them to take vows to abstain from any profit that is not shared by all the rest, and from all indulgences which might blunt their consciences or subject them to the family influences so bitterly deprecated by Jesus.

This natural "called" minority was never elected in the scandalous way we call democratic. Its members were in the first instance self-elected: that is, they voluntarily lived holy lives and devoted themselves to the public welfare in obedience to the impulse of the Holy Ghost within them. This impulse was their vocation. They were called from above, not chosen by the uncalled. To protect themselves and obtain the necessary power, they organized themselves, and called their organization The Church. After that, the genuineness and sufficiency of the vocation of the new recruits were judged by The Church. If the judgment was favorable, and the candidates took certain vows, they were admitted to the official priesthood and set to govern as priests in the parish and spiritual directors in the family, all of them being eligible, if they had the requisite ability, for promotion to the work of governing the Church itself as bishops or cardinals, or to the supreme rank of Pope or Vicar of Christ on earth. And all this without the smallest reference to the opinions of the uncalled and unordained.

Need for a Common Faith

Now comes the question, why should persons of genuine vocation be asked to take vows before being placed in authority? Is not the vocation a sufficient guarantee of their wisdom?

No. Before priests can govern they must have a common faith as to the fundamental conditions of a stable human society. Otherwise the result might be an assembly of random men of genius unable to agree on a single legislative measure or point of policy. An ecumenical council consisting of Einstein and Colonel Lynch, Aquinas and Francis Bacon, Dante and Galileo, Lenin and Lloyd George, could seldom come to a unanimous decision, if indeed to any decision except in the negative against a minority of one, on any point beyond the capacity of a coroner's jury. The Pope must not be an eccentric genius presiding over a conclave of variously disposed cardinals: he must have an absolutely closed mind on what Herbert Spencer called Social Statics; and in this the cardinals must resemble and agree with him. What is more, they must to some extent represent the conscience of the common people; for it is evident that if they made laws and gave personal directions which would produce general horror or be taken as proofs of insanity their authority would collapse. Hence the need for vows committing all who take them to definite articles of faith on social statics, and to their logical consequences in law and custom. Such vows automatically exclude revolutionary geniuses, who, being uncommon, are not representative, more especially scientific geniuses, with whom it is a point of honor to have unconditionally open minds even on the most apparently sacred subjects.

Russia Rediscovers the Church System

A tremendous importance is given to a clear understanding of the Catholic system at this moment by the staggering fact that the biggest State in the modern world, having made a clean sweep of its Church by de-

nouncing its religion as dope, depriving its priests and
bishops of any greater authority than a quack can pick
up at a fair, encouraging its most seriously minded children to form a League of the Godless, shooting its pious
Tsar, turning its cathedrals into historical museums il-
lustrating the infamies of ecclesiastical history and expressly entitling them anti-religious: in short, addressing
itself solemnly and implacably to a root-and-branch extermination of everything that we associate with priesthood, has, under pressure of circumstances, unconsciously
and spontaneously established as its system of government an as-close-as-possible reproduction of the hierarchy
of the Catholic Church. The nomenclature is changed,
of course: the Church is called the Communist Party;
and the Holy Office and its familiars are known as the
Komintern and the Gay Pay Oo. There is the popular
safeguard of having the symptoms of the priestly vocation verified in the first instance by the group of peasants
or industrial workers with whom the postulant's daily
life has been passed, thus giving a genuine democratic
basis to the system; and the hierarchy elected on this
basis is not only up to date for the moment, but ame-
nable to the daily lessons of trial and error in its practical
operations and in no way pledged against change and
innovation as such. But essentially the system is that of
the old Christian Catholic Church, even to its fundamental vow of Communism and the death penalty on
Ananias and Sapphira for violating it.

If our newspapers knew what is really happening in
the world, or could discriminate between the news value
of a bicycle accident in Clapham and that of a capsize
of civilization, their columns would be full of this literally
epoch-making event. And the first question they would

address to Russia would be "Why, seeing that the Christian system has been such a hopeless failure, do you go back to it, and invite us to go back to it?"

WHY THE CHRISTIAN SYSTEM FAILED

The answer is that the Christian system failed, not because it was wrong in its psychology, its fundamental postulate of equality, or its anticipation of Lenin's principle that the rulers must be as poor as the ruled so that they can raise themselves only by raising their people, but because the old priests' ignorance of economics and political science blinded them to the mischief latent in the selfishness of private property in the physical earth. Before the Church knew where it was (it has not quite located itself yet) it found itself so prodigiously rich that the Pope was a secular Italian prince with armies and frontiers, enjoying not only the rent of Church lands, but selling salvation on such a scale that when Torquemada began burning Jews instead of allowing them to ransom their bodies by payments to the Roman treasury, and leaving their souls to God, a first-rate quarrel between the Church and the Spanish Inquisition was the result.

But the riches of the Church were nothing compared to the riches of the Church's great rival, the Empire. And the poverty of the priest was opulence compared to the poverty of the proletarian. Whilst the Church was being so corrupted by its own property, and by the influence on it of the lay proprietors, that it lost all its moral prestige, the warriors and robbers of the Empire had been learning from experience that a pirate ship needs a hierarchy of officers and an iron discipline even more than police boats, and that the work of robbing the poor all the time involves a very elaborate system of government to ensure that the poor shall, like bees, continue to produce not only their own subsistence but the surplus that can be robbed from them without bringing on them the doom of the goose that lays the golden eggs. Naked coercion is so expensive that it became necessary to practise on the imaginations of the poor to the extent of making them believe that it is a pious duty to be robbed, and that their moment of life in this world is only a prelude to an eternity in which the poor will be blest and happy, and the rich horribly tortured.

Matters at last reached a point at which there was more law and order in the Empire than in The Church. Emperor Philip of Spain was enormously more respectable and pious, if less amiable, than Pope Alexander Borgia. The Empire gained moral prestige as The Church lost it until the Empire, virtuously indignant, took it on itself to reform The Church, all the more readily as the restoration of priestly poverty was a firstrate excuse for plundering it.

Now The Church could not with any decency allow itself to be reformed by a plutocracy of pirate kings, robber barons, commercial adventurers, moneylenders, and deserters from its own ranks. It reformed itself from within by its own saints and the Orders they founded, and thus "dished" the Reformation; whilst the Reformers set up national Churches and free Churches of their own under the general definition of Protestants, and thereby found themselves committed to a curious adulteration of their doctrine of Individualism, or the right of private judgment, with most of the ecclesiastical corruptions against which they had protested. And as neither Church nor Empire would share the government of mankind with the other nor allow the common people any say in the matter, the Catholics and Protestants set to work to exterminate one another with rack and stake, fire, sword, and gunpowder, aided by the poison gas of scurrilous calumny, until the very name of religion began to stink in the nostrils of all really charitable and faithful people.

GOVERNMENT BY EVERYBODY

The moral drawn from all this was that as nobody could be trusted to govern the people the people must govern themselves, which was nonsense. Nevertheless it was assumed that by inscribing every man's name on a register of voters we could realize the ideal of every man his own Solon and his own Plato, as to which one could only ask why not every man his own Shakespear and his own Einstein? But this assumption suited the pluto-crats very well, as they had only to master the easy art of stampeding elections by their newspapers to do anything they liked in the name of the people. Votes for every-body (called for short, Democracy) ended in govern-ment neither of the best nor of the worst, but in an official government which could do nothing but talk, and an actual government of landlords, employers, and financiers at war with an Opposition of trade unionists, strikers, pickets, and—occasionally—rioters. The result-ant disorder, indiscipline, and breakdown of distribu-tion, produced a reaction of pure disappointment and distress in which the people looked wildly round for a Savior, and were ready to give a hopeful trial to anyone bold enough to assume dictatorship and kick aside the

impotent official government until he had completely
muzzled and subjugated it.

Failure All Round

That is the history of Catholicism and Protestantism.
Church and Empire, Liberalism and Democracy, up to
date. Clearly a ghastly failure, both positively as an
attempt to solve the problem of government and
negatively as an attempt to secure freedom of thought
and facility of change to keep pace with thought.

Now this does not mean in the least that the original
Catholic plan was wrong. On the contrary, all the disasters to which it has led have been demonstrations of
the eternal need for it. The alternative to vocational
government is a mixture of a haporth of very incom-
petent official government with an intolerable deal of
very competent private tyranny. Providence, or Nature
if you prefer that expression, has not ordained that all
men shall have a vocation for being "servants of all the
rest" as saints or rulers. Providence knows better than to
provide armies consisting exclusively of commanders-in-
chief or factories staffed exclusively with managing
directors; and to that inexorable natural fact we shall
always have to come back, just as the Russian revolutionists, who were reeking with Protestant Liberal
superstitions at the beginning, have had to come back to
it. But we have now thought out much more carefully
than St Peter the basic articles of faith, without which
the vocation of the priest is inevitably pushed out by
the vocation of the robbers and the racketeers, self-
elected as gentlemen and ladies. We know that private

property distributes wealth, work, and leisure so un-
evenly that a wretchedly poor and miserably overworked majority are forced to maintain a minority in-
ordinately rich and passionately convinced that labor is
so disgraceful to them that they dare not be seen carrying
a parcel down Bond Street. We know that the strains
set up by such a division of interests also destroy peace,
justice, religion, good breeding, honor, reasonable freedom, and everything that government exists to secure,
and that all this iniquity arises automatically when we
thoughtlessly allow a person to own a thousand acres
of land in the middle of London much more completely
than he owns the pair of boots in which he walks over
it; for he may not kick me out of my house into the street
with his boots; but he may do so with his writ of ejectment. And so we are driven to the conclusion that the
modern priesthood must utterly renounce, abjure, abhor,
abominate and annihilate private property as the very
worst of all the devil's inventions for the demoralization
and damnation of mankind. Civilized men and women
must live by their ordered and equal share in the work
needed to support the community, and must find their
freedom in their ordered and equal share of the leisure
produced by scientific economy in producing that support.
It still takes some conviction to repudiate an institution
so well spoken of as private property; but the facts must
be faced: our clandestine methods of violating it by
income tax and surtax, which mean only "What a thief
stole steal thou from the thief," will no longer serve;
for a modern government, as the Russians soon found
out, must not take money, even from thieves, until it
is ready to employ it productively. To throw it away in
doles as our governing duffers do, is to burn the candle

at both ends and precipitate the catastrophe they are
trying to avert.

Obsolete Vows

As to the vows, some of the old ones must go. The
Catholic Church and our Board of Education insist on
celibacy, the one for priests and the other for school-
mistresses. That is a remnant of the cynical superstition of original sin. Married people have a right to
married rulers; mothers have a right to have their children taught and handled by mothers; and priests and
pastors who meddle with family affairs should know
what they are talking about.

Another important modern discovery is that government is not a whole-time job for all its agents. A council
of peasants derives its ancient wisdom from its normal
day's work on the land, without which it would be a
council of tramps and village idiots. It is not desirable
that an ordinary parish priest should have no other occupation, nor an abnormal occupation, even that of a
scholar. Nor is it desirable that his uniform should be
too sacerdotal; for that is the method of idolatry, which
substitutes for rational authority the superstitious awe
produced by a contrived singularity. St Vincent de Paul
knew thoroughly well what he was about when he constituted his Sisterhood of Charity on the rule that the
sister should not be distinguishable from an ordinary
respectable woman. Unfortunately, the costume prescribed under this rule has in the course of the centuries
become as extraordinary as that of the Bluecoat boy;
and St Vincent's idea is consequently lost; but modern
industrial experience confirms it; for the latest re-

discovery of the Vincentian principle has been made by
Mr Ford, who has testified that if you want a staff of
helpful persons who will turn their hands to anything
at need you must not give them either title, rank, or
uniform, as the immediate result will be their partial
disablement by the exclusion from their activities of many
of the most necessary jobs as beneath their dignity.

Another stipulation made by St Vincent, who already
in the sixteenth century was far ahead of us, was that
no sister may pledge herself for longer than a year at a
time, however often she may renew her vows. Thus the
sisters can never lose their freedom nor suffer from cold
feet. If he were alive today St Vincent would probably
propose a clean sweep of all our difficulties about marriage and divorce by forbidding people to marry for
longer than a year, and make them renew their vows
every twelve months. In Russia the members of the
Communist Party cannot dedicate themselves eternally:
they can drop out into the laity when they please, and
if they do not please and nevertheless have become slack
in their ministry, they are pushed out.

Supernatural Pretensions

Furthermore, modern priests must not make supernatural pretensions. They must not be impostors. A
vocation for politics, though essentially a religious vocation, must be on the same footing as a vocation for music
or mathematics or cooking or nursing or acting or
architecture or farming or billiards or any other born
aptitude. The authority which must attach to all public
officials and councils must rest on their ability and efficiency. In the Royal Navy every mishap to a ship in-

volves a court martial on the responsible officer: if the officer makes a mistake he forfeits his command unless he can convince the court that he is still worthy it. In no other way can our hackneyed phrase "responsible government" acquire any real meaning. When a Catholic priest goes wrong (or too right) he is silenced: when a Russian Commissar goes wrong, he is expelled from the Party. Such responsibility necessarily makes official authority very authoritative and frightens off the unduly nervous. Stalin and Mussolini are the most responsible statesmen in Europe because they have no hold on their places except their efficiency; and their authority is consequently greater than that of any of the monarchs, presidents, and prime ministers who have to deal with them. Stalin is one of the higher functionaries with whom governing is necessarily a whole-time job. But he is no richer than his neighbors, and can "better himself" only by bettering them, not by bettering them like a British demagogue.

ECLECTIC DEMOCRACY

I think my views on intellectual aristocracy and democracy and all the rest of it are now plain enough. As between the intentions of The Church and the intentions of The Empire (unrealized ideals both) I am on the side of The Church. As to the evil done by The Church with the best intentions and the good done by The Empire with the worst, I am an Eclectic: there is much to be learnt from each. I harp on Russia because the Moscow experiment is the only really new departure from Tweedledum and Tweedledee: Fascism is still wavering between Empire and Church, between private property and Communism. Years ago, I said that what democracy needed was a trustworthy anthropometric machine for the selection of qualified rulers. Since then I have elaborated this by demanding the formation of panels of tested persons eligible for the different grades in the governmental hierarchy. Panel A would be for diplomacy and international finance, Panel B for national affairs, Panel C for municipal and county affairs, Panel D for the village councils, and so forth. Under such a panel system the voters would lose their present liberty to return such candidates as the late Horatio Bottomley to parliament by enormous majorities; but they would gain the advantage of at least knowing that their rulers know how to read and write, which they do not enjoy at present.

Nobody ventured to disagree with me when I urged the need for such panels; but when I was challenged to produce my anthropometric machine or my endocrine or phrenological tests, I was obliged to confess that they had not yet been invented, and that such existing attempts at them as competitive examinations are so irrelevant and misleading as to be worse than useless as tests of vocation. But the Soviet system, hammered out under the sternest pressure of circumstances, supplies an excellent provisional solution, which turns out to be the solution of the old Catholic Church purged of supernatural pretension, assumption of final perfection, and the poison of private property with its fatal consequences. Mr Stalin is not in the least like an Emperor, nor an Archbishop, nor a Prime Minister, nor a Chancellor; but he would be strikingly like a Pope, claiming for form's sake an apostolic succession from Marx, were it not for his frank method of Trial and Error, his entirely human

footing, and his liability to removal at a moment's notice
if his eminence should upset his mental balance. At the
other end of the scale are the rank and file of the Communist Party, doing an ordinary day's work with the
common folk, and giving only their leisure to the Party.
For their election as representatives of the commons they
must depend on the votes of their intimate and equal
neighbors and workmates. They have no incentive to
seek election except the vocational incentive; for success,
in the first instance, means, not release from the day's
ordinary work, but the sacrifice of all one's leisure to
politics, and, if promotion to the whole-time-grades be
achieved, a comparatively ascetic discipline and virtually
no pecuniary gain.

If anyone can suggest a better practically tested plan,
now is the time to do it; for it is all up with the old
Anarchist-Liberal parliamentary systems in the face of
thirty millions of unemployed, and World Idiotic Conferences at which each nation implores all the others to
absorb its unemployed by a revival of international trade.
Mr Chesterton says truly that a government, if it is to
govern, "cannot select one ruler to do something and
another to undo it, one intellectual to restore the nation and another to ruin the nation." But that is precisely
what our parliamentary party system does. Mr Chesterton has put it in a nutshell; and I hope he will appreciate
the sound Catholicism with which I have cracked it.

AYOT ST LAWRENCE,
     1933.

TOO TRUE TO BE GOOD

ACT I

Night. One of the best bedrooms in one of the best suburban villas in one of the richest cities in England. A young lady with an unhealthy complexion is asleep in the bed. A small table at the head of the bed, convenient to her right hand, and crowded with a medicine bottle, a measuring glass, a pill box, a clinical thermometer in a glass of water, a half read book with the place marked by a handkerchief, a powder puff and handmirror, and an electric bell handle on a flex, shews that the bed is a sick bed and the young lady an invalid.

The furniture includes a very handsome dressing table with silver-backed hairbrushes and toilet articles, a dainty pincushion, a stand of rings, a jewel box of black steel with the lid open and a rope of pearls heaped carelessly half in and half out, a Louis Quinze writing table and chair with inkstand, blotter, and cabinet of stationery, a magnificent wardrobe, a luxurious couch, and a tall screen of Chinese workmanship which, like the expensive carpet and everything else in the room, proclaims that the owner has money enough to buy the best things at the best shops in the best purchaseable taste.

The bed is nearly in the middle of the room, so that the patient's nurses can pass freely between the wall and the head of it. If we contemplate the room from the foot of the bed, with the patient's toes pointing straight at us, we have the door (carefully sandbagged lest a draught of fresh air should creep underneath) level with us in the

*righthand wall, the couch against the same wall farther
away, the window (every ray of moonlight excluded by
closed curtains and a dark green spring blind) in the
middle of the left wall with the wardrobe on its right and
the writing table on its left, the screen at right angles
to the wardrobe, and the dressing table against the wall
facing us half way between the bed and the couch.*

*Besides the chair at the writing table there is an easy
chair at the medicine table, and a chair at each side of the
dressing table.*

*The room is lighted by invisible cornice lights, and by
two mirror lights on the dressing table and a portable
one on the writing table; but these are now switched off;
and the only light in action is another portable one on
the medicine table, very carefully subdued by a green
shade.*

*The patient is sleeping heavily. Near her, in the easy
chair, sits a Monster. In shape and size it resembles a
human being; but in substance it seems to be made of a
luminous jelly with a visible skeleton of short black rods.
It droops forward in the chair with its head in its hands,
and seems in the last degree wretched.*

THE MONSTER. Oh! Oh!! Oh!!! I am so ill! so miserable! Oh, I wish I were dead. Why doesnt she die and
release me from my sufferings? What right has she to
get ill and make me ill like this? Measles: thats what
she's got. Measles! German measles! And she's given
them to me, a poor innocent microbe that never did
her any harm. And she says that *I* gave them to her.
Oh, is this justice? Oh, I feel so rotten. I wonder what
my temperature is: they took it from under her tongue
half an hour ago. [*Scrutinizing the table and discovering*

the thermometer in the glass]. Here's the thermometer: theyve left it for the doctor to see instead of shaking it down. If it's over a hundred I'm done for: I darent look. Oh, can it be that I'm dying? I must look. [*It looks, and drops the thermometer back into the glass with a gasping scream*]. A hundred and three! It's all over. [*It collapses*].

The door opens; and an elderly lady and a young doctor come in. The lady steals along on tiptoe, full of the deepest concern for the invalid. The doctor is indifferent, but keeps up his bedside manner carefully, though he evidently does not think the case so serious as the lady does. She comes to the bedside on the invalid's left. He comes to the other side of the bed and looks attentively at his patient.

THE ELDERLY LADY [*in a whisper sibillant enough to wake the dead*] She is asleep.

THE MONSTER. I should think so. This fool here, the doctor, has given her a dose of the latest fashionable opiate that would keep a cock asleep til half past eleven on a May morning.

THE ELDERLY LADY. Oh doctor, do you think there is any chance? Can she possibly survive this last terrible complication?

THE MONSTER. Measles! He mistook it for influenza.

THE ELDERLY LADY. It was so unexpected! such a crushing blow! And I have taken such care of her. She is my only surviving child: my pet: my precious one. Why do they all die? I have never neglected the smallest symptom of illness. She has had doctors in attendance on her almost constantly since she was born.

THE MONSTER. She has the constitution of a horse or she'd have died like the others.

THE ELDERLY LADY. Oh, dont you think, dear doctor—of course you know best; but I am so terribly anxious—dont you think you ought to change the prescription? I had such hopes of that last bottle; but you know it was after that that she developed measles.

THE DOCTOR. My dear Mrs Mopply, you may rest assured that the bottle had nothing to do with the measles. It was merely a gentle tonic—

THE MONSTER. Strychnine!

THE DOCTOR. —to brace her up.

THE ELDERLY LADY. But she got measles after it.

THE DOCTOR. That was a specific infection: a germ, a microbe.

THE MONSTER. Me! Put it all on me.

THE ELDERLY LADY. But how did it get in? I keep the windows closed so carefully. And there is a sheet steeped in carbolic acid always hung over the door.

THE MONSTER [in tears] Not a breath of fresh air for me!

THE DOCTOR. Who knows? It may have lurked here since the house was built. You never can tell. But you must not worry. It is not serious: a light rubeola: you can hardly call it measles. We shall pull her through, believe me.

THE ELDERLY LADY. It is such a comfort to hear you say so, doctor. I am sure I shall never be able to express my gratitude for all you have done for us.

THE DOCTOR. Oh, that is my profession. We do what we can.

THE ELDERLY LADY. Yes; but some doctors are dreadful. There was that man at Folkstone: he was impossible. He tore aside the curtain and let the blazing sunlight into the room, though she cannot bear it without green spectacles. He opened the windows and let in all the cold morning air. I told him he was a murderer; and he only said "One guinea, please". I am sure he let in that microbe.

THE DOCTOR. Oh, three months ago! No: it was not that.

THE ELDERLY LADY. Then what was it? Oh, are you quite quite sure that it would not be better to change the prescription?

THE DOCTOR. Well, I have already changed it.

THE MONSTER. Three times!

THE ELDERLY LADY. Oh, I know you have, doctor: nobody could have been kinder. But it really did not do her any good. She got worse.

THE DOCTOR. But, my dear lady, she was sickening for measles. That was not the fault of my prescription.

THE ELDERLY LADY. Oh, of course not. You mustnt think that I ever doubted for a moment that everything you did was for the best. Still—

THE DOCTOR. Oh, very well, very well: I will write another prescription.

THE ELDERLY LADY. Oh, thank you, thank you: I felt sure you would. I have so often known a change of medicine work wonders.

THE DOCTOR. When we have pulled her through this attack I think a change of air—

THE ELDERLY LADY. Oh no: dont say that. She must be near a doctor who knows her constitution. Dear old Dr Newland knew it so well from her very birth.

THE DOCTOR. Unfortunately, Newland is dead.

THE ELDERLY LADY. Yes; but you bought his practice. I should never be easy in my mind if you were not within call. You persuaded me to take her to Folkstone; and see what happened! No: never again.

THE DOCTOR. Oh, well! [*He shrugs his shoulders resignedly, and goes to the bedside table*]. What about the temperature?

THE ELDERLY LADY. The day nurse took it. I havnt dared to look.

THE DOCTOR [*looking at the thermometer*] Hm!

THE ELDERLY LADY [*trembling*] Has it gone up? Oh, doctor!

THE DOCTOR [*hastily shaking the mercury down*] No. Nothing. Nearly normal.

THE MONSTER. Liar.

THE ELDERLY LADY. What a relief!

THE DOCTOR. You must be careful, though. Dont fancy she's well yet: she isnt. She must not get out of bed for a moment. The slightest chill might be serious.

THE ELDERLY LADY. Doctor: are you sure you are not concealing something from me? Why does she never get well in spite of the fortune I have spent on her illnesses? There must be some deep-rooted cause. Tell me the worst: I have dreaded it all my life. Perhaps I should have told you the whole truth; but I was afraid. Her uncle's step-father died of an enlarged heart. Is that what it is?

THE DOCTOR. Good gracious, NO! What put that into your head?

THE ELDERLY LADY. But even before this rash broke out there were pimples.

THE MONSTER. Boils! Too many chocolate creams.

THE DOCTOR. Oh, that! Nothing. Her blood is not quite what it should be. But we shall get that right.

THE ELDERLY LADY. You are sure it is not her lungs?

THE DOCTOR. My good lady, her lungs are as sound as a seagull's.

THE ELDERLY LADY. Then it must be her heart. Dont deceive me. She has palpitations. She told me the other day that it stopped for five minutes when that horrid nurse was rude to her.

THE DOCTOR. Nonsense! She wouldnt be alive now if her heart had stopped for five seconds. There is nothing constitutionally wrong. A little below par: that is all. We shall feed her up scientifically. Plenty of good fresh meat. A half bottle of champagne at lunch and a glass of port after dinner will make another woman of her. A chop at breakfast, rather underdone, is sometimes very helpful.

THE MONSTER. I shall die of overfeeding. So will she too: thats one consolation.

THE DOCTOR. Dont worry about the measles. It's really quite a light case.

THE ELDERLY LADY. Oh, you can depend on me for that. Nobody can say that I am a worrier. You wont forget the new prescription?

THE DOCTOR. I will write it here and now [*he takes out his pen and book, and sits down at the writing table*].

THE ELDERLY LADY. Oh, thank you. And I will go and see what the new night nurse is doing. They take so long with their cups of tea [*she goes to the door and is about to go out when she hesitates and comes back*]. Doctor: I know you dont believe in inoculations; but I cant help thinking she ought to have one. They do so much good.

THE DOCTOR [*almost at the end of his patience*] My dear Mrs Mopply: I never said that I dont believe in inoculations. But it is no use inoculating when the patient is already fully infected.

THE ELDERLY LADY. But I have found it so necessary myself. I was inoculated against influenza three years ago; and I have had it only four times since. My sister

has it every February. Do, to please me, give her an
inoculation. I feel such a responsibility if anything is left
undone to cure her.

THE DOCTOR. Oh very well, very well: I will see what
can be done. She shall have both an inoculation and a
new prescription. Will that set your mind at rest?

THE ELDERLY LADY. Oh, thank you. You have lifted
such a weight from my conscience. I feel sure they will
do her the greatest good. And now excuse me a moment
while I fetch the nurse. [*She goes out*].

THE DOCTOR. What a perfectly maddening woman!

THE MONSTER [*rising and coming behind him*] Yes:
aint she?

THE DOCTOR [*starting*] What! Who is that?

THE MONSTER. Nobody but me and the patient. And
you have dosed her so that she wont speak again for ten
hours. You will overdo that some day.

THE DOCTOR. Rubbish! She thought it was an opiate;
but it was only an aspirin dissolved in ether. But who am
I talking to? I must be drunk.

THE MONSTER. Not a bit of it.

THE DOCTOR. Then who are you? What are you? Where
are you? Is this a trick?

THE MONSTER. I'm only an unfortunate sick bacillus.

THE DOCTOR. A sick bacillus!

THE MONSTER. Yes. I suppose it never occurs to you
that a bacillus can be sick like anyone else.

THE DOCTOR. Whats the matter with you?

THE MONSTER. Measles.

THE DOCTOR. Rot! The microbe of measles has never
been discovered. If there is a microbe it cannot be measles:
it must be parameasles.

THE MONSTER. Great Heavens! what are parameasles?

THE DOCTOR. Something so like measles that nobody can see any difference.

THE MONSTER. If there is no measles microbe why did you tell the old girl that her daughter caught measles from a microbe?

THE DOCTOR. Patients insist on having microbes nowadays. If I told her there is no measles microbe she wouldnt believe me; and I should lose my patient. When there is no microbe I invent one. Am I to understand that you are the missing microbe of measles, and that you have given them to this patient here?

THE MONSTER. No: she gave them to me. These humans are full of horrid diseases: they infect us poor microbes with them; and you doctors pretend that it is we that infect them. You ought all to be struck off the register.

THE DOCTOR. We should be, if we talked like that.

THE MONSTER. Oh, I feel so wretched! Please cure my measles.

THE DOCTOR. I cant. I cant cure any disease. But I get the credit when the patients cure themselves. When she cures herself she will cure you too.

THE MONSTER. But she cant cure herself because you and her mother wont give her a dog's chance. You wont let her have even a breath of fresh air. I tell you she's naturally as strong as a rhinoceros. Curse your silly bottles and inoculations! Why dont you chuck them and turn faith healer?

THE DOCTOR. I am a faith healer. You dont suppose I believe the bottles cure people? But the patient's faith in the bottle does.

THE MONSTER. Youre a humbug: thats what you are.

THE DOCTOR. Faith is humbug. But it works.

THE MONSTER. Then why do you call it science?

THE DOCTOR. Because people believe in science. The Christian Scientists call their fudge science for the same reason.

THE MONSTER. The Christian Scientists let their patients cure themselves. Why dont you?

THE DOCTOR. I do. But I help them. You see, it's easier to believe in bottles and inoculations than in oneself and in that mysterious power that gives us our life and that none of us knows anything about. Lots of people believe in the bottles and wouldnt know what you were talking about if you suggested the real thing. And the bottles do the trick. My patients get well as often as not. That is, unless their number's up. Then we all have to go.

THE MONSTER. No girl's number is up until she's worn out. I tell you this girl could cure herself and cure me if youd let her.

THE DOCTOR. And I tell you that it would be very hard work for her. Well, why should she work hard when she can afford to pay other people to work for her? She doesnt black her own boots or scrub her own floors. She pays somebody else to do it. Why should she cure herself, which is harder work than blacking boots or scrubbing floors, when she can afford to pay the doctor to cure her? It pays her and it pays me. That's logic, my friend. And now, if you will excuse me, I shall take myself off before the old woman comes back and provokes me to wring her neck. [*Rising*] Mark my words: someday somebody will fetch her a clout over the head. Somebody who can afford to. Not the doctor. She has driven me mad already: the proof is that I hear voices and talk to them. [*He goes out*].

THE MONSTER. Youre saner than most of them, you fool. They think I have the keys of life and death in my pocket; but I have nothing but a horrid headache. Oh dear! oh dear!

The Monster wanders away behind the screen. The patient, left alone, begins to stir in her bed. She turns over and calls querulously for somebody to attend to her.

THE PATIENT. Nurse! Mother! Oh, is anyone there? [*Crying*] Selfish beasts! to leave me like this. [*She snatches angrily at the electric bell which hangs within her reach and presses the button repeatedly*].

The Elderly Lady and the night nurse come running in. The nurse is young, quick, active, resolute, and decidedly pretty. Mrs Mopply goes to the bedside table, the nurse going to the patient's left.

THE ELDERLY LADY. What is it, darling? Are you awake? Was the sleeping draught no good? Are you worse? What has happened? What has become of the doctor?

THE PATIENT. I am in the most frightful agony. I have been lying here ringing for ages and ages, and no one has come to attend to me. Nobody cares whether I am alive or dead.

THE ELDERLY LADY. Oh, how can you say such things, darling? I left the doctor here. I was away only for a minute. I had to receive the new night nurse and give her her instructions. Here she is. And oh, do cover up your arm, darling. You will get a chill; and then it will be all over. Nurse: see that she is never uncovered for a moment. Do you think it would be well to have another hot water bottle against her arm until it is quite warm again? Do you feel it cold, darling?

THE PATIENT [*angrily*] Yes, deadly cold.

THE ELDERLY LADY. Oh, dont say that. And there is so much pneumonia about. I wish the doctor had not gone.

He could sound your lungs—

NIGHT NURSE [*feeling the patient's arm*] She is quite warm enough.

THE PATIENT [*bursting into tears*] Mother: take this hateful woman away. She wants to kill me.

THE ELDERLY LADY. Oh no, dear: she has been so highly recommended. I cant get a new nurse at this hour. Wont you try, for my sake, to put up with her until the day nurse comes in the morning?

THE NURSE. Come! Let me arrange your pillows and make you comfortable. You are smothered with all this bedding. Four thick blankets and an eiderdown! No wonder you feel irritable.

THE PATIENT [*screaming*] Dont touch me. Go away. You want to murder me. Nobody cares whether I am alive or dead.

THE ELDERLY LADY. Oh, darling, dont keep on saying that. You know it's not true; and it does hurt me so.

THE NURSE. You must not mind what a sick person says, madam. You had better go to bed and leave the patient to me. You are quite worn out. [*She comes to Mrs Mopply and takes her arm coaxingly but firmly*].

THE ELDERLY LADY. I know I am: I am ready to drop. How sympathetic of you to notice it! But how can I leave her at such a moment?

THE NURSE. She ought not to have more than one person in the room at a time. You see how it excites and worries her.

THE ELDERLY LADY. Oh, thats very true. The doctor said she was to be kept as quiet as possible.

THE NURSE [*leading her to the door*] You need a good night's sleep. You may trust me to do what is right and necessary.

THE ELDERLY LADY [*whispering*] I will indeed. How kind of you! You will let me know if anything—

THE NURSE. Yes, yes. I promise to come for you and wake you if anything happens. Good night, madam.

THE ELDERLY LADY [*sotto voce*] Good night. [*She steals out*].

The nurse, left alone with her patient, pays no attention to her, but goes to the window. She opens the curtains and raises the blind, admitting a flood of moonlight. She unfastens the sash and throws it right up. She then makes for the door, where the electric switch is.

THE PATIENT [*huddling herself up in the bedclothes*] What are you doing? Shut that window and pull down that blind and close those curtains at once. Do you want to kill me?

The nurse turns all the lights full on.

THE PATIENT [*hiding her eyes*] Oh! Oh! I cant bear it: turn it off.

The nurse switches the lights off.

THE PATIENT. So inconsiderate of you!

The nurse switches the lights on again.

THE PATIENT. Oh, please, please. Not all that light.

The nurse switches off.

THE PATIENT. No, no. Leave me something to read by. My bedside lamp is not enough, you stupid idiot.

The nurse switches on again, and calmly returns to the bedside.

THE PATIENT. I cant imagine how anyone can be so thoughtless and clumsy when I am so ill. I am suffering horribly. Shut that window and switch off half those lights at once: do you hear?

The nurse snatches the eiderdown and one of the pillows rudely from the bed, letting the patient down with a jerk, and arranges them comfortably in the bedside chair.

THE PATIENT. How dare you touch my pillow? The audacity!

The nurse sits down; takes out a leaf cut from an illustrated journal; and proceeds to study it attentively.

THE PATIENT. Well! How much longer are you going to sit there neglecting me? Shut that window instantly.

THE NURSE [*insolently, in her commonest dialect*] Oh go to—to sleep [*she resumes her study of the document*].

THE PATIENT. Dont dare address me like that. I dont believe you are a properly qualified nurse.

THE NURSE [*calmly*] I should think not. I wouldnt take five thousand a year to be a nurse. But I know how to deal with you and your like, because I was once a patient in a hospital where the women patients were a rough lot, and the nurses had to treat them accordingly. I kept my eyes open there, and learnt a little of the game. [*She takes a paper packet from her pocket and opens it on the bedside table. It contains about half a pound of kitchen salt*]. Do you know what that is and what it's for?

THE PATIENT. Is it medicine?

THE NURSE. Yes. It's a cure for screaming and hysterics and tantrums. When a woman starts making a row, the first thing she does is to open her mouth. A nurse who knows her business just shoves a handful of this into it. Common kitchen salt. No more screaming. Understand?

THE PATIENT [*hardily*] No I dont [*she reaches for the bell*].

THE NURSE [*intercepting her quickly*] No you dont. [*She throws the bell cord with its button away on the floor behind the bed*]. Now we shant be disturbed. No bell.

And if you open your mouth too wide, youll get the salt. See?

THE PATIENT. And do you think I am a poor woman in a hospital whom you can illtreat as you please? Do you know what will happen to you when my mother comes in the morning?

THE NURSE. In the morning, darling, I shall be over the hills and far away.

THE PATIENT. And you expect me, sick as I am, to stay here alone with you!

THE NURSE. We shant be alone. I'm expecting a friend.

THE PATIENT. A friend!

THE NURSE. A gentleman friend. I told him he might drop in when he saw the lights switched off twice.

THE PATIENT. So that was why—

THE NURSE. That was why.

THE PATIENT. And you calmly propose to have your young man here in my room to amuse yourself all night before my face.

THE NURSE. You can go to sleep.

THE PATIENT. I shall do nothing of the sort. You will have to behave yourself decently before me.

THE NURSE. Oh, dont worry about that. He's coming on business. He's my business partner, in fact: not my best boy.

THE PATIENT. And can you not find some more suitable place for your business than in my room at night?

THE NURSE. You see, you dont know the nature of the business yet. It's got to be done here and at night. Here he is, I think.

A burglar, well dressed, wearing rubber gloves and a small white mask over his nose, clambers in. He is still in his early thirties, and quite goodlooking. His voice is disarmingly pleasant.

THE BURGLAR. All right, Sweetie?

THE NURSE. All right, Popsy.

The burglar closes the window softly; draws the curtains; and comes past the nurse to the bedside.

THE BURGLAR. Damn it, she's awake. Didn't you give her a sleeping draught?

THE PATIENT. Do you expect me to sleep with you in the room? Who are you? and what are you wearing that mask for?

THE BURGLAR. Only so that you will not recognize me if we should happen to meet again.

THE PATIENT. I have no intention of meeting you again. So you may just as well take it off.

THE NURSE. I havnt broken to her what we are here for, Popsy.

THE PATIENT. I neither know nor care what you are here for. All I can tell you is that if you dont leave the room at once and send my mother to me, I will give you both measles.

THE BURGLAR. We have both had them, dear invalid. I am afraid we must intrude a little longer. [*To the nurse*] Have you found out where it is?

THE NURSE. No: I havnt had time. The dressing table's over there. Try that.

The burglar crosses to the other side of the bed, coming round by the foot of it, and is making for the dressing table when—

THE PATIENT. What do you want at my dressing table?

THE BURGLAR. Obviously, your celebrated pearl necklace.

THE PATIENT [*escaping from her bed with a formidable*

bound and planting herself with her back to the dressing table as a bulwark for the jewel case] Not if I know it, you shant.

THE BURGLAR [*approaching her*] You really must allow me.

THE PATIENT. Take that.

Holding on to the table edge behind her, she lifts her foot vigorously waist high, and shoots it hard into his solar plexus. He curls up on the bed with an agonized groan and rolls off on to the carpet at the other side. The nurse rushes across behind the head of the bed and tackles the patient. The patient swoops at her knees, lifts her; and sends her flying. She comes down with a thump flat on her back on the couch. The patient pants hard; sways giddily; staggers to the bed and falls on it, exhausted. The nurse, dazed by the patient's very unexpected athleticism, but not hurt, springs up.

THE NURSE. Quick, Popsy: tie her feet. She's fainted.

THE BURGLAR [*utters a lamentable groan and rolls over on his face*]!!

THE NURSE. Be quick, will you?

THE BURGLAR [*trying to rise*] Ugh! Ugh!

THE NURSE [*running to him and shaking him*] My God, you are a fool, Popsy. Come and help me before she comes to. She's too strong for me.

THE BURGLAR. Ugh! Let me die.

THE NURSE. Are you going to lie there for ever? Has she killed you?

THE BURGLAR [*rising slowly to his knees*] As nearly as doesnt matter. Oh, Sweetiest, why did you tell me that this heavyweight champion was a helpless invalid?

THE NURSE. Shut up. Get the pearls.

THE BURGLAR [*rising with difficulty*] I dont seem to

want any pearls. She got me just in the wind. I am sorry
to have been of so little assistance; but oh, my Sweetie-
Weetie, Nature never intended us to be burglars. Our
first attempt has been a hopeless failure. Let us apologize
and withdraw.

THE NURSE. Fathead! Dont be such a coward. [*Looking closely at the patient*] I say, Popsy: I believe she's
asleep.

THE BURGLAR. Let her sleep. Wake not the lioness's
wrath.

THE NURSE. You maddening fool, dont you see that
we can tie her feet and gag her before she wakes, and get
away with the pearls. It's quite easy if we do it quick
together. Come along.

THE BURGLAR. Do not deceive yourself, my pet: we
should have about as much chance as if we tried to take a
female gorilla to the Zoo. No: I am not going to steal
those jewels. Honesty is the best policy. I have another
idea, and a much better one. You leave this to me. [*He
goes to the dressing table. She follows him*].

THE NURSE. Whatever have you got into your silly
head now?

THE BURGLAR. You shall see. [*Handling the jewel
case*] One of these safes that open by a secret arrangement
of letters. As they are as troublesome as an automatic telephone nobody ever locks them. Here is the necklace. By
Jove! If they are all real, it must be worth about twenty
thousand pounds. Gosh! here's a ring with a big blue
diamond in it. Worth four thousand pounds if it's worth
a penny. Sweetie: we are on velvet for the rest of our
lives.

THE NURSE. What good are blue diamonds to us if we
dont steal them?

THE BURGLAR. Wait. Wait and see. Go and sit down in that chair and look as like a nice gentle nurse as you can.

THE NURSE. But—

THE BURGLAR. Do as you are told. Have faith—faith in your Popsy.

THE NURSE [obeying] Well, I give it up. Youre mad.

THE BURGLAR. I was never saner in my life. Stop. How does she call people? Hasnt she an electric bell? Where is it?

THE NURSE [picking it up] Here. I chucked it out of her reach when she was grabbing at it.

THE BURGLAR. Put it on the bed close to her hand.

THE NURSE. Popsy: youre off your chump. She—

THE BURGLAR. Sweetie: in our firm I am the brains: you are the hand. This is going to be our most glorious achievement. Obey me instantly.

THE NURSE [resignedly] Oh, very well. [She places the handle of the bell as desired]. I wash my hands of this job. [She sits down doggedly].

THE BURGLAR [coming to the bedside] By the way, she is hardly a success as The Sleeping Beauty. She has a wretched complexion; and her breath is not precisely ambrosial. But if we can turn her out to grass she may put up some good looks. And if her punch is anything like her kick she will be an invaluable bodyguard for us two weaklings—if I can persuade her to join us.

THE NURSE. Join us! What do you mean?

THE BURGLAR. Shshshshsh. Not too much noise: we must wake her gently. [He stoops to the patient's ear and whispers] Miss Mopply.

THE PATIENT [in a murmur of protest] Mmmmmmmm-mmmmmmmmmm.

THE NURSE. What does she say?

THE BURGLAR. She says, in effect, "You have waked me too soon: I must slumber again." [*To the patient, more distinctly*] It is not your dear mother, Miss Mopply: it is the burglar. [*The patient springs half up, threateningly. He falls on his knees and throws up his hands.*] Kamerad, Miss Mopply: Kamerad! I am utterly at your mercy. The bell is on your bed, close to your hand: look at it. You have only to press the button to bring your mother and the police in upon me [*she seizes the handle of the bell*] and be a miserable invalid again for the rest of your life. [*She drops the bell thoughtfully*]. Not an attractive prospect, is it? Now listen. I have something to propose to you of the greatest importance: something that may make another woman of you and change your entire destiny. You can listen to me in perfect security: at any moment you can ring your bell, or throw us out of the window if you prefer it. I ask you for five minutes only.

THE PATIENT [*still dangerously on guard*] Well?

THE BURGLAR [*rising*] Let me give you one more proof of my confidence. [*He takes off his mask*]. Look. Can you be afraid of such a face? Do I look like a burglar?

THE PATIENT [*relaxing, and even shewing signs of goodhumor*] No: you look like a curate.

THE BURGLAR [*a little hurt*] Oh, not a curate. I hope I look at least like a beneficed clergyman. But it is very clever of you to have found me out. The fact is, I am a clergyman. But I must ask you to keep it a dead secret; for my father, who is an atheist, would disinherit me if he knew. I was secretly ordained when I was up at Oxford.

THE PATIENT. Oh, this is ridiculous. I'm dreaming. It must be that new sleeping draught the doctor gave me.

But it's delicious, because I'm dreaming that I'm perfectly well. Ive never been so happy in my life. Go on with the dream, Pops: the nicest part of it is that I am in love with you. My beautiful Pops, my own, my darling, you are a perfect film hero, only more like an English gentleman. [*She waves him a kiss*].

THE NURSE. Well I'll be da—

THE BURGLAR. Shshshshs. Break not the spell.

THE PATIENT [*with a deep sigh of contentment*] Let nobody wake me. I'm in heaven. [*She sinks back blissfully on her pillows*]. Go on, Pops. Tell me another.

THE BURGLAR. Splendid. [*He takes a chair from beside the dressing table and seats himself comfortably at the bedside*]. We are going to have an ideal night. Now listen. Picture to yourself a heavenly afternoon in July: a Scottish loch surrounded by mirrored mountains, and a boat—may I call it a shallop?—

THE PATIENT [*ecstatically*] A shallop! Oh, Popsy!

THE BURGLAR.—with Sweetie sitting in the stern, and I stretched out at full length with my head pillowed on Sweetie's knees.

THE PATIENT. You can leave Sweetie out, Pops. Her amorous emotions do not interest me.

THE BURGLAR. You misunderstand. Sweetie's thoughts were far from me. She was thinking about you.

THE PATIENT. Just like her impudence! How did she know about me?

THE BURGLAR. Simply enough. In her lily hand was a copy of The Lady's Pictorial. It contained an illustrated account of your jewels. Can you guess what Sweetie said to me as she gazed at the soft majesty of the mountains and bathed her soul in the beauty of the sunset?

THE PATIENT. Yes. She said "Popsy: we must pinch that

necklace."

THE BURGLAR. Exactly. Word for word. But now can you guess what *I* said?

THE PATIENT. I suppose you said "Right you are, Sweetie" or something vulgar like that.

THE BURGLAR. Wrong. I said, "If that girl had any sense she'd steal the necklace herself."

THE PATIENT. Oh! This is getting interesting. How could I steal my own necklace?

THE BURGLAR. Sell it; and have a glorious spree with the price. See life. Live. You dont call being an invalid living, do you?

THE PATIENT. Why shouldnt I call it living? I am not dead. Of course when I am awake I am terribly delicate—

THE BURGLAR. Delicate! It's not five minutes since you knocked me out, and threw Sweetie all over the room. If you can fight like that for a string of pearls that you never have a chance of wearing, why not fight for freedom to do what you like, with your pocket full of money and all the fun in the wide world at your command? Hang it all, dont you want to be young and goodlooking and have a sweet breath and be a lawn tennis champion and enjoy everything that is to be enjoyed instead of frowsting here and being messed about by your silly mother and all the doctors that live on her folly? Have you no conscience, that you waste God's gifts so shamefully? You think you are in a state of illness. Youre not: youre in a state of sin. Sell the necklace and buy your salvation with the proceeds.

THE PATIENT. Youre a clergyman all right, Pops. But I dont know how to sell the necklace.

THE BURGLAR. I do. Let me sell it for you. You will of course give us a fairly handsome commission on the transaction.

THE PATIENT. Theres some catch in this. If I trust you with it how do I know that you will not keep the whole price for yourself?

THE BURGLAR. Sweetie: Miss Mopply has the makings of a good business woman in her. [*To the patient*] Just reflect, Mops (Let us call one another Mops and Pops for short). If I steal that necklace, I shall have to sell it as a burglar to a man who will know perfectly well that I have stolen it. I shall be lucky if I get a fiftieth of its value. But if I sell it on the square, as the agent of its lawful owner, I shall be able to get its full market value. The payment will be made to you; and I will trust you to pay me the commission. Sweetie and I will be more than satisfied with fifty per cent.

THE PATIENT. Fifty! Oh!

THE BURGLAR [*firmly*] I think you will admit that we deserve it for our enterprise, our risk, and the priceless boon of your emancipation from this wretched home. Is it a bargain, Mops?

THE PATIENT. It's a monstrous overcharge; but in dreamland generosity costs nothing. You shall have your fifty. Lucky for you that I'm asleep. If I wake up I shall never get loose from my people and my social position. It's all very well for you two criminals: you can do what you like. If you were ladies and gentlemen, youd know how hard it is not to do what everybody else does.

THE BURGLAR. Pardon me; but I think you will feel more at ease with us if I inform you that we are ladies and gentlemen. My own rank—not that I would presume on it for a moment—is, if you ask Burke or Debrett, higher than your own. Your people's money was made in trade: my people have always lived by owning property or governing Crown Colonies. Sweetie would be a woman of the highest position but for the unfortunate fact that her parents, though united in the sight of Heaven, were not legally married. At least so she tells me.

THE NURSE [*hotly*] I tell you what is true. [*To the patient*] Popsy and I are as good company as ever you kept.

THE PATIENT. No, Sweetie: you are a common little devil and a liar. But you amuse me. If you were a real lady you wouldnt amuse me. Youd be afraid to be so unladylike.

THE BURGLAR. Just so. Come! confess! we are better fun than your dear anxious mother and the curate and all the sympathizing relatives, arnt we? Of course we are.

THE PATIENT. I think it perfectly scandalous that you two, who ought to be in prison, are having all the fun while I, because I am respectable and a lady, might just as well be in prison.

THE BURGLAR. Dont you wish you could come with us?

THE PATIENT [*calmly*] I fully intend to come with you. I'm going to make the most of this dream. Do you forget that I love you, Pops? The world is before us. You and Sweetie have had a week in the land of the mountain and the flood for seven guineas, tips included. Now you shall have an eternity with your Mops in the loveliest earthly paradise we can find, for nothing.

THE NURSE. And where do I come in?

THE PATIENT. You will be our chaperone.

THE NURSE. Chaperone! Well, you have a nerve, you have.

THE PATIENT. Listen. You will be a Countess. We shall go abroad, where nobody will know the difference. You shall have a splendid foreign title. The Countess Valbrioni: doesnt that tempt you?

THE NURSE. Tempt me hell! I'll see you further first.

THE BURGLAR. Stop. Sweetie: I have another idea. A regular dazzler. Lets stage a kidnap.

THE NURSE. What do you mean? stage a kidnap.

THE BURGLAR. It's quite simple. We kidnap Mops: that is, we shall hide her in the mountains of Corsica or Istria or Dalmatia or Greece or in the Atlas or where you please that is out of reach of Scotland Yard. We shall pretend to be brigands. Her devoted mother will cough up five thousand to ransom her. We shall share the ransom fifty-fifty: fifty for Mops, twentyfive for you, twentyfive for me. Mops: you will realize not only the value of the pearls, but of yourself. What a stroke of finance!

THE PATIENT [excited] Greece! Dalmatia! Kidnapped! Brigands! Ransomed! [Collapsing a little] Oh, dont tantalize me, you two fools: you have forgotten the measles.

The Monster suddenly reappears from behind the screen. It is transfigured. The bloated moribund Caliban has become a dainty Ariel.

THE MONSTER [picking up the last remark of the patient] So have you. No more measles: that scrap for the jewels cured you and cured me. Ha ha! I am well, I am well, I am well. [It bounds about ecstatically, and finally perches on the pillows and gets into bed beside the patient].

THE NURSE. If you could jump out of bed to knock out Popsy and me you can jump out to dress yourself and hop it from here. Wrap yourself up well: we have a car waiting.

THE BURGLAR. It's no worse than being taken to a nursing home, Mops. Strike for freedom. Up with you!

They pull her out of bed.

THE PATIENT. But I cant dress myself without a maid.

THE NURSE. Have you ever tried?

THE BURGLAR. We will give you five minutes. If you are not ready we go without you [*he looks at his watch*].

The patient dashes at the wardrobe and tears out a fur cloak, a hat, a walking dress, a combination, a pair of stockings, black silk breeches, and shoes, all of which she flings on the floor. The nurse picks up most of them; the patient snatches up the rest; the two retire behind the screen. Meanwhile the burglar comes forward to the foot of the bed and comments oratorically, half auctioneer, half clergyman.

THE BURGLAR. Fur cloak. Seal. Old fashioned but worth forty-five guineas. Hat. Quiet and ladylike. Tailor made frock. Combination: silk and wool. Real silk stockings without ladders. Knickers: how daringly modern! Shoes: heels only two inches but no use for the mountains. What a theme for a sermon! The well brought up maiden revolts against her respectable life. The aspiring soul escapes from home, sweet home, which, as a wellknown author has said, is the girl's prison and the woman's workhouse. The intrusive care of her anxious parents, the officious concern of the family clergyman for her salvation and of the family doctor for her health, the imposed affection of uninteresting brothers and sisters, the outrage of being called by her Christian name by distant cousins who will not keep their distance, the invasion of her privacy and independence at every turn by questions as to where she has been and what she has been doing, the whispering behind her back about her chances of marriage, the continual violation of that sacred aura which surrounds every living soul like the halo surrounding the heads of saints in religious pictures: against all these devices for worrying her to death the innermost uppermost life in her rises like milk in a boiling saucepan and cries "Down with you! away with you! henceforth my gates are open to real life, bring what it may. For what sense is there in this world of hazards, disasters, elations and victories, except as a field for the adventures of the life everlasting? In vain do we disfigure our streets with scrawls of Safety First: in vain do the nations clamor for Security, security, security. They who cry Safety First never cross the street: the empires which sacrifice life to security find it in the grave. For me Safety Last; and Forward, Forward, always For—"

THE NURSE [*coming from behind the screen*] Dry up, Popsy: she's ready.

The patient, cloaked, hatted, and shoed, follows her breathless, and comes to the burglar, on his left.

THE PATIENT. Here I am, Pops. One kiss; and then— Lead on.

THE BURGLAR. Good. Your complexion still leaves something to be desired; but [*kissing her*] your breath is sweet: you breathe the air of freedom.

THE MONSTER. Never mind her complexion: look at mine!

THE BURGLAR [*releasing the patient and turning to the nurse*] Did you speak?

THE NURSE. No. Hurry up, will you.

THE BURGLAR. It must have been your mother snoring, Mops. It will be long before you hear that music again. Drop a tear.

THE PATIENT. Not one. A woman's future is not with her mother.

THE NURSE. If you are going to start preaching like

Popsy, the milkman will be here before we get away. Remember, I have to take off this uniform and put on my walking things downstairs. Popsy: there may be a copper on his beat outside. Spy out and see. Safety First [*she hurries out*].

THE BURGLAR. Well, for just this once, safety first [*he makes for the window*].

THE PATIENT [*stopping him*] Idiot: the police cant touch you if I back you up. It's I who run the risk of being caught by my mother.

THE BURGLAR. True. You have an unexpectedly powerful mind. Pray Heaven that in kidnapping you I am not biting off more than I can chew. Come along. [*He runs out*].

THE PATIENT. He's forgotten the pearls!!! Thank Heaven he's a fool, a lovely fool: I shall be able to do as I like with him. [*She rushes to the dressing table; bundles the jewels into their case; and carries it out*].

THE MONSTER [*sitting up*] The play is now virtually over; but the characters will discuss it at great length for two acts more. The exit doors are all in order. Goodnight. [*It draws up the bedclothes round its neck and goes to sleep*].

ACT II

A sea beach in a mountainous country. Sand dunes rise to a brow which cuts off the view of the plain beyond, only the summits of the distant mountain range which bounds it being visible. An army hut on the hither side, with a klaxon electric horn projecting from a board on the wall, shews that we are in a military cantoonment. Opposite the hut is a particolored canvas bathing pavilion with a folding stool beside the entrance. As seen from the sand dunes the hut is on the right and the pavilion on the left. From the neighborhood of the hut a date palm throws a long shadow; for it is early morning.

In this shadow sits a British colonel in a deck chair, peacefully reading the weekly edition of The Times, but with a revolver in his equipment. A light cane chair for use by his visitors is at hand by the hut. Though well over fifty, he is still slender, handsome, well set up, and every inch a commanding officer. His full style and title is Colonel Tallboys V.C., D.S.O. He won his cross as a company-officer, and has never looked back since then.

He is disturbed by a shattering series of explosions announcing the approach of a powerful and very imperfectly silenced motor bicycle from the side opposite to the huts.

TALLBOYS. Damn that noise!

The unseen rider dismounts and races his engine with a hideous clatter.

TALLBOYS [*angrily*] Stop that motorbike, will you?

The noise stops; and the bicyclist, having hoiked his machine up on to its stand, taken off his goggles and gloves, and extracted a letter from his carrier, comes past the pavilion into the colonel's view with the letter in his hand.

He is an insignificant looking private soldier, dusty as to his clothes and a bit gritty as to his windbeaten face. Otherwise there is nothing to find fault with: his tunic and puttees are smart and correct, and his speech ready and rapid. Yet the colonel, already irritated by the racket of the bicycle and the interruption to his newspaper, contemplates him with stern disfavor; for there is something exasperatingly and inexplicably wrong about him. He wears a pith helmet with a pagri; and in profile this pagri suggests a shirt which he has forgotten to tuck in behind, whilst its front view as it falls on his shoulders gives him a feminine air of having ringlets and a veil which is in the last degree unsoldierly. His figure is that of a boy of seventeen; but he seems to have borrowed a long head and Wellingtonian nose and chin from somebody else for the express purpose of annoying the colonel. Fortunately for him these are offences which cannot be stated on a charge sheet and dealt with by the provo-marshal; and of this the colonel is angrily aware. The dispatch rider seems conscious of his incongruities; for, though very prompt, concise, and soldierly in his replies, he somehow suggests that there is an imprescriptible joke somewhere by an invisible smile which unhappily produces at times an impression of irony.

He salutes; hands the letter to the colonel; and stands at attention.

TALLBOYS [*taking the letter*] Whats this?

THE RIDER. I was sent with a letter to the headman of native village in the mountains, sir. That is his answer, sir.

TALLBOYS. I know nothing about it. Who sent you?

THE RIDER. Colonel Saxby, sir.

TALLBOYS. Colonel Saxby has just returned to the base, seriously ill. I have taken over from him. I am Colonel Tallboys.

THE RIDER. So I understand, sir.

TALLBOYS. Well, is this a personal letter to be sent on to him, or is it a dispatch?

THE RIDER. Dispatch, sir. Service document, sir. You may open it.

TALLBOYS [*turning in his chair and concentrating on him with fierce sarcasm*] Thank you. [*He surveys him from his instep to his nose*]. What is your name?

THE RIDER. Meek, sir.

TALLBOYS [*with disgust*] What!

THE RIDER. Meek, sir. M, double e, k.

The colonel looks at him with loathing, and tears open the letter. There is a painful silence whilst he puzzles over it.

TALLBOYS. In dialect. Send the interpreter to me.

MEEK. It's of no consequence, sir. It was only to impress the headman.

TALLBOYS. INNdeed. Who picked you for this duty?

MEEK. Sergeant, sir.

TALLBOYS. He should have selected a capable responsible person, with sufficient style to impress the native headman to whom Colonel Saxby's letter was addressed. How did he come to select you?

MEEK. I volunteered, sir.

TALLBOYS. Did you indeed? You consider yourself an impressive person, eh? You think you carry about with you the atmosphere of the British Empire, do you?

MEEK. No, sir. I know the country. I can speak the dialects a little.

TALLBOYS. Marvellous! And why, with all these accomplishments, are you not at least a corporal?

MEEK. Not educationally qualified, sir.

TALLBOYS. Illiterate! Are you not ashamed?

MEEK. No, sir.

TALLBOYS. Proud of it, eh?

MEEK. Cant help it, sir.

TALLBOYS. Where did you pick up your knowledge of the country?

MEEK. I was mostly a sort of tramp before I enlisted, sir.

TALLBOYS. Well, if I could get hold of the recruiting sergeant who enlisted you, I'd have his stripes off. Youre a disgrace to the army.

MEEK. Yessir.

TALLBOYS. Go and send the interpreter to me. And dont come back with him. Keep out of my sight.

MEEK [*hesitates*] Er—

TALLBOYS [*peremptorily*] Now then! Did you hear me give you an order? Send me the interpreter.

MEEK. The fact is, Colonel—

TALLBOYS [*outraged*] How dare you say Colonel and tell me that the fact is? Obey your order and hold your tongue.

MEEK. Yessir. Sorry, sir. *I* am the interpreter.

Tallboys bounds to his feet; towers over Meek, who looks smaller than ever; and folds his arms to give emphasis to a terrible rejoinder. On the point of delivering it, he suddenly unfolds them again and sits down resignedly.

TALLBOYS [*wearily and quite gently*] Very well. If you are the interpreter you had better interpret this for me. [*He proffers the letter*].

MEEK [*not accepting it*] No need, thank you, sir. The headman couldnt compose a letter, sir. I had to do it for him.

TALLBOYS. How did you know what was in Colonel Saxby's letter?

MEEK. I read it to him, sir.

TALLBOYS. Did he ask you to?

MEEK. Yessir.

TALLBOYS. He had no right to communicate the contents of such a letter to a private soldier. He cannot have known what he was doing. You must have represented yourself as being a responsible officer. Did you?

MEEK. It would be all the same to him, sir. He addressed me as Lord of the Western Isles.

TALLBOYS. You! You worm! If my letter was sent by the hands of an irresponsible messenger it should have contained a statement to that effect. Who drafted it?

MEEK. Quartermaster's clerk, sir.

TALLBOYS. Send him to me. Tell him to bring his note of Colonel Saxby's instructions. Do you hear? Stop making idiotic faces; and get a move on. Send me the quartermaster's clerk.

MEEK. The fact is—

TALLBOYS [*thundering*] Again!!

MEEK. Sorry, sir. *I* am the quartermaster's clerk.

TALLBOYS. What! You wrote both the letter and the headman's answer?

MEEK. Yessir.

TALLBOYS. Then either you are lying now or you were lying when you said you were illiterate. Which is it?

MEEK. I dont seem to be able to pass the examination when they want to promote me. It's my nerves, sir, I suppose.

TALLBOYS. Your nerves! What business has a soldier with nerves? You mean that you are no use for fighting, and have to be put to do anything that can be done without it.

MEEK. Yessir.

TALLBOYS. Well, next time you are sent with a letter I hope the brigands will catch you and keep you.

MEEK. There are no brigands, sir.

TALLBOYS. No brigands! Did you say no brigands?

MEEK. Yessir.

TALLBOYS. You are acquainted with the Articles of War, are you not?

MEEK. I have heard them read out, sir.

TALLBOYS. Do you understand them?

MEEK. I think so, sir.

TALLBOYS. You think so! Well, do a little more thinking. You are serving on an expeditionary force sent out to suppress brigandage in this district and to rescue a British lady who is being held for ransom. You know that. You dont think it: you know it, eh?

MEEK. So they say, sir.

TALLBOYS. You know also that under the Articles of War any soldier who knowingly does when on active service any act calculated to imperil the success of his Majesty's forces or any part thereof shall be liable to suffer death. Do you understand? Death!

MEEK. Yessir. Army Act, Part One, Section Four, Number Six. I think you mean Section Five, Number Five, sir.

TALLBOYS. Do I? Perhaps you will be good enough to quote Section Five, Number Five.

MEEK. Yessir. "By word of mouth spreads reports

calculated to create unnecessary alarm or despondency."

TALLBOYS. It is fortunate for you, Private Meek, that the Act says nothing about private soldiers who create despondency by their personal appearance. Had it done so your life would not be worth half an hour's purchase.

MEEK. No, sir. Am I to file the letter and the reply with a translation, sir?

TALLBOYS [*tearing the letter to pieces and throwing them away*] Your folly has made a mockery of both. What did the headman say?

MEEK. Only that the country has very good roads now, sir. Motor coaches ply every day all the year round. The last active brigand retired fifteen years ago, and is ninety years old.

TALLBOYS. The usual tissue of lies. That headman is in league with the brigands. He takes a turn himself occasionally, I should say.

MEEK. I think not, sir. The fact is—

TALLBOYS. Did I hear you say "The fact is"?

MEEK. Sorry, sir. That old brigand was the headman himself. He is sending you a present of a sheep and six turkeys.

TALLBOYS. Send them back instantly. Take them back on your damned bicycle. Inform him that British officers are not orientals, and do not accept bribes from officials in whose districts they have to restore order.

MEEK. He wont understand, sir. He wont believe you have any authority unless you take presents. Besides, they havnt arrived yet.

TALLBOYS. Well, when his messengers arrive pack them back with their sheep and their turkeys and a note to say that my favor can be earned by honesty and diligence, but not purchased.

MEEK. They wont dare take back either the presents or the note, sir. Theyll steal the sheep and turkeys and report gracious messages from you. Better keep the meat and the birds, sir: they will be welcome after a long stretch of regulation food.

TALLBOYS. Private Meek.

MEEK. Yessir.

TALLBOYS. If you should be at any future time entrusted with the command of this expedition you will no doubt give effect to your own views and moral standards. For the present will you be good enough to obey my orders without comment?

MEEK. Yessir. Sorry, sir.

As Meek salutes and turns to go, he is confronted by the nurse, who, brilliantly undressed for bathing under a variegated silk wrap, comes from the pavilion, followed by the patient in the character of a native servant. All traces of the patient's illness have disappeared: she is sunburnt to the color of terra cotta; and her muscles are hard and glistening with unguent. She is disguised en belle sauvage *by headdress, wig, ornaments, and girdle proper to no locality on earth except perhaps the Russian ballet. She carries a sun umbrella and a rug.*

TALLBOYS [*rising gallantly*] Ah, my dear Countess, delighted to see you. How good of you to come!

THE COUNTESS [*giving him her finger tips*] How do, Colonel? Hot, isn't it? [*Her dialect is now a spirited amalgamation of the foreign accents of all the waiters she has known*].

TALLBOYS. Take my chair. [*He goes behind it and moves it nearer to her*].

THE COUNTESS. Thanks. [*She throws off her wrap,*

which the patient takes, and flings herself with careless elegance into the chair, calling] Mr. Meek. Mr. Mee-e-e-eek!

Meek returns smartly, and touches the front of his cap.

THE COUNTESS. My new things from Paris have arrived at last. If you would be so very sweet as to get them to my bungalow somehow. Of course I will pay anything necessary. And could you get a letter of credit cashed for me. I'd better have three hundred pounds to go on with.

MEEK [*quite at his ease: unconsciously dropping the soldier and assuming the gentleman*] How many boxes, Countess?

THE COUNTESS. Six, I am afraid. Will it be a lot of trouble?

MEEK. It will involve a camel.

THE COUNTESS. Oh, strings of camels if necessary. Expense is no object. And the letter of credit?

MEEK. Sorry, Countess: I have only two hundred on me. You shall have the other hundred tomorrow. [*He hands her a roll of notes; and she gives him the letter of credit*].

THE COUNTESS. You are never at a loss. Thanks. So good of you.

TALLBOYS. Chut! Dismiss.

Meek comes to attention, salutes, left-turns, and goes out at the double.

TALLBOYS [*who has listened to this colloquy in renewed stupefaction*] Countess: that was very naughty of you.

THE COUNTESS. What have I done?

TALLBOYS. In camp you must never forget discipline. We keep it in the background; but it is always there and always necessary. That man is a private soldier. Any sort of social relation—any hint of familiarity with him—is impossible for you.

THE COUNTESS. But surely I may treat him as a human being.

TALLBOYS. Most certainly not. Your intention is natural and kindly; but if you treat a private soldier as a human being the result is disastrous to himself. He presumes. He takes liberties. And the consequence of that is that he gets into trouble and has a very bad time of it until he is taught his proper place by appropriate disciplinary measures. I must ask you to be particularly careful with this man Meek. He is only half-witted: he carries all his money about with him. If you have occasion to speak to him, make him feel by your tone that the relation between you is one of a superior addressing a very distant inferior. Never let him address you on his own initiative, or call you anything but "my lady." If there is anything we can do for you we shall be delighted to do it; but you must always ask me.

The patient, greatly pleased with the colonel for snubbing Sweetie, deposits her rug and umbrella on the sand, and places a chair for him on the lady's right with grinning courtesy. She then seats herself on the rug, and listens to them, hugging her knees and her umbrella, and trying to look as indigenous as possible.

TALLBOYS. Thank you. [*He sits down*].

THE COUNTESS. I am so sorry. But if I ask anyone else they only look helpless and say "You had better see Meek about it."

TALLBOYS. No doubt they put everything on the poor fellow because he is not quite all there. Is it understood that in future you come to me, and not to Meek?

THE COUNTESS. I will indeed, Colonel. I am so sorry, and I thoroughly understand. I am scolded and forgiven, arnt I?

TALLBOYS [*smiling graciously*] Admonished, we call it. But of course it is not your fault: I have no right to scold you. It is I who must ask your forgiveness.

THE COUNTESS. Granted.

THE PATIENT [*in waiting behind them, coughs significantly*]!!

THE COUNTESS [*hastily*] A vulgar expression, Colonel, isnt it? But so simple and direct. I like it.

TALLBOYS. I didnt know it was vulgar. It is concise.

THE COUNTESS. Of course it isnt really vulgar. But a little lower middle class, if you follow me.

THE PATIENT [*pokes the chair with the sun umbrella*]!

THE COUNTESS [*as before*] Any news of the brigands, Colonel?

TALLBOYS. No; but Miss Mopply's mother, who is in a distracted condition—very naturally of course, poor woman!—has actually sent me the ransom. She implores me to pay it and release her child. She is afraid that if I make the slightest hostile demonstration the brigands will cut off the girl's fingers and send them in one by one until the ransom is paid. She thinks they may even begin with her ears, and disfigure her for life. Of course that is a possibility: such things have been done; and the poor lady points out very justly that I cannot replace her daughter's ears by exterminating the brigands afterwards, as I shall most certainly do if they dare lay a hand on a British lady. But I cannot countenance such a concession to deliberate criminality as the payment of a ransom. [*The two conspirators exchange dismayed glances*]. I have sent a message to the old lady by wireless to say that payment of a ransom is out of the question, but that the British Government is offering a substantial reward for information.

THE COUNTESS [*jumping up excitedly*] Wotjesoy? A reward on top of the ransom?

THE PATIENT [*pokes her savagely with the umbrella*]!!!

TALLBOYS [*surprised*] No. Instead of the ransom.

THE COUNTESS [*recollecting herself*] Of course. How silly of me! [*She sits down and adds, reflectively*] If this native girl could find out anything would she get the reward?

TALLBOYS. Certainly she would. Good idea that: what?

THE COUNTESS. Yes, Colonel, isn't it?

TALLBOYS. By the way, Countess, I met three people yesterday who know you very well.

THE PATIENT [*forgetting herself and scrambling forward to her knees*] But you—

THE COUNTESS [*stopping her with a backhanded slap on the mouth*] Silence, girl. How dare you interrupt the colonel? Go back to your place and hold your tongue.

The patient obeys humbly until the Colonel delicately turns his head away, when she shakes her fist threateningly at the smiter.

TALLBOYS. One of them was a lady. I happened to mention your brother's name; and she lit up at once and said "Dear Aubrey Bagot! I know his sister intimately. We were all three children together."

THE COUNTESS. It must have been dear Florence Dorchester. I hope she wont come here. I want to have an absolute holiday. I dont want to see anybody—except you, Colonel.

TALLBOYS. Haw! Very good of you to say so.

The burglar comes from the bathing tent, very elegant in black and white bathing costume and black silken wrap with white silk lapels: a clerical touch.

TALLBOYS [*continuing*] Ah, Bagot! Ready for your dip? I was just telling the Countess that I met some friends of yours yesterday. Fancy coming on them out here of all places! Shews how small the world is, after all. [*Rising*] And now I am off to inspect stores. There is a shortage of maroons that I dont understand.

THE COUNTESS. What a pity! I love maroons. They have such nice ones at that confectioner's near the Place Vendôme.

TALLBOYS. Oh, youre thinking of marrons glacés. No: maroons are fireworks: things that go off with a bang. For signalling.

THE COUNTESS. Oh! the things they used to have in the war to warn us of an air raid?

TALLBOYS. Just so. Well, au revoir.

THE COUNTESS. Au revoir. Au revoir.

The Colonel touches his cap gallantly and bustles off past the hut to his inspection.

THE PATIENT [*rising vengefully*] You dare smack me in the face again, my girl, and I'll lay you out flat, even if I have to give away the whole show.

THE COUNTESS. Well, you keep that umbrella to yourself next time. What do you suppose I'm made of? Leather?

AUBREY [*coming between them*] Now! now! now! Children! children! Whats wrong?

THE PATIENT. This silly bitch—

AUBREY. Oh no, no, no, Mops. Damn it, be a lady. Whats the matter, Sweetie?

THE COUNTESS. You shouldnt talk like that, dearie. A low girl might say a thing like that; but youre expected to know better.

AUBREY. Mops: youve shocked Sweetie.

THE PATIENT. Well: do you think she never shocks me? She's a walking earthquake. And now what are we to do if these people the colonel has met turn up? There must be a real Countess Valbrioni.

THE COUNTESS. Not much there isnt. Do you suppose we three are the only liars in the world? All you have to do is to give yourself a swell title, and all the snobs within fifty miles will swear that you are their dearest friend.

AUBREY. The first lesson a crook has to learn, darling, is that nothing succeeds like lying. Make any statement that is so true that it has been staring us in the face all our lives, and the whole world will rise up and passionately contradict you. If you dont withdraw and apologize, it will be the worse for you. But just tell a thundering silly lie that everyone knows is a lie, and a murmur of pleased assent will hum up from every quarter of the globe. If Sweetie had introduced herself as what she obviously is: that is, an ex-hotel chambermaid who became a criminal on principle through the preaching of an ex-army chaplain —me!—with whom she fell in love deeply but transitorily, nobody would have believed her. But she has no sooner made the impossible statement that she is a countess, and that the ex-chaplain is her half step-brother the Honorable Aubrey Bagot, than clouds of witnesses spring up to assure Colonel Tallboys that it is all gospel truth. So have no fear of exposure, darling; and do you, my Sweetie, lie and lie and lie until your imagination bursts.

THE PATIENT [throwing herself moodily into the deck chair] I wonder are all crooks as fond of preaching as you are.

AUBREY [bending affectionately over her] Not all,

dearest. I dont preach because I am a crook, but because I have a gift—a divine gift—that way.

THE PATIENT. Where did you get it? Is your father a bishop?

AUBREY [*straightening himself up to declaim*] Have I not told you that he is an atheist, and, like all atheists, an inflexible moralist? He said I might become a preacher if I believed what I preached. That, of course, was nonsense: my gift of preaching is not confined to what I believe: I can preach anything, true or false. I am like a violin, on which you can play all sorts of music, from jazz to Mozart. [*Relaxing*] But the old man never could be brought to see it. He said the proper profession for me was the bar. [*He snatches up the rug; replaces it on the patient's left; and throws himself down lazily on it*].

THE COUNTESS. Aint we going to bathe?

AUBREY. Oh, dash it, dont lets go into the water. Lets sun-bathe.

THE COUNTESS. Lazy devil! [*She takes the folding stool from the pavilion, and sits down discontentedly*].

THE PATIENT. Your father was right. If you have no conscience about what you preach, your proper job is at the bar. But as you have no conscience about what you do, you will probably end in the dock.

AUBREY. Most likely. But I am a born preacher, not a pleader. The theory of legal procedure is that if you set two liars to expose one another, the truth will emerge. That would not suit me. I greatly dislike being contradicted; and the only place where a man is safe from contradiction is in the pulpit. I detest argument: it is unmannerly, and obscures the preacher's message. Besides, the law is too much concerned with crude facts and too little with spiritual things; and it is in spiritual things that

I am interested: they alone call my gift into full play.

THE PATIENT. You call preaching things you dont believe spiritual, do you?

AUBREY. Put a sock in it, Mops. My gift is divine: it is not limited by my petty personal convictions. It is a gift of lucidity as well as of eloquence. Lucidity is one of the most precious of gifts: the gift of the teacher: the gift of explanation. I can explain anything to anybody; and I love doing it. I feel I must do it if only the doctrine is beautiful and subtle and exquisitely put together. I may feel instinctively that it is the rottenest nonsense. Still, if I can get a moving dramatic effect out of it, and preach a really splendid sermon about it, my gift takes possession of me and obliges me to sail in and do it. Sweetie: go and get me a cushion for my head: there's a dear.

THE PATIENT. Do nothing of the kind, Sweetie. Let him wait on himself.

THE COUNTESS [rising] He'd only mess everything about looking for it. I like to have my rooms left tidy. [She goes into the pavilion].

THE PATIENT. Isnt that funny, Pops? She has a conscience as a chambermaid and none as a woman.

AUBREY. Very few people have more than one point of honor, Mops. And lots of them havnt even one.

THE COUNTESS [returning with a silk cushion, which she hurls hard at Aubrey's head] There! And now I give you both notice. I'm getting bored with this place.

AUBREY [making himself comfortable with his cushion] Oh, you are always getting bored.

THE PATIENT. I suppose that means that you are tired of Tallboys.

THE COUNTESS [moving restlessly about] I am fed up with him to that degree that I sometimes feel I could

almost marry him, just to put him on the list of the in-
evitables that I must put up with willynilly, like getting
up in the morning, and washing and dressing and eating
and drinking: things you darent let yourself get tired of
because if you did theyd drive you mad. Lets go and have
a bit of real life somewhere.

THE PATIENT. Real life! I wonder where thats to be
found! Weve spent nearly six thousand pounds in two
months looking for it. The money we got for the necklace
wont last for ever.

AUBREY. Sweetie: you will have to stick it in this spot
until we touch that ransom; and that's all about it.

THE COUNTESS. I'll do as I like, not what you tell
me. And I tell you again—the two of you—you can
take a week's notice. I'm bored with this business. I
need a change.

AUBREY. What are we to do with her, Mops? Always change! change! change!

THE COUNTESS. Well, I like to see new faces.

AUBREY. I could be happy as a Buddha in a temple,
eternally contemplating my own middle and having
the same old priest to polish me up every day. But
Sweetie wants a new face every fortnight. I have
known her fall in love with a new face twice in the
same week. [*Turning to her*] Woman: have you any
sense of the greatness of constancy?

COUNTESS. I might be constant if I were a real countess. But I'm only a hotel chambermaid; and a hotel
chambermaid gets so used to new faces that at last they
become a necessity. [*She sits down on the stool*].

AUBREY. And the oftener the faces change the more
the tips come to, eh?

COUNTESS. Oh, it's not that, though of course that

counts. The real secret of it is that though men are awfully nice for the first few days, it doesnt last. You get the best out of men by having them always new. What I say is that a love affair should always be a honeymoon. And the only way to make sure of that is to keep changing the man; for the same man can never keep it up. In all my life I have known only one man that kept it up til he died.

THE PATIENT [*interested*] Ah! Then the thing is possible?

COUNTESS. Yes: it was a man that married my sister: that was how I came to know about it.

AUBREY. And his ardor never palled? Day in and day out, until death did them part, he was the same as on the wedding day? Is that really true, Sweetie?

THE COUNTESS. It is. But then he beat her on their wedding day; and he beat her just as hard every day afterwards. I made her get a separation order; but she went back to him because nobody else paid her any attention.

AUBREY. Why didn't you tell me that before? I'd have beaten you black and blue sooner than lose you. [*Sitting up*] Would you believe it, Mops, I was in love with this woman: madly in love with her. She was not my intellectual equal; and I had to teach her table manners. But there was an extraordinary sympathy between our lower centres; and when after ten days she threw me over for another man I was restrained from murder and suicide only by the most resolute exercise of my reasoning powers, my determination to be a civilized man, and fear of the police.

THE COUNTESS. Well, I gave you a good time for the ten days, didnt I? Lots of people dont get that much to look back on. Besides, you know it was for your own good, Popsy. We werent really suited, were we?

AUBREY. You had acquired an insatiable taste for commercial travellers. You could sample them at the rate of three a week. I could not help admiring such amazing mobility of the affections. I had heard operatic tenors bawling Woman Is Fickle; but it always seemed to me that what was to be dreaded in women was their implacable constancy. But you! Fickle! I should think so.

THE COUNTESS. Well, the travellers were just as bad, you know.

AUBREY. Just as bad! Say just as good. Fickleness means simply mobility, and mobility is a mark of civilization. You should pride yourself on it. If you dont you will lose your self-respect; and I cannot endure a woman who has no self-respect.

THE COUNTESS. Oh, whats the use of us talking about self-respect? You are a thief and so am I. I go a little further than that, myself; and so would you if you were a woman. Dont you be a hypocrite, Popsy: at least not with me.

AUBREY. At least not with you! Sweetie: that touch of concern for my spiritual welfare almost convinces me that you still love me.

THE COUNTESS. Not me. Not much. I'm through with you, my lad. And I cant quite fancy the colonel: he's too old, and too much the gentleman.

AUBREY. He's better than nobody. Who else is there?

THE COUNTESS. Well, there's the sergeant. I daresay I have low tastes; but he's my sort, and the colonel isnt.

THE PATIENT. Have you fallen in love with Sergeant

Fielding, Sweetie?

THE COUNTESS. Well, yes; if you like to call it that.

AUBREY. May I ask have you sounded him on the subject?

THE COUNTESS. How can I? I'm a countess; and he's only a sergeant. If I as much as let on that I'm conscious of his existence I give away the show to the colonel. I can only look at him. And I cant do even that when anyone else is looking. And all the time I want to hug him [*she breaks down in tears*].

AUBREY. Oh for Heaven's sake dont start crying.

THE PATIENT. For all you know, Sweetie, the sergeant may be a happily married man.

THE COUNTESS. What difference does that make to my feelings? I am so lonely. The place is so dull. No pictures. No dances. Nothing to do but be ladylike. And the one really lovable man going to waste! I'd rather be dead.

THE PATIENT. Well, it's just as bad for me.

THE COUNTESS. No it isnt. Youre a real lady: youre broken in to be dull. Besides, you have Popsy. And youre supposed to be our servant. That gives you the run of the whole camp when youre tired of him. You can pick up a private when you like. Whats to prevent you?

THE PATIENT. My ladylike morals, I suppose.

THE COUNTESS. Morals your grandmother! I thought youd left all that flapdoodle behind you when you came away with us.

THE PATIENT. I meant to. Ive tried to. But you shock me in spite of myself every second time you open your mouth.

THE COUNTESS. Dont you set up to be a more moral

woman than I am, because youre not.

THE PATIENT. I dont pretend to be. But I may tell you that my infatuation for Popsy, which I now see was what really nerved me to this astonishing breakaway, has been, so far, quite innocent. Can you believe that, you clod?

THE COUNTESS. Oh yes I can: Popsy's satisfied as long as you let him talk. What I mean is—and I tell it to you straight—that with all my faults I'm content with one man at a time.

THE PATIENT. Do you suggest that I am carrying on with two men?

THE COUNTESS. I dont suggest anything. I say what I mean straight out; and if you dont like it you can lump it. You may be in love with Popsy; but youre interested in Private Meek, though what you see in that dry little worm beats me.

THE PATIENT. Have you noticed, my Sweetie, that your big strapping splendid sergeant is completely under the thumb of that dry little worm?

THE COUNTESS. He wont be when I get him under my thumb. But you just be careful. Take this tip from me: one man at a time. I am advising you for your good, because youre only a beginner; and what you think is love, and interest, and all that, is not real love at all: three quarters of it is only unsatisfied curiosity. Ive lived at that address myself; and I know. When I love a man now it's all love and nothing else. It's the real thing while it lasts. I havnt the least curiosity about my lovely sergeant: I know just what he'll say and what he'll do. I just want him to do it.

THE PATIENT [*rising, revolted*] Sweetie: I really cannot bear any more of this. No doubt it's perfectly true.

It's quite right that you should say it frankly and plainly. I envy and admire the frightful coolness with which you plump it all out. Perhaps I shall get used to it in time. But at present it knocks me to pieces. I shall simply have to go away if you pursue the subject. [*She sits down in the cane chair with her back to them*].

AUBREY. Thats the worst of Sweetie. We all have— to put it as nicely as I can—our lower centres and our higher centres. Our lower centres act: they act with a terrible power that sometimes destroys us; but they dont talk. Speech belongs to the higher centres. In all the great poetry and literature of the world the higher centres speak. In all respectable conversation the higher centres speak, even when they are saying nothing or telling lies. But the lower centres are there all the time: a sort of guilty secret with every one of us, though they are dumb. I remember asking my tutor at college whether, if anyone's lower centres began to talk, the shock would not be worse than the one Balaam got when his donkey began talking to him. He only told me half a dozen improper stories to shew how open-minded he was. I never mentioned the subject again until I met Sweetie. Sweetie is Balaam's ass.

THE COUNTESS. Keep a civil tongue in your head, Popsy. I—

AUBREY [*springing to his feet*] Woman: I am paying you a compliment: Balaam's ass was wiser than Balaam. You should read your Bible. That is what makes Sweetie almost superhuman. Her lower centres speak. Since the war the lower centres have become vocal. And the effect is that of an earthquake. For they speak truths that have never been spoken before—truths that the makers of our domestic institutions have tried to ignore. And now that Sweetie goes shouting them all over the place, the institutions are rocking and splitting and sundering. They leave us no place to live, no certainties, no workable morality, no heaven, no hell, no commandments, and no God.

THE PATIENT. What about the light in our own souls that you were so eloquent about the day before yesterday at lunch when you drank a pint of champagne?

AUBREY. Most of us seem to have no souls. Or if we have them, they have nothing to hang on to. Meanwhile, Sweetie goes on shouting. [*He takes refuge in the deck chair*]

THE COUNTESS [*rising*] Oh, what are you gassing about? I am not shouting. I should be a good woman if it wasnt so dull. If youre goodnatured, you just get put upon. Who are the good women? Those that enjoy being dull and like being put upon. Theyve no appetites. Life's thrown away on them: they get nothing out of it.

THE PATIENT. Well, come, Sweetie! What do you get out of it?

THE COUNTESS. Excitement: thats what I get out of it. Look at Popsy and me! We're always planning robberies. Of course I know it's mostly imagination; but the fun is in the planning and the expectation. Even if we did them and were caught, there would be the excitement of being tried and being in all the papers. Look at poor Harry Smiler that murdered the cop in Croydon! When he came and told us what he'd done Popsy offered to go out and get him some cyanide to poison himself; for it was a dead sure thing that he'd be caught and bumped off. "What!" says Harry; "and lose the excitement of being tried for my life! I'd rather be hanged" he says; and hanged he was. And I say it must have been almost worth it. After all, he'd have died anyhow: perhaps of something really painful. Harry wasnt a bad man really; but he couldnt bear dullness. He had a wonderful collection of pistols that he had begun as a boy: he picked up a lot in the war. Just for the romance of it, you know: he meant no harm. But he'd never shot anyone with them; and at last the temptation was too great and he went out and shot the cop. Just for nothing but the feeling that he'd fired the thing off and done somebody in with it. When Popsy asked him why he'd done it, all he could say was that it was a sort of fulfilment. But it gives you an idea, doesnt it, of what I mean? [*She sits down again, relieved by her outburst*].

AUBREY. All it means is a low vitality. Here is a man with all the miracles of the universe to stagger his imagination and all the problems of human destiny to employ his mind, and he goes out and shoots an innocent policeman because he can think of nothing more interesting to do. Quite right to hang him. And all the people who can find nothing more exciting to do than to crowd into the court to watch him being sentenced to death should have been hanged too. You will be hanged someday, Sweetie, because you have not what people call a richly stored mind. I have tried to educate you—

THE COUNTESS. Yes: you gave me books to read. But I couldnt read them: they were as dull as ditchwater. Ive tried crossword puzzles to occupy my mind and keep me off planning robberies; but what crossword puzzle is half the fun and excitement of picking somebody's pocket, let alone that you cant live by it? You

wanted me to take to drink to keep me quiet. But I
dont like being drunk; and what would become of my
good looks if I did? Ten bottles of champagne couldnt
make you feel as you do when you walk past a policeman who has only to stop you and search you to put
you away for three years.

THE PATIENT. Pops: did you really try to set her
drinking? What a thoroughpaced blackguard you are!

AUBREY. She is much better company when she's half
drunk. Listen to her now, when she is sober!

THE PATIENT. Sweetie: are you really having such a
jolly time after all? You began by threatening to give
up our exciting enterprise because it is so dull.

AUBREY. She is free. There is the sergeant. And there
is always the hope of something turning up and the
sense of being ready for it without having to break all
the shackles and throw down all the walls that im-
prison a respectable woman.

THE PATIENT. Well, what about me?

AUBREY [puzzled] Well, what about you? You are
free, arnt you?

THE PATIENT [rising very deliberately, and going behind him to his left hand, which she picks up and
fondles as she sermonizes, seated on the arm of his
chair] My angel love, you have rescued me from respectability so completely that I have for a month past
been living the life of a mountain goat. I have got rid
of my anxious worrying mother as completely as a
weaned kid, and I no longer hate her. My slavery to
cooks stuffing me with long meals of fish, flesh, and
fowl is a thing of the miserable past: I eat dates and
bread and water and raw onions when I can get them;
and when I cant get them I fast, with the result that I

have forgotten what illness means; and if I ran away from you two neither of you could catch me; and if you did I could fight the pair of you with one hand tied behind me. I revel in all your miracles of the universe: the delicious dawns, the lovely sunsets, the changing winds, the cloud pictures, the flowers, the animals and their ways, the birds and insects and reptiles. Every day is a day of adventure with its cold and heat, its light and darkness, its cycles of exultant vigor and exhaustion, hunger and satiety, its longings for action that change into a longing for sleep, its thoughts of heavenly things that change so suddenly into a need for food.

AUBREY. What more could any mortal desire?

THE PATIENT [*seizing him by the ears*] Liar.

AUBREY. Thank you. You mean, I presume, that these things do not satisfy you: you want me as well.

THE PATIENT. You!! You!!! you selfish lazy sugary tongued blackguard. [*Releasing him*] No: I included you with the animals and their ways, just as I included Sweetie and the sergeant.

THE COUNTESS. You let Sweetie and her sergeant alone: d'y'hear? I have had enough of that joke on me.

THE PATIENT [*rising and taking her by the chin to turn her face up*] It is no joke, Sweetiest: it is the dead solemn earnest. I called Pops a liar, Sweetie, because all this is not enough. The glories of nature dont last any decently active person a week, unless theyre professional naturalists or mathematicians or a painter or something. I want something sensible to do. A beaver has a jolly time because it has to build its dam and bring up its family. I want my little job like the beaver. If I do nothing but contemplate the universe there is so much in it that is cruel and terrible and wantonly evil, and so much more that is oppressively astronomical and endless and inconceivable and impossible, that I shall just go stark raving mad and be taken back to my mother with straws in my hair. The truth is, I am free; I am healthy; I am happy; and I am utterly miserable. [*Turning on Aubrey*] Do you hear? Utterly miserable.

AUBREY [*losing his temper*] And what do you suppose I am? Here with nothing to do but drag about two damn' silly women and talk to them.

THE COUNTESS. It's worse for them. They have to listen to you.

THE PATIENT. I despise you. I hate you. You—you—you—you gentleman thief. What right has a thief to be a gentleman? Sweetie is bad enough, heaven knows, with her vulgarity and her low cunning: always trying to get the better of somebody or to get hold of a man; but at least she's a woman; and she's real. Men are not real: theyre all talk, talk, talk—

THE COUNTESS [*half rising*] You keep a civil tongue in your head: do you hear?

THE PATIENT. Another syllable of your cheek, Sweetie; and I'll give you a hiding that will keep you screaming for half an hour. [*Sweetie subsides*]. I want to beat somebody: I want to kill somebody. I shall end by killing the two of you. What are we, we three glorious adventurers? Just three inefficient fertilizers.

AUBREY. What on earth do you mean by that?

THE PATIENT. Yes: inefficient fertilizers. We do nothing but convert good food into bad manure. We are walking factories of bad manure: thats what we are.

THE COUNTESS [*rising*] Well, I am not going to sit here and listen to that sort of talk. You ought to be ashamed of yourself.

AUBREY [*rising also, shocked*] Miss Mopply: there are certain disgusting truths that no lady would throw in the teeth of her fellow creatures—

THE PATIENT. I am not a lady: I am free now to say what I please. How do you like it?

THE COUNTESS [*relenting*] Look here, dearie. You mustnt go off at the deep end like this. You— [*The patients turns fiercely on her: she screams*]. Ah-a-a-ah! Popsy: she's mad. Save me. [*She runs away, out past the pavilion*].

AUBREY. What is the matter with you? Are you out of your senses? [*He tries to hold her; but she sends him sprawling*].

THE PATIENT. No. I am exercising my freedom. The freedom you preached. The freedom you made possible for me. You dont like to hear Sweetie's lower centres shouting. Well, now you hear my higher centres shouting. You dont seem to like it any better.

AUBREY. Mops: youre hysterical. You felt splendid an hour ago; and you will feel splendid again an hour from now. You will always feel splendid if you keep yourself fit.

THE PATIENT. Fit for what? A lost dog feels fit: thats what makes him stray; but he's the unhappiest thing alive. I am a lost dog: a tramp, a vagabond. Ive got nothing to do. Ive got nowhere to go. Sweetie's miserable; and youre miserable; and I'm miserable; and I shall just kick you and beat you to a jelly.

She rushes at him. He dodges her and runs off past the hut. At that moment Tallboys returns with Meek past the other side of the hut; and the patient, unable to check herself, crashes into his arms.

TALLBOYS [*sternly*] Whats this? What are you doing here? Why are you making this noise? Dont clench your fists in my presence. [*She droops obsequiously*]. Whats the matter?

THE PATIENT [*salaaming and chanting*] Bmal elttil a dah yram, Tuan.

TALLBOYS. Can you speak English?

THE PATIENT. No Engliss.

TALLBOYS. Or French?

THE PATIENT. No Frennss, Tuan. Wons sa etihw saw eceelf sti.

TALLBOYS. Very well: dont do it again. Now off with you.

She goes out backward into the pavilion, salaaming. Tallboys sits down in the deck chair.

TALLBOYS [*to Meek*] Here, you. You say youre the interpreter. Did you understand what that girl said to me?

MEEK. Yessir.

TALLBOYS. What dialect was it? It didnt sound like what the natives speak here.

MEEK. No sir. I used to speak it at school. English back slang, sir.

TALLBOYS. Back slang? What do you mean?

MEEK. English spelt backwards. She reversed the order of the words too, sir. That shews that she has those two little speeches off by heart.

TALLBOYS. But how could a native girl do such a thing? I couldnt do it myself.

MEEK. That shews that she's not a native girl, sir.

TALLBOYS. But this must be looked into. Were you able to pick up what she said?

MEEK. Only bmal elttil, sir. That was quite easy. It

put me on to the rest.

TALLBOYS. But what does bmal elttil mean?

MEEK. Little lamb, sir.

TALLBOYS. She called me a little lamb!

MEEK. No sir. All she said was "Mary had a little lamb." And when you asked her could she speak French she said, of course, "Its fleece was white as snow."

TALLBOYS. But that was insolence.

MEEK. It got her out of her difficulty, sir.

TALLBOYS. This is very serious. The woman is passing herself off on the Countess as a native servant.

MEEK. Do you think so, sir?

TALLBOYS. I dont think so: I know so. Dont be a fool, man. Pull yourself together, and dont make silly answers.

MEEK. Yessir. No sir.

TALLBOYS [*angrily bawling at him*] "Ba Ba black sheep: have you any wool? Yes sir, no sir, three bags full." Dont say yessir no sir to me.

MEEK. No sir.

TALLBOYS. Go and fetch that girl back. Not a word to her about my finding her out, mind. When I have finished with her you will explain to me about those maroons.

MEEK. Yessir. [*He goes into the pavilion*].

TALLBOYS. Hurry up. [*He settles himself comfortably and takes out his cigaret case*].

The Countess peers round the corner of the pavilion to see whether she may safely return. Aubrey makes a similar reconnaissance round the corner of the hut.

THE COUNTESS. Here I am again, you see. [*She smiles fascinatingly at the Colonel and sits down on her stool*].

AUBREY. Moi aussi. May I— [*he stretches himself on*

the rug].

TALLBOYS [*sitting up and putting the cigaret case back in his pocket*] Just in the nick of time. I was about to send for you. I have made a very grave discovery. That native servant of yours is not a native. Her lingo is a ridiculous fraud. She is an English-woman.

AUBREY. You dont say so!

THE COUNTESS. Oh, impossible.

TALLBOYS. Not a doubt of it. She's a fraud: take care of your jewels. Or else—and this is what I suspect —she's a spy.

AUBREY. A spy! But we are not at war.

TALLBOYS. The League of Nations has spies everywhere. [*To the Countess*] You must allow me to search her luggage at once, before she knows that I have found her out.

THE COUNTESS. But I have missed nothing. I am sure she hasnt stolen anything. What do you want to search her luggage for?

TALLBOYS. For maroons.

THE COUNTESS } [*together*] {Maroons!
AUBREY } {Maroons!

TALLBOYS. Yes, maroons. I inspected the stores this morning; and the maroons are missing. I particularly wanted them to recall me at lunch time when I go sketching. I am rather a dab at water-colors. And there is not a single maroon left. There should be fifteen.

AUBREY. Oh, I can clear that up. It's one of your men: Meek. He goes about on a motor bicycle with a sack full of maroons and a lot of wire. He said he was surveying. He was evidently very anxious to get rid of me; so I did not press my inquiries. But that accounts for the maroons.

TALLBOYS. Not at all. This is very serious. Meek is a half witted creature who should never have been enlisted. He is like a child: this woman could do anything she pleases with him.

THE COUNTESS. But what could she possibly want with maroons?

TALLBOYS. I dont know. This expedition has been sent out without the sanction of the League of Nations. We always forget to consult it when there is anything serious in hand. The woman may be an emissary of the League. She may be working against us.

THE COUNTESS. But even so, what harm can she do us?

TALLBOYS [*tapping his revolver*] My dear lady, do you suppose I am carrying this for fun? Dont you realize that the hills here are full of hostile tribes who may try to raid us at any moment? Look at that electric horn there. If it starts honking, look out; for it will mean that a body of tribesmen has been spotted advancing on us.

THE COUNTESS [*alarmed*] If I'd known that, you wouldnt have got me here. Is that so, Popsy?

AUBREY. Well, yes; but it doesnt matter: they're afraid of us.

TALLBOYS. Yes, because they dont know that we are a mere handful of men. But if this woman is in communication with them and has got hold of that idiot Meek, we may have them down on us like a swarm of hornets. I dont like this at all. I must get to the bottom of it at once. Ah! here she comes.

Meek appears at the entrance to the pavilion. He stands politely aside to let the patient pass him, and remains there.

MEEK. The colonel would like a word with you, Miss.

AUBREY. Go easy with her, Colonel. She can run like a deer. And she has muscles of iron. You had better turn out the guard before you tackle her.

TALLBOYS. Pooh! Here, you!

The patient comes to him past the Countess with an air of disarming innocence; falls on her knees; lifts her palms; and smites the ground with her forehead.

TALLBOYS. They tell me you can run fast. Well, a bullet can run faster. [*He taps his revolver*]. Do you understand that?

THE PATIENT [*salaaming*] Bmal elttil a dah yram wons sa etihw saw eceelf tsi—

TALLBOYS [*tonitruant*] And everywhere that Mary went—

THE PATIENT [*adroitly cutting in*] That lamb was sure to go. Got me, Colonel. How clever of you! Well, what of it?

TALLBOYS. That is what I intend to find out. You are not a native.

THE PATIENT. Yes, of Somerset.

TALLBOYS. Precisely. Well, why are you disguised? Why did you try to make me believe that you dont understand English?

THE PATIENT. For a lark, Colonel.

TALLBOYS. Thats not good enough. Why have you passed yourself off on this lady as a native servant? Being a servant is no lark. Answer me. Dont stand there trying to invent a lie. Why did you pretend to be a servant?

THE PATIENT. One has so much more control of the house as a servant than as a mistress nowadays, Colonel.

TALLBOYS. Very smart, that. You will tell me next that one controls a regiment much more effectively as a private than as a colonel, eh?

The klaxon sounds stridently. The Colonel draws his revolver and makes a dash for the top of the sandhill, but is outraced by Meek, who gets there first and takes the word of command with irresistible authority, leaving him stupent. Aubrey, who has scrambled to his feet, moves towards the sand dunes to see what is happening. Sweetie clutches the patient's arm in terror and drags her towards the pavilion. She is fiercely shaken off; and Mops stands her ground defiantly and runs towards the sound of the guns when they begin.

MEEK. Stand to. Charge your magazines. Stand by the maroons. How many do you make them, sergeant? How far off?

SERGEANT FIELDING [*invisible*] Forty horse. Nine hundred yards, about, I make it.

MEEK. Rifles at the ready. Cut-offs open. Sights up to eighteen hundred, right over their heads: no hitting. Ten rounds rapid: fire. [*Fusillade of rifles*]. How is that?

SERGEANT'S VOICE. Theyre coming on, sir.

MEEK. Number one maroons: ready. Contact. [*Formidable explosions on the right*]. How is that?

SERGEANT'S VOICE. Theyve stopped.

MEEK. Number two maroons ready. Contact. [*Explosions on the left*]. How is that?

SERGEANT'S VOICE. Bolted, sir, every man of them.

Meek returns from the hill in the character of an insignificant private, followed by Aubrey, to the Colonel's left and right respectively.

MEEK. Thats all right, sir. Excuse interruption.

TALLBOYS. Oh! You call this an interruption?

MEEK. Yessir: theres nothing in it to trouble you

about. Shall I draw up the report, sir? Important engagement: enemy routed: no British casualties. D.S.O. for you, perhaps, sir.

TALLBOYS. Private Meek: may I ask—if you will pardon my presumption—who is in command of this expedition, you or I?

MEEK. You, sir.

TALLBOYS [*repouching the revolver*] You flatter me. Thank you. May I ask, further, who the devil gave you leave to plant the entire regimental stock of maroons all over the hills and explode them in the face of the enemy?

MEEK. It was the duty of the intelligence orderly, sir. I'm the intelligence orderly. I had to make the enemy believe that the hills are bristling with British cannon. They think that now, sir. No more trouble from them.

TALLBOYS. Indeed! Quartermaster's clerk, interpreter, intelligence orderly. Any further rank of which I have not been informed?

MEEK. No sir.

TALLBOYS. Quite sure youre not a fieldmarshal, eh?

MEEK. Quite sure, sir. I never was anything higher than a colonel.

TALLBOYS. You a colonel? What do you mean?

MEEK. Not a real colonel, sir. Mostly a brevet, sir, to save appearances when I had to take command.

TALLBOYS. And how do you come to be a private now?

MEEK. I prefer the ranks, sir. I have a freer hand. And the conversation in the officers' mess doesnt suit me. I always resign a commission and enlist again.

TALLBOYS. Always! How many commissions have you held?

MEEK. I dont quite remember, sir. Three, I think.

TALLBOYS. Well, I am dashed!

THE PATIENT. Oh, Colonel! And you mistook this great military genius for a half wit!!!

TALLBOYS [*with aplomb*] Naturally. The symptoms are precisely the same. [*To Meek*] Dismiss.

Meek salutes and trots smartly out past the hut.

AUBREY. By Jove!!

THE COUNTESS. Well I ne— [*Correcting herself*] Tiens, tiens, tiens, tiens!

THE PATIENT. What are you going to do about him, Colonel?

TALLBOYS. Madam: the secret of command, in the army and elsewhere, is never to waste a moment doing anything that can be delegated to a subordinate. I have a passion for sketching in watercolors. Hitherto the work of commanding my regiment has interfered very seriously with its gratification. Henceforth I shall devote myself almost entirely to sketching, and leave the command of the expedition to Private Meek. And since you all seem to be on more intimate terms with him than I can claim, will you be good enough to convey to him— casually, you understand—that I already possess the D.S.O. and that what I am out for at present is a K.C.B. Or rather, to be strictly accurate, that is what my wife is out for. For myself, my sole concern for the moment is whether I should paint that sky with Prussian blue or with cobalt.

THE COUNTESS. Fancy you wasting your time on painting pictures!

TALLBOYS. Countess: I paint pictures to make me feel sane. Dealing with men and women makes me feel mad. Humanity always fails me: Nature never.

ACT III

A narrow gap leading down to the beach through masses of soft brown sandstone, pitted with natural grottoes. Sand and big stones in the foreground. Two of the grottoes are accessible from the beach by mounting from the stones, which make rough platforms in front of them. The soldiers have amused themselves by hewing them into a rude architecture and giving them fancy names. The one on your right as you descend the rough path through the gap is taller than it is broad, and has a natural pillar and a stone like an altar in it, giving a Gothic suggestion which has been assisted by knocking the top of the opening into something like a pointed arch, and surmounting it with the inscription SN PAULS. *The grotto to the left is much wider. It contains a bench long enough to accommodate two persons; its recesses are illuminated rosily by bulbs wrapped in pink paper; and some scholarly soldier has carved above it in Greek characters the word* Αγαπεμονε, *beneath which is written in red chalk* THE ABODE OF LOVE, *under which again some ribald has added in white chalk,* NO NEED TO WASTE THE ELECTRIC LIGHT.*

For the moment The Abode of Love has been taken possession of by the sergeant, a wellbuilt handsome man, getting on for forty. He is sitting on the bench, and is completely absorbed in two books, comparing them with rapt attention.

St Pauls is also occupied. A vary tall gaunt elder, by his dress and bearing a well-to-do Englishman, sits on a stone at the altar, resting his elbows on it with his chin in his hands. He is in the deepest mourning; and his attitude is one of hopeless dejection.

Sweetie, now fully and brilliantly dressed, comes slowly down the path through the gap, moody and bored. On the beach she finds nothing to interest her until the sergeant unconsciously attracts her notice by finding some remarkable confirmation or contradiction between his two books, and smiting one of them appreciatively with his fist. She instantly brightens up; climbs to the mouth of the grotto eagerly; and posts herself beside him, on his right. But he is so rapt in his books that she waits in vain to be noticed.

SWEETIE [*contemplating him ardently*] Ahem!

The sergeant looks up. Seeing who it is, he springs to his feet and stands to attention.

SWEETIE [*giving herself no airs*] You neednt stand up for me, you know.

THE SERGEANT [*stiffly*] Beg pardon, your ladyship. I was not aware of your ladyship's presence.

SWEETIE. Can all that stuff, Sergeant. [*She sits on the bench on his right*]. Dont lets waste time. This place is as dull for me as it is for you. Dont you think we two could amuse ourselves a bit if we were friends?

THE SERGEANT [*with stern contempt*] No, my lady, I dont. I saw a lot of that in the war: pretty ladies brightening up the hospitals and losing their silly heads, let alone upsetting the men; and I dont hold with it. Keep to your class: I'll keep to mine.

SWEETIE. My class! Garn! I'm no countess; and I'm fed up with pretending to be one. Didnt you guess?

THE SERGEANT [*resuming his seat and treating her as*

one of his own class] Why should I trouble to start guessing about you? Any girl can be a countess nowadays if she's goodlooking enough to pick up a count.

SWEETIE. Oh! You think I'm goodlooking, do you?

THE SERGEANT. Come! If youre not a countess what are you? Whats the game, eh?

SWEETIE. The game, darling, is that youre my fancy. I love you.

THE SERGEANT. Whats that to me? A man of my figure can have his pick.

SWEETIE. Not here, dear. Theres only one other white woman within fifty miles; and she's a real lady. She wouldn't look at you.

THE SERGEANT. Well, thats a point. Thats a point, certainly.

SWEETIE [*snuggling to him*] Yes, isnt it?

THE SERGEANT [*suffering the advance but not responding*] This climate plays the devil with a man, no matter how serious minded he is.

SWEETIE [*slipping her arm through his*] Well, isnt it natural? Whats the use of pretending.

THE SERGEANT. Still, I'm not a man to treat a woman as a mere necessity. Many soldiers do: to them a woman is no more than a jar of marmalade, to be consumed and put away. I dont take that view. I admit that there is that side to it, and that for people incapable of anything better—mere animals as you might say—thats the beginning and the end of it. But to me thats only the smallest part of it. I like getting a woman's opinions. I like to explore her mind as well as her body. See these two little books I was deep in when you accosted me? I carry them with me wherever I go. I put the problems they raise for me to every woman I meet.

SWEETIE [*with growing misgiving*] What are they?

THE SERGEANT [*pointing to them successively*] The Bible. The Pilgrim's Progress from this world to that which is to come.

SWEETIE [*dismayed, trying to rise*] Oh, my God!

SERGEANT [*holding her ruthlessly in the crook of his elbow*] No you dont. Sit quiet; and dont take the name of the Lord your God in vain. If you believe in him, it's blasphemy: if you dont, it's nonsense. You must learn to exercise your mind: what is a woman without an active mind to a man but a mere convenience?

SWEETIE. I have plenty to exercise my mind looking after my own affairs. What I look to you for, my lad, is a bit of fun.

THE SERGEANT. Quite. But when men and women pick one another up just for a bit of fun, they find theyve picked up more than they bargained for, because men and women have a top storey as well as a ground floor; and you cant have the one without the other. Theyre always trying to; but it doesnt work. Youve picked up my mind as well as my body; and youve got to explore it. You thought you could have a face and a figure like mine with the limitations of a gorilla. Youre finding out your mistake: thats all.

SWEETIE. Oh, let me go: I have had enough of this. If I'd thought you were religious I'd have given you a wide berth, I tell you. Let me go, will you?

THE SERGEANT. Wait a bit. Nature may be using me as a sort of bait to draw you to take an interest in things of the mind. Nature may be using your pleasant animal warmth to stimulate my mind. I want your advice. I dont say I'll take it; but it may suggest something to me. You see, I'm in a mess.

SWEETIE. Well, of course. Youre in the sergeants' mess.

THE SERGEANT. Thats not the mess I mean. My mind's in a mess—a muddle. I used to be a religious man; but I'm not so clear about it as I was.

SWEETIE. Thank goodness for that, anyhow.

THE SERGEANT. Look at these two books. I used to believe every word of them because they seemed to have nothing to do with real life. But war brought those old stories home quite real; and then one starts asking questions. Look at this bit here [*he points to a page of The Pilgrim's Progress*]. It's on the very first page of it. "I am for certain informed that this our city will be burned with fire from heaven, in which fearful over-throw both myself, with thee my wife, and you my sweet babes, shall miserably come to ruin, except some way of escape can be found whereby we may be deliv-ered." Well, London and Paris and Berlin and Rome and the rest of them will be burned with fire from heaven all right in the next war: thats certain. Theyre all Cities of Destruction. And our Government chaps are running about with a great burden of corpses and debts on their backs, crying "What must we do to be saved?" There it is: not a story in a book as it used to be, but God's truth in the real actual world. And all the comfort they get is "Flee from the wrath to come." But where are they to flee to? There they are, meeting at Geneva or hobnobbing at Chequers over the weekend, asking one another, like the man in the book, "Whither must we flee?" And nobody can tell them. The man in the book says "Do you see yonder shining light?" Well, today the place is blazing with shining lights: shining lights in parliament, in the papers, in the churches, and in the books that they call Outlines—Outlines of History and Science and what not—and in spite of all their ballyhoo here we are waiting in the City of Destruction like so many sheep for the wrath to come. This uneducated tinker tells me the way is straight before us and so narrow that we cant miss it. But he starts by calling the place the wilderness of this world. Well, theres no road in a wilderness: you have to make one. All the straight roads are made by soldiers; and the soldiers didnt get to heaven along them. A lot of them landed up in the other place. No, John: you could tell a story well; and they say you were a soldier; but soldiers that try to make storytelling do for service end in the clink; and thats where they put you. Twelve years in Bedford Gaol, he got. He used to read the Bible in gaol; and—

SWEETIE. Well, what else was there to read there? It's all they give you in some gaols.

THE SERGEANT. How do you know that?

SWEETIE. Never you mind how I know it. It's nothing to do with you.

THE SERGEANT. Nothing to do with me! You dont know me, my lass. Some men would just order you off; but to me the most interesting thing in the world is the experience of a woman thats been shut up in a cell for years at a time with nothing but a Bible to read.

SWEETIE. Years! What are you talking about? The longest I ever did was nine months; and if anyone says I ever did a day longer she's a liar.

THE SERGEANT [laying his hand on the Bible] You could read that book from cover to cover in nine months.

SWEETIE. Some of it would drive you melancholy mad. It only got me into trouble: it did. The chaplain asked me what I was in for. Spoiling the Egyptians, I says; and heres chapter and verse for it. He went and reported me, the swine; and I lost seven days remission for it.

THE SERGEANT. Serve you right! I dont hold with spoiling the Egyptians. Before the war, spoiling the Egyptians was something holy. Now I see plainly it's nothing but thieving.

SWEETIE [*shocked*] Oh, you shouldnt say that. But what I say is, if Moses might do it why maynt I?

THE SERGEANT. If thats the effect it had on your mind, it's a bad effect. Some of this scripture is all right. Do justice; love mercy; and walk humbly before your God. That appeals to a man if only it could be set out in plain army regulations. But all this thieving, and slaughtering your enemies without giving quarter, and offering up human sacrifices, and thinking you can do what you like to other people because youre the chosen people of God, and you are in the right and everyone else is in the wrong: how does that look when you have had four years of the real thing instead of merely reading about it. No: damn it, we're civilized men; and though it may have gone down with those old Jews it isnt religion. And, if it isnt, where are we? Thats what I want to know.

SWEETIE. And is this all you care about? Sitting here and thinking of things like that?

THE SERGEANT. Well, somebody must think about them, or whats going to become of us all? The officers wont think about them. The colonel goes out sketching: the lootnants go out and kill the birds and animals, or play polo. They wont flee from the wrath to come, not they. When they wont do their military duties I have to do them. It's the same with our religious duties. It's the chaplain's job, not mine; but when you get a real religious chaplain you find he doesnt believe any of the old stuff; and if you get a gentleman, all he cares about is to shew you that he's a real sport and not a mealy mouthed parson. So I have to puzzle it out for myself.

SWEETIE. Well, God help the woman that marries you: thats all I have to say to you. I dont call you a man. [*She rises quickly to escape from him*].

THE SERGEANT [*also rising, and seizing her in a very hearty embrace*] Not a man, eh? [*He kisses her*] How does that feel, Judy?

SWEETIE [*struggling, but not very resolutely*] You let me go, will you. I dont want you now.

THE SERGEANT. You will if I kiss you half a dozen times, more than you ever wanted anything in your life before. Thats a hard fact of human nature; and it's one of the facts that religion has to make room for.

SWEETIE. Oh, well, kiss me and have done with it. You cant kiss and talk about religion at the same time.

THE ELDER [*springing from his cell to the platform in front of it*] Forbear this fooling, both of you. You, sir, are not an ignorant man: you know that the universe is wrecked.

SWEETIE [*clinging to the sergeant*] He's mad.

THE ELDER. I am sane in a world of lunatics.

THE SERGEANT [*putting Sweetie away*] It's a queer thing, isnt it, that though there is a point at which I'd rather kiss a woman than do anything else in the world, yet I'd rather be shot than let anyone see me doing it?

THE ELDER. Sir: women are not, as they suppose, more interesting than the universe. When the universe is crumbling let women be silent; and let men rise to something nobler than kissing them.

The Sergeant, interested and overawed, sits down quietly and makes Sweetie sit beside him as before. The Elder continues to declaim with fanatical intensity.

THE ELDER. Yes, sir: the universe of Isaac Newton, which has been an impregnable citadel of modern civilization for three hundred years, has crumbled like the walls of Jericho before the criticism of Einstein. Newton's universe was the stronghold of rational Determinism: the stars in their orbits obeyed immutably fixed laws; and when we turned from surveying their vastness to study the infinite littleness of the atoms, there too we found the electrons in their orbits obeying the same universal laws. Every moment of time dictated and determined the following moment, and was itself dictated and determined by the moment that came before it. Everything was calculable: everything happened because it must: the commandments were erased from the tables of the law; and in their place came the cosmic algebra: the equations of the mathematicians. Here was my faith: here I found my dogma of infallibility: I, who scorned alike the Catholic with his vain dream of responsible Free Will, and the Protestant with his pretence of private judgment. And now—now—what is left of it? The orbit of the electron obeys no law: it chooses one path and rejects another: it is as capricious as the planet Mercury, who wanders from his road to warm his hands at the sun. All is caprice: the calculable world has become incalculable: Purpose and Design, the pretexts for all the vilest superstitions, have risen from the dead to cast down the mighty from their seats and put paper crowns on presumptuous fools. Formerly, when differences with my wife, or business worries, tried me too hard, I sought consolation and reassurance in our natural history museums, where I could forget all common cares in wondering at the diversity of forms and colors in the birds and fishes and animals, all produced without the agency of any designer by the operation of Natural Selection. Today I dare not enter an aquarium, because I can see nothing in those grotesque monsters of the deep but the caricatures of some freakish demon artist: some Zeus-Mephistopheles with paintbox and plasticine, trying to surpass himself in the production of fantastic and laughable creatures to people a Noah's ark for his baby. I have to rush from the building lest I go mad, crying, like the man in your book, "What must I do to be saved?" Nothing can save us from a perpetual headlong fall into a bottomless abyss but a solid footing of dogma; and we no sooner agree to that than we find that the only trustworthy dogma is that there is no dogma. As I stand here I am falling into that abyss, down, down, down. We are all falling into it; and our dizzy brains can utter nothing but madness. My wife has died cursing me. I do not know how to live without her: we were unhappy together for forty years. My son, whom I brought up to be an incorruptible Godfearing atheist, has become a thief and a scoundrel; and I can say nothing to him but "Go, boy: perish in your villainy; for neither your father nor anyone else can now give you a good reason for being a man of honor."

He turns from them and is rushing distractedly away when Aubrey, in white tropicals, comes strolling along the beach from the St Pauls side, and hails him nonchalantly.

AUBREY. Hullo, father, is it really you? I thought I heard the old trombone: I couldnt mistake it. How the dickens did you turn up here?

THE ELDER [*to the sergeant*] This is my prodigal son.

AUBREY. I am not a prodigal son. The prodigal son was a spendthrift and neer-do-weel who was reduced to eating the husks that the swine did eat. I am not ruined: I am rolling in money. I have never owed a farthing to any man. I am a model son; but I regret to say that you are very far from being a model father.

THE ELDER. What right have you to say that, sir? In what way have I fallen short?

AUBREY. You tried to thwart my manifest destiny. Nature meant me for the Church. I had to get ordained secretly.

THE ELDER. Ordained! You dared to get ordained without my knowledge!

AUBREY. Of course. You objected. How could I have done it with your knowledge? You would have stopped my allowance.

THE ELDER [*sitting down on the nearest stone, overwhelmed*] My son a clergyman! This will kill me.

AUBREY [*coolly taking another stone, on his father's right*] Not a bit of it: fathers are not so easily killed. It was at the university that I became what was then called a sky pilot. When the war took me it seemed natural that I should pursue that avocation as a member of the air force. As a flying ace I won a very poorly designed silver medal for committing atrocities which were irreconcilable with the profession of a Christian clergyman. When I was wounded and lost my nerve for flying, I became an army chaplain. I then found myself obliged to tell mortally wounded men that they were dying in a state of grace and were going straight to heaven when as a matter of fact they were dying in mortal sin and going elsewhere. To expiate this blasphemy I kept as much under fire as possible; but my nerve failed again: I had to take three months leave and go into a nursing home. In that home I met my doom.

THE ELDER. What do you mean by your doom? You are alive and well, to my sorrow and shame.

AUBREY. To be precise, I met Sweetie. Thats Sweetie.

SWEETIE. Very pleased to meet Popsy's father, I'm sure.

THE ELDER. My son was called Popsy in his infancy, I put a stop to it, on principle, when he entered on his sixth year. It is strange to hear the name from your lips after so long an interval.

SWEETIE. I always ask a man what his mother called him, and call him that. It takes the starch out of him, somehow.

AUBREY [resuming his narrative] Sweetie was quite the rottenest nurse that ever raised the mortality of a hospital by ten per cent. But—

SWEETIE. Oh, what a lie! It was the other nurses that killed the men: waking them up at six in the morning and washing them! Half of them died of chills.

AUBREY. Well, you will not deny that you were the prettiest woman in the place.

SWEETIE. You thought so, anyhow.

THE ELDER. Oh, cease—cease this trifling. I cannot endure this unending sex appeal.

AUBREY. During the war it was found that sex appeal was as necessary for wounded or shellshocked soldiers as skilled nursing; so pretty girls were allowed to pose as nurses because they could sit about on beds and prevent the men from going mad. Sweetie did not prevent me going mad: on the contrary, she drove me mad. I saw in Sweetie not only every charm, but every virtue. And she returned my love. When I left that nursing home, she left it too. I was discharged as cured on the third of the month: she had been kicked out on the first. The trained staff could stand a good deal; but they could not stand Sweetie.

SWEETIE. They were jealous; and you know it.

AUBREY. I daresay they were. Anyhow, Sweetie and I took the same lodgings; and she was faithful to me for ten days. It was a record for her.

SWEETIE. Popsy: are you going to give the whole show away, or only part of it? The Countess Valbrioni would like to know.

AUBREY. We may as well be frank up to the point at which we should lose money by it. But perhaps I am boring the company.

THE ELDER. Complete your confession, sir. You have just said that you and this lady took the same lodging. Am I to understand that you are husband and wife?

SWEETIE. We might have been if we could have depended on you for a good time. But how could I marry an army chaplain with nothing but his pay and an atheist for his father?

AUBREY. So that was the calculation, Sweetie, was it? I never dreamt that the idea of marriage had occurred to either of us. It certainly never occurred to me. I went to live with you quite simply because I felt I could not live without you. The improbability of that statement is the measure of my infatuation.

SWEETIE. Dont you be so spiteful. Did I give you a good time or did I not?

AUBREY. Heavenly. That also seems improbable; but it is gospel truth.

THE ELDER. Wretched boy: do not dare to trifle with me. You said just now that you owe no man anything, and that you are rolling in money. Where did you get that money?

AUBREY. I stole a very valuable pearl necklace and restored it to the owner. She rewarded me munificently. Hence my present opulence. Honesty is the best policy —sometimes.

THE ELDER. Worse even than a clergyman! A thief!

AUBREY. Why make such a fuss about nothing?

THE ELDER. Do you call the theft of a pearl necklace nothing?

AUBREY. Less than nothing, compared to the things I have done with your approval. I was hardly more than a boy when I first dropped a bomb on a sleeping village. I cried all night after doing that. Later on I swooped into a street and sent machine gun bullets into a crowd of civilians: women, children, and all. I was past crying by that time. And now you preach to me about stealing a pearl necklace! Doesnt that seem a little ridiculous?

THE SERGEANT. That was war, sir.

AUBREY. It was me, Sergeant: ME. You cannot divide my conscience into a war department and a peace department. Do you suppose that a man who will commit murder for political ends will hesitate to commit theft for personal ends? Do you suppose you can make a man the mortal enemy of sixty millions of his fellow creatures without making him a little less scrupulous about his next door neighbor?

THE ELDER. I did not approve. Had I been of military age I should have been a conscientious objector.

AUBREY. Oh, you were a conscientious objector to

everything, even to God. But my mother was an enthusiast for everything: that was why you never could get on with her. She would have shoved me into the war if I had needed any shoving. She shoved my brother into it, though he did not believe a word of all the lies we were stuffed with, and didnt want to go. He was killed; and when it came out afterwards that he was right, and that we were all a parcel of fools killing one another for nothing, she lost the courage to face life, and died of it.

THE SERGEANT. Well, sir, I'd never let a son of mine talk to me like that. Let him have a bit of your Determinism, sir.

THE FATHER [*rising impulsively*] Determinism is gone, shattered, buried with a thousand dead religions, evaporated with the clouds of a million forgotten winters. The science I pinned my faith to is bankrupt: its tales were more foolish than all the miracles of the priests, its cruelties more horrible than all the atrocities of the Inquisition. Its spread of enlightenment has been a spread of cancer: its counsels that were to have established the millennium have led straight to European suicide. And I—I who believed in it as no religious fanatic has ever believed in his superstition! For its sake I helped to destroy the faith of millions of worshippers in the temples of a thousand creeds. And now look at me and behold the supreme tragedy of the atheist who has lost his faith—his faith in atheism, for which more martyrs have perished than for all the creeds put together. Here I stand, dumb before my scoundrel of a son; for that is what you are, boy, a common scoundrel and nothing else.

AUBREY. Well, why not? If I become an honest man

I shall become a poor man; and then nobody will respect me: nobody will admire me: nobody will say thank you to me. If on the contrary I am bold, unscrupulous, acquisitive, successful and rich, everyone will respect me, admire me, court me, grovel before me. Then no doubt I shall be able to afford the luxury of honesty. I learnt that from my religious education.

THE ELDER. How dare you say that you had a religious education. I shielded you from that, at least.

AUBREY. You thought you did, old man; but you reckoned without my mother.

THE ELDER. What!

AUBREY. You forbad me to read the Bible; but my mother made me learn three verses of it every day, and whacked me if I could not repeat them without misplacing a word. She threatened to whack me still worse if I told you.

THE ELDER [*thunderstruck*] Your mother!!!

AUBREY. So I learnt my lesson. Six days on the make, and on the seventh shalt thou rest. I shall spend another six years on the make, and then I shall retire and be a saint.

THE ELDER. A saint! Say rather the ruined son of an incorrigibly superstitious mother. Retire now—from the life you have dishonored. There is the sea. Go. Drown yourself. In that graveyard there are no lying epitaphs. [*He mounts to his chapel and again gives way to utter dejection*].

AUBREY [*unconcerned*] I shall do better as a saint. A few thousands to the hospitals and the political party funds will buy me a halo as large as Sweetie's sun hat. That is my program. What have any of you to say against it?

THE SERGEANT. Not the program of a gentleman, as I understand the word, sir.

AUBREY. You cannot be a gentleman on less than fifty thousand a year nowadays, sergeant.

THE SERGEANT. You can in the army, by God.

AUBREY. Yes: because you drop bombs on sleeping villages. And even then you have to be an officer. Are you a gentleman?

THE SERGEANT. No, sir: it wouldnt pay me. I couldnt afford it.

Disturbance. A voice is heard in complaint and lamentation. It is that of the Elderly Lady, Mrs Mopply. She is pursuing Colonel Tallboys down the path through the gap, the lady distracted and insistent, the colonel almost equally distracted: she clutching him and stopping him: he breaking loose and trying to get away from her. She is dressed in black precisely as if she were in Cheltenham, except that she wears a sun helmet. He is equipped with a box of sketching materials slung over his shoulder, an easel, which he has tucked under his left arm, and a sun umbrella, a substantial affair of fawn lined with red, podgily rolled up, which he carries in his right hand.

MRS MOPPLY. I wont be patient. I wont be quiet. My child is being murdered.

TALLBOYS. I tell you she is not being murdered. Will you be good enough to excuse me whilst I attend to my business.

MRS MOPPLY. Your business is to save my child. She is starving.

TALLBOYS. Nonsense. Nobody starves in this country. There are plenty of dates. Will you be good enough—

MRS MOPPLY. Do you think my child can live on

dates? She has to have a sole for breakfast, a cup of nourishing soup at eleven, a nice chop and a sweet-bread for lunch, a pint of beef-tea with her ordinary afternoon tea, and a chicken and some lamb or veal—

TALLBOYS. Will you be good enough—

MRS MOPPLY. My poor delicate child with nothing to eat but dates! And she is the only one I have left: they were all delicate—

TALLBOYS. I really must— [*He breaks away and hurries off along the beach past the Abode of Love*].

MRS MOPPLY [*running after him*] Colonel, Colonel: you might have the decency to listen to a distracted mother for a moment. Colonel: my child is dying. She may be dead for all I know. And nobody is doing anything: nobody cares. Oh dear, wont you listen— [*Her voice is lost in the distance*].

Whilst they are staring mutely after the retreating pair, the patient, still in her slave girl attire, but with some brilliant variations, comes down the path.

THE PATIENT. My dream has become a nightmare. My mother has pursued me to these shores. I cannot shake her off. No woman can shake off her mother. There should be no mothers: there should be only women, strong women able to stand by themselves, not clingers. I would kill all the clingers. Mothers cling: daughters cling: we are all like drunken women clinging to lamp posts: none of us stands upright.

THE ELDER. There is great comfort in clinging, and great loneliness in standing alone.

THE PATIENT. Hallo! [*She climbs to the St Pauls platform and peers into the cell*]. A sententious anchorite! [*To Aubrey*]. Who is he?

AUBREY. The next worst thing to a mother: a father.

THE ELDER. A most unhappy father.

AUBREY. My father, in fact.

THE PATIENT. If only I had had a father to stand between me and my mother's care. Oh, that I had been an orphan!

THE SERGEANT. You will be, miss, if the old lady drives the colonel too hard. She has been at him all the morning, ever since she arrived; and I know the colonel. He has a temper; and when it gives way, it's a bit of high explosive. He'll kill her if she pushes him too far.

THE PATIENT. Let him kill her. I am young and strong: I want a world without parents: there is no room for them in my dream. I shall found a sisterhood.

AUBREY. All right, Mops. Get thee to a nunnery.

THE PATIENT. It need not be a nunnery if men will come in without spoiling everything. But all the women must be rich. There must be no chill of poverty. There are plenty of rich women like me who hate being devoured by parasites.

AUBREY. Stop. You have the most disgusting mental pictures. I really cannot stand intellectual coarseness. Sweetie's vulgarity I can forgive and even enjoy. But you say perfectly filthy things that stick in my mind, and break my spirit. I can bear no more of it. [*He rises angrily and tries to escape by the beach past the Abode of Love*].

SWEETIE. Youre dainty, arnt you? If chambermaids were as dainty as you, youd have to empty your own slops.

AUBREY [*recoiling from her with a yell of disgust*] You need not throw them in my teeth, you beast. [*He sits in his former place, sulking*].

THE ELDER. Silence, boy. These are home truths.

They are good for you. [*To the patient*]. May I ask, young woman, what are the relations between you and my son, whom you seem to know.

THE PATIENT. Popsy stole my necklace, and got me to run away with him by a wonderful speech he made about freedom and sunshine and lovely scenery. Sweetie made me write it all down and sell it to a tourist agency as an advertisement. And then I was devoured by parasites: by tourist agencies, steamboat companies, railways, motor car people, hotel keepers, dressmakers, servants, all trying to get my money by selling me things I dont really want; shoving me all over the globe to look at what they call new skies, though they know as well as I do that it is only the same old sky everywhere; and disabling me by doing all the things for me that I ought to do for myself to keep myself in health. They preyed on me to keep themselves alive: they pretended they were making me happy when it was only by drinking and drugging—cocktails and cocaine—that I could endure my life.

AUBREY. I regret to have to say it, Mops; but you have not the instincts of a lady. [*He sits down moodily on a stone a little way up the path*].

THE PATIENT. You fool, there is no such thing as a lady. I have the instincts of a good housekeeper: I want to clean up this filthy world and keep it clean. There must be other women who want it too. Florence Nightingale had the same instinct when she went to clean up the Crimean war. She wanted a sisterhood; but there wasnt one.

THE ELDER. There were several. But steeped in superstition, unfortunately.

THE PATIENT. Yes, all mixed up with things that I

dont believe. Women have to set themselves apart to
join them. I dont want to set myself apart. I want to
have every woman in my sisterhood, and to have all
the others strangled.

THE ELDER. Down! down! down! Even the young,
the strong, the rich, the beautiful, feel that they are
plunging into a bottomless pit.

THE SERGEANT. Your set, miss, if you will excuse me
saying so, is only a small bit of the world. If you dont
like the officers' mess, the ranks are open to you. Look
at Meek! That man could be an emperor if he laid his
mind to it: but he'd rather be a private. He's happier so.

THE PATIENT. I dont belong to the poor, and dont
want to. I always knew that there were thousands of
poor people; and I was taught to believe that they were
poor because God arranged it that way to punish them
for being dirty and drunken and dishonest, and not
knowing how to read and write. But I didnt know that
the rich were miserable. I didnt know that I was miserable. I didn't know that our respectability was uppish
snobbery and our religion gluttonous selfishness, and
that my soul was starving on them. I know now. I have
found myself out thoroughly—in my dream.

THE ELDER. You are young. Some good man may
cure you of this for a few happy years. When you fall
in love, life will seem worth living.

THE PATIENT. I did fall in love. With that thing.
And though I was never a hotel chambermaid I got
tired of him sooner than Sweetie did. Love gets people
into difficulties, not out of them. No more lovers for
me: I want a sisterhood. Since I came here I have been
wanting to join the army, like Joan of Arc. It's a
brotherhood, of a sort.

THE SERGEANT. Yes, miss: that is so; and there used to be a peace of mind in the army that you could find nowhere else. But the war made an end of that. You see, miss, the great principle of soldiering, I take it, is that the world is kept going by the people who want the right thing killing the people who want the wrong thing. When the soldier is doing that, he is doing the work of God, which my mother brought me up to do. But thats a very different thing from killing a man because he's a German and he killing you because youre an Englishman. We were not killing the right people in 1915. We werent even killing the wrong people. It was innocent men killing one another.

THE PATIENT. Just for the fun of it.

THE SERGEANT. No, miss: it was no fun. For the misery of it.

THE PATIENT. For the devilment of it, then.

THE SERGEANT. For the devilment of the godless rulers of this world. Those that did the killing hadnt even the devilment to comfort them: what comfort is there in screwing on a fuse or pulling a string when the devilment it makes is from three to forty miles off, and you dont know whether you have only made a harmless hole in the ground or blown up a baby in its cradle that might have been your own? That wasnt devilment: it was damnation. No, miss: the bottom has come out of soldiering. What the gentleman here said about our all falling into a bottomless pit came home to me. I feel like that too.

THE ELDER. Lost souls, all of us.

THE PATIENT. No: only lost dogs. Cheer up, old man: the lost dogs always find their way home. [*The voice of the Elderly Lady is heard returning*]. Oh! here she comes again!

Mrs Mopply is still pursuing the colonel, who is walking doggedly and steadily away from her, with closed lips and a dangerous expression on his set features.

MRS MOPPLY. You wont even speak to me. It's a disgrace. I will send a cable message home to the Government about it. You were sent out here to rescue my daughter from these dreadful brigands. Why is nothing being done? What are the relations between yourself and that disgraceful countess who ought to have her coronet stripped off her back? You are all in a conspiracy to murder my poor lost darling child. You are in league with the brigands. You are—

The colonel turns at bay, and brings down his umbrella whack on poor Mrs Mopply's helmet.

MRS MOPPLY. Oh! Oh! Oh! Oh! [*With a series of short, dry, detached screams she totters and flutters back along the beach out of sight like a wounded bird*].

General stupefaction. All stare at the colonel aghast. The sergeant rises in amazement, and remains standing afterwards as a matter of military etiquette.

THE PATIENT. Oh, if only someone had done that to her twenty years ago, how different my childhood would have been! But I must see to the poor old dear. [*She runs after her mother*].

AUBREY. Colonel: you have our full, complete, unreserved sympathy. We thank you from the bottom of our hearts. But that does not alter the fact that the man who would raise his hand to a woman, save in the way of kindness, is unworthy the name of Briton.

TALLBOYS. I am perfectly aware of that, sir. I need no reminder. The lady is entitled to an apology. She shall have it.

THE ELDER. But have you considered the possibility of a serious injury—

TALLBOYS [*cutting him short*] My umbrella is quite uninjured, thank you. The subject is now closed. [*He sits down on the stone below St Pauls recently vacated by Aubrey. His manner is so decisive that nobody dares carry the matter further*].

As they sit uneasily seeking one another's eyes and avoiding them again, dumbfounded by the violence of the catastrophe, a noise like that of a machine gun in action reaches their ears from afar. It increases to shattering intensity as it approaches. They all put their fingers to their ears. It diminishes slightly, then suddenly rises to a climax of speed and uproar, and stops.

TALLBOYS. Meek.

AUBREY. Meek.

SWEETIE. Meek.

THE ELDER. What is this? Why do you all say Meek?

Meek, dusty and gritty, but very alert, comes down the path through the gap with a satchel of papers.

TALLBOYS. My dear Meek, can you not be content with a motor cycle of ordinary horse power? Must you always travel at eighty miles an hour?

MEEK. I have good news for you, Colonel; and good news should travel fast.

TALLBOYS. For me?

MEEK. Your K.C.B., sir. [*Presenting a paper*] Honors list by wireless.

TALLBOYS [*rising joyously to take the paper*] Ah! Congratulate me, my friends. My dear Sarah is Lady Tallboys at last. [*He resumes his seat and pores over the paper*].

AUBREY ⎫

THE SERGEANT ⎬ [*together*] ⎰ Splendid!

You deserve it, sir, if I may say so.

SWEETIE ⎭ ⎱ Delighted, I am sure.

THE ELDER. May I crave to know the nature of the distinguished service which has won this official recognition, sir?

TALLBOYS. I have won the battle of the maroons. I have suppressed brigandage here. I have rescued a British lady from the clutches of the brigands. The Government is preparing for a general election, and has had to make the most of these modest achievements.

THE ELDER. Brigands! Are there any here?

TALLBOYS. None.

THE ELDER. But—? The British lady? In their clutches?

TALLBOYS. She has been in my clutches, and perfectly safe, all the time.

THE ELDER [*more and more puzzled*] Oh! Then the battle of the—

TALLBOYS. Won by Private Meek. I had nothing whatever to do with it.

AUBREY. I invented the brigands and the British lady. [*To Tallboys*]. By the way, Colonel, the impressive old party in the shrine is my father.

TALLBOYS. Indeed! Happy to meet you, sir, though I cannot congratulate you on your son, except in so far as you have brought into the world the most abandoned liar I have ever met.

THE ELDER. And may I ask, sir, is it your intention not only to condone my son's frauds, but to take advantage of them to accept a distinction which you have in no way earned?

TALLBOYS. I have earned it, sir, ten times over. Do you suppose, because the brigandage which I am honored for suppressing has no existence, that I have never suppressed real brigands? Do you forget that though this battle of which I am crowned victor was won by a subordinate, I, too, have won real battles, and seen all the honors go to a brigadier who did not even know what was happening? In the army these things average themselves out: merit is rewarded in the long run. Justice is none the less justice though it is always delayed, and finally done by mistake. My turn today: Private Meek's tomorrow.

THE FATHER. And meanwhile Mr Meek—this humble and worthy soldier—is to remain in obscurity and poverty whilst you are strutting as a K.C.B.

TALLBOYS. How I envy him! Look at me and look at him! I, loaded with responsibilities whilst my hands are tied, my body disabled, my mind crippled because a colonel must not do anything but give orders and look significant and profound when his mind is entirely vacant! he, free to turn his hand to everything and to look like an idiot when he feels like one! I have been driven to sketching in watercolors because I may not use my hands in life's daily useful business. A commanding officer must not do this, must not do that, must not do the other, must not do anything but tell other men to do it. He may not even converse with them. I see this man Meek doing everything that is natural to a complete man: carpentering, painting, digging, pulling and hauling, fetching and carrying, helping himself and everybody else, whilst I, with a bigger body to exercise and quite as much energy, must loaf and loll, allowed to do nothing but read the papers and drink brandy and water to prevent myself going mad. I should have become a drunkard had it not been for the colors.

THE SERGEANT. Ah yes, sir, the colors. The fear of disgracing them has kept me off the drink many a time.

TALLBOYS. Man: I do not mean the regimental colors, but the watercolors. How willingly would I exchange my pay, my rank, my K.C.B., for Meek's poverty, his obscurity!

MEEK. But, my dear Colonel—sorry, sir: what I mean to say is that you can become a private if you wish. Nothing easier: I have done it again and again. You resign your commission; take a new and very common name by deed poll; dye your hair and give your age to the recruiting sergeant as twenty-two; and there you are! You can select your own regiment.

TALLBOYS. Meek: you should not tantalize your commanding officer. No doubt you are an extraordinary soldier. But have you ever passed the extreme and final test of manly courage?

MEEK. Which one is that, sir?

TALLBOYS. Have you ever married?

MEEK. No, sir.

TALLBOYS. Then do not ask me why I do not resign my commission and become a free and happy private. My wife would not let me.

THE COUNTESS. Why dont you hit her on the head with your umbrella?

TALLBOYS. I dare not. There are moments when I wish some other man would. But not in my presence. I should kill him.

THE ELDER. We are all slaves. But at least your son is an honest man.

TALLBOYS. Is he? I am glad to hear it. I have not spoken to him since he shirked military service at the beginning of the war and went into trade as a contractor. He is now so enormously rich that I cannot afford to keep up his acquaintance. Neither need you keep up that of your son. By the way, he passes here as the half step-brother of this lady, the Countess Valbrioni.

SWEETIE. Valbrioni be blowed! My name is Susan Simpkins. Being a countess isnt worth a damn. There's no variety in it: no excitement. What I want is a month's leave for the sergeant. Wont you give it to him, Colonel?

TALLBOYS. What for?

SWEETIE. Never mind what for. A fortnight might do; but I dont know for certain yet. There's something steadying about him; and I suppose I will have to settle down some day.

TALLBOYS. Nonsense! The sergeant is a pious man, not your sort. Eh, Sergeant?

SERGEANT. Well, sir, a man should have one woman to prevent him from thinking too much about women in general. You cannot read your Bible undisturbed if visions and wandering thoughts keep coming between you and it. And a pious man should not marry a pious woman: two of a trade never agree. Besides, it would give the children a onesided view of life. Life is very mixed, sir: it is not all piety and it is not all gaiety. This young woman has no conscience; but I have enough for two. I have no money; but she seems to have enough for two. Mind: I am not committing myself; but I will go so far as to say that I am not dead set against it. On the plane of this world and its vanities—and weve got to live in it, you know, sir—she appeals to me.

AUBREY. Take care, Sergeant. Constancy is not Sweet-ie's strong point.

THE SERGEANT. Neither is it mine. As a single man and a wandering soldier I am fair game for every woman. But if I settle down with this girl she will keep the others off. I'm a bit tired of adventures.

SWEETIE. Well, if the truth must be told, so am I. We were made for one another, Sergeant. What do you say?

THE SERGEANT. Well, I dont mind keeping company for a while, Susan, just to see how we get along to-gether.

The voice of Mrs Mopply is again heard. Its tone is hardy and even threatening; and its sound is approach-ing rapidly.

MRS MOPPLY'S VOICE. You just let me alone, will you? Nobody asked you to interfere. Get away with you.

General awe and dismay. Mrs Mopply appears strid-ing resolutely along the beach. She walks straight up to the colonel, and is about to address him when he rises firmly to the occasion and takes the word out of her mouth.

TALLBOYS. Mrs Mopply: I have a duty to you which I must discharge at once. At our last meeting, I struck you.

MRS MOPPLY. Struck me! You bashed me. Is that what you mean?

TALLBOYS. If you consider my expression inadequate I am willing to amend it. Let us put it that I bashed you. Well, I apologize without reserve, fully and amply. If you wish, I will give it to you in writing.

MRS MOPPLY. Very well. Since you express your re-gret, I suppose there is nothing more to be said.

TALLBOYS [*darkening ominously*] Pardon me. I apologized. I did not express my regret.

AUBREY. Oh, for heaven's sake, Colonel, dont start her again. Dont qualify your apology in any way.

MRS MOPPLY. You shut up, whoever you are.

TALLBOYS. I do not qualify my apology in the least. My apology is complete. The lady has a right to it. My action was inexcusable. But no lady—no human being —has a right to impose a falsehood on me. I do not regret my action. I have never done anything which gave me more thorough and hearty satisfaction. When I was a company officer I once cut down an enemy in the field. Had I not done so he would have cut me down. It gave me no satisfaction: I was half ashamed of it: I have never before spoken of it. But this time I struck with unmixed enjoyment. In fact I am grateful to Mrs. Mopply. I owe her one of the very few delightfully satisfactory moments of my life.

MRS MOPPLY. Well, thats a pretty sort of apology, isnt it?

TALLBOYS [*firmly*] I have nothing to add, madam.

MRS MOPPLY. Well, I forgive you, you peppery old blighter.

Sensation. They catch their breaths, and stare at one another in consternation. The patient arrives.

THE PATIENT. I am sorry to say, Colonel Tallboys, that you have unsettled my mother's reason. She wont believe that I am her daughter. She's not a bit like herself.

MRS MOPPLY. Isnt she? What do you know about myself? my real self? They told me lies; and I had to pretend to be somebody quite different.

TALLBOYS. Who told you lies, madam? It was not

with my authority.

MRS MOPPLY. I wasnt thinking of you. My mother told me lies. My nurse told me lies. My governess told me lies. Everybody told me lies. The world is not a bit like what they said it was. I wasnt a bit like what they said I ought to be. I thought I had to pretend. And I neednt have pretended at all.

THE ELDER. Another victim! She, too, is falling through the bottomless abyss.

MRS MOPPLY. I dont know who you are or what you think you mean; but you have just hit it: I dont know my head from my heels. Why did they tell me that children couldnt live without medicine and three meat meals a day? Do you know that I have killed two of my children because they told me that? My own children! Murdered them, just!

THE ELDER. Medea! Medea!

MRS MOPPLY. It isn't an idea: it's the truth. I will never believe anything again as long as I live. I'd have killed the only one I had left if she hadnt run away from me. I was told to sacrifice myself—to live for others; and I did it if ever a woman did. They told me that everyone would love me for it; and I thought they would; but my daughter ran away when I had sacrificed myself to her until I found myself wishing she would die like the others and leave me a little to myself. And now I find it was not only my daughter that hated me but that all my friends, all the time they were pretending to sympathize, were just longing to bash me over the head with their umbrellas. This poor man only did what all the rest would have done if theyd dared. When I said I forgave you I meant it: I am greatly obliged to you. [*She kisses him*]. But now what am I to do?

How am I to behave in a world thats just the opposite of everything I was told about it?

THE PATIENT. Steady, mother! steady! steady! Sit down. [*She picks up a heavy stone and places it near the Abode of Love for Mrs Mopply to sit on*].

MRS MOPPLY [*seating herself*] Dont you call me mother. Do you think my daughter could carry rocks about like that? she that had to call the nurse to pick up her Pekingese dog when she wanted to pet it! You think you can get round me by pretending to be my daughter; but that just shews what a fool you are; for I hate my daughter and my daughter hates me, because I sacrificed myself to her. She was a horrid selfish girl, always ill and complaining, and never satisfied, no matter how much you did for her. The only sensible thing she ever did was to steal her own necklace and sell it and run away to spend the money on herself. I expect she's in bed somewhere with a dozen nurses and six doctors all dancing attendance on her. Youre not a bit like her, thank goodness: thats why Ive taken a fancy to you. You come with me, darling. I have lots of money, and sixty years of a misspent life to make up for; so you will have a good time with me. Come with me as my companion; and lets forget that there are such miserable things in the world as mothers and daughters.

THE PATIENT. What use shall we be to one another?

MRS MOPPLY. None, thank God. We can do without one another if we dont hit it off.

THE PATIENT. Righto! I'll take you on trial until Ive had time to look about me and see what I'm going to do. But only on trial, mind.

MRS MOPPLY. Just so, darling. We'll both be on trial.

So thats settled.

THE PATIENT. And now, Mr Meek, what about the little commission you promised to do for me? Have you brought back my passport?

THE COUNTESS. Your passport! Whatever for?

AUBREY. What have you been up to, Mops? Are you going to desert me?

Meek advances and empties a heap of passports from his satchel on the sand, kneeling down to sort out the patient's.

TALLBOYS. What is the meaning of this? Whose passports are these? What are you doing with them? Where did you get them?

MEEK. Everybody within fifty miles is asking me to get a passport visa'd.

TALLBOYS. Visa'd! For what country?

MEEK. For Beotia, sir.

TALLBOYS. Beotia?

MEEK. Yessir. The Union of Federated Sensible Societies, sir. The U.F.S.S. Everybody wants to go there now, sir.

THE COUNTESS. Well I never!

THE ELDER. And what is to become of our unhappy country if all its inhabitants desert it for an outlandish place in which even property is not respected?

MEEK. No fear, sir: they wont have us. They wont admit any more English, sir: they say their lunatic asylums are too full already. I couldn't get a single visa, except [*to the Colonel*] for you, sir.

TALLBOYS. For me! Damn their impudence! I never asked for one.

MEEK. No, sir; but their people have so much leisure that they are at their wits' end for some occupation to keep them out of mischief. They want to introduce the only institution of ours that they admire.

THE ELDER. And pray which one is that?

MEEK. The English school of watercolor painting, sir. Theyve seen some of the Colonel's work; and theyll make him head of their centres of repose and culture if he'll settle there.

TALLBOYS. This cannot be true, Meek. It indicates a degree of intelligence of which no Government is capable.

MEEK. It's true, sir, I assure you.

TALLBOYS. But my wife—

MEEK. Yessir: I told them. [*He repacks his satchel*].

TALLBOYS. Well, well: there is nothing for it but to return to our own country.

THE ELDER. Can our own country return to its senses, sir? that is the question.

TALLBOYS. Ask Meek.

MEEK. No use, sir: all the English privates want to be colonels: there's no salvation for snobs. [*To Tallboys*]. Shall I see about getting the expedition back to England, sir?

TALLBOYS. Yes. And get me two tubes of rose madder and a big one of Chinese White, will you?

MEEK [*about to go*] Yessir.

THE ELDER. Stop. There are police in England. What is to become of my son there?

SWEETIE [*rising*] Make Popsy a preacher, old man. But dont start him until weve gone.

THE ELDER. Preach, my son, preach to your heart's content. Do anything rather than steal and make your military crimes an excuse for your civil ones. Let men call you the reverend. Let them call you anything rather than thief.

AUBREY [*rising*] If I may be allowed to improve the occasion for a moment—

General consternation. All who are seated rise in alarm, except the patient, who jumps up and claps her hands in mischievous encouragement to the orator.

MRS MOPPLY		You hold your tongue, young man.
SWEETIE		Oh Lord! we're in for it now.
THE ELDER	[*together*]	Shame and silence would better become you, sir.
THE PATIENT		Go on, Pops. It's the only thing you do well.

AUBREY [*continuing*]—it is clear to me that though we seem to be dispersing quietly to do very ordinary things: Sweetie and the sergeant to get married [*the sergeant hastily steals down from his grotto, beckoning to Sweetie to follow him. They both escape along the beach*] the colonel to his wife, his watercolors, and his K.C.B. [*the colonel hurries away noiselessly in the opposite direction*] Napoleon Alexander Trotsky Meek to his job of repatriating the expedition [*Meek takes to flight up the path through the gap*] Mops, like Saint Teresa, to found an unladylike sisterhood with her mother as cook-housekeeper [*Mrs Mopply hastily follows the sergeant, dragging with her the patient, who is listening to Aubrey with signs of becoming rapt in his discourse*] yet they are all, like my father here, falling, falling, falling endlessly and hopelessly through a void in which they can find no footing. [*The Elder vanishes into the recesses of St Pauls, leaving his son to preach in solitude*]. There is something fantastic about them, something unreal and perverse, something profoundly unsatisfactory. They are too absurd to be believed in; yet they are not fictions: the newspapers are full of them: what storyteller, however reckless a liar, would dare to invent figures so improbable as men and women with their minds stripped naked? Naked bodies no longer shock us: our sunbathers, grinning at us from every illustrated summer number of our magazines, are nuder than shorn lambs. But the horror of the naked mind is still more than we can bear. Throw off the last rag of your bathing costume; and I shall not blench nor expect you to blush. You may even throw away the outer garments of your souls: the manners, the morals, the decencies. Swear; use dirty words; drink cocktails; kiss and caress and cuddle until girls who are like roses at eighteen are like battered demireps at twenty-two: in all these ways the bright young things of the victory have scandalized their dull old prewar elders and left nobody but their bright young selves a penny the worse. But how are we to bear this dreadful new nakedness: the nakedness of the souls who until now have always disguised themselves from one another in beautiful impossible idealisms to enable them to bear one another's company. The iron lightning of war has burnt great rents in these angelic veils, just as it has smashed great holes in our cathedral roofs and torn great gashes in our hillsides. Our souls go in rags now; and the young are spying through the holes and getting glimpses of the reality that was hidden. And they are not horrified: they exult in having found us out: they expose their own souls; and when we their elders desperately try to patch our torn clothes with scraps of the old material, the young lay violent hands on us and tear from us even the rags that were left to us. But when they have stripped themselves and us utterly naked, will they be able to bear the spectacle? You have seen me try to strip my soul before my father; but when these two young women stripped themselves more boldly than I—when the old woman had the mask struck from her soul and revelled in it instead of dying of it—I shrank from the revelation as from a wind bringing from the unknown regions of the future a breath which may be a breath of life, but of a life too keen for me to bear, and therefore for me a blast of death. I stand midway between youth and age like a man who has missed his train: too late for the last and too early for the next. What am I to do? What am I? A soldier who has lost his nerve, a thief who at his first great theft has found honesty the best policy and restored his booty to its owner. Nature never intended me for soldiering or thieving: I am by nature and destiny a preacher. I am the new Ecclesiastes. But I have no Bible, no creed: the war has shot both out of my hands. The war has been a fiery forcing house in which we have grown with a rush like flowers in a late spring following a terrible winter. And with what result? This: that we have outgrown our religion, outgrown our political system, outgrown our own strength of mind and character. The fatal word NOT has been miraculously inserted into all our creeds: in the desecrated temples where we knelt murmuring "I believe" we stand with stiff knees and stiffer necks shouting "Up, all! the erect posture is the mark of the man: let lesser creatures kneel and crawl: we will not kneel and we do not believe." But what next? Is NO enough? For a boy, yes: for a man, never. Are we any the less obsessed with a belief when we are denying it than when we were affirming it? No: I must have affirmations to preach. Without them the young will not listen to me; for even the young grow tired of denials. The negative-monger falls before the soldiers, the men of action, the fighters, strong in the old uncompromising affirmations which give them status, duties, certainty of consequences; so that the pugnacious spirit of man in them can reach out and strike deathblows with steadfastly closed minds. Their way is straight and sure; but it is the way of death; and the preacher must preach the way of life. Oh, if I could only find it! [*A white sea fog swirls up from the beach to his feet, rising and thickening round him*]. I am ignorant: I have lost my nerve and am intimidated: all I know is that I must find the way of life, for myself and all of us, or we shall surely perish. And meanwhile my gift has possession of me: I must preach and preach and preach no matter how late the hour and how short the day, no matter whether I have nothing to say—

The fog has enveloped him; the gap with its grottoes is lost to sight; the ponderous stones are wisps of shifting white cloud; there is left only fog: impenetrable fog; but the incorrigible preacher will not be denied his peroration, which, could we only hear it distinctly, would probably run—

—or whether in some pentecostal flame of revelation the Spirit will descend on me and inspire me with a message the sound whereof shall go out unto all lands and realize for us at last the Kingdom and the Power and the Glory for ever and ever. Amen.

The audience disperses (or the reader puts down the book) impressed in the English manner with the Pentecostal flame and the echo from the Lord's Prayer. But fine words butter no parsnips. A few of the choicer spirits will know that the Pentecostal flame is always alight at the service of those strong enough to bear its terrible intensity. They will not forget that it is accompanied by a rushing mighty wind, and that any rascal who happens to be also a windbag can get a prodigious volume of talk out of it without ever going near enough to be shrivelled up. The author, though himself a professional talk maker, does not believe that the world can be saved by talk alone. He has given the rascal the last word; but his own favorite is the woman of action, who begins by knocking the wind out of the rascal, and ends with a cheerful conviction that the lost dogs always find their way home. So they will, perhaps, if the women go out and look for them.

VILLAGE WOOING

A COMEDIETTINA FOR TWO VOICES

1933

VILLAGE WOOING

FIRST CONVERSATION

The lounge deck of the Empress of Patagonia, a pleasure ship. Two of the deck chairs are occupied by A, a literary looking pale gentleman under forty in green spectacles, a limp black beard, and a tropical suit of white silk, who is writing and does not wish to be disturbed, and Z, a young woman, presentable but not aristocratic, who is bored with her book. She is undressed for bathing, but is very modestly covered up with a not too flamboyant wrap.

z. Excuse me. Could you tell me the time?

A. [*curtly*] Eleven.

z. My watch makes it half past ten.

A. The clocks were put on half an hour last night. We are going east.

z. I always think it adds to the interest of a voyage having to put on your watch.

A. I am glad you are so easily interested [*he resumes his writing pointedly*].

z. The steward will be round with the soup in half an hour. I thought we should have to wait an hour.

A. I never take it. It interrupts my work.

z. Why do you work all the time? It's not what one comes on a pleasure cruise for, is it?

A. Work is my only pleasure.

z. Oh, thats not good sense, is it? It gives me the pip to see you always sitting there over your writing,

139

and never enjoying yourself, nor even taking a drop of soup. You should get up and have a game of deck quoits: you will feel ever so much better after it.

A. I feel perfectly well, thank you. And I loathe deck games, especially deck quoits. The slapping of those silly things on the deck destroys the quiet of the ship.

Z. Oh, I see. That is why you select this end of the deck. I often wondered why.

A. Within the last fortnight you have inspected the priceless antiquities of Naples, Athens, Egypt, and the Holy Land. Please occupy your mind with them until the soup comes.

Z. I never cared much for geography. Where are we now?

A. We are on the Red Sea.

Z. But it's blue.

A. What did you expect it to be?

Z. Well, I didnt know what color the sea might be in these parts. I always thought the Red Sea would be red.

A. Well, it isnt.

Z. And isnt the Black Sea black?

A. It is precisely the color of the sea at Margate.

Z. [*eagerly*] Oh, I am so glad you know Margate. Theres no place like it in the season, is there?

A. I dont know: I have never been there.

Z. [*disappointed*] Oh, you ought to go. You could write a book about it.

A. [*shudders, sighs, and pretends to write very hard*]!
. *A pause.*

Z. I wonder why they call it the Red Sea.

A. Because their fathers did. Why do you call America America?

z. Well, because it is America. What else would you call it?

a. Oh, call it what you like, dear lady; but I have five hundred words to write before lunch; and I cannot do that if I talk to you.

z. [*sympathetically*] Yes: it is awful to have to talk to people, isnt it? Oh, that reminds me: I have something really interesting to tell you. I believe the man in the cabin next mine beats his wife.

a. I feel a little like him myself. Some women would provoke any men to beat them.

z. I will say this for him, that she always begins it.

a. No doubt.

z. I hate a nagger: dont you?

a. It is your privilege as a woman to have the last word. Please take it and dont end all your remarks with a question.

z. You are funny.

a. Am I? I never felt less funny in my life.

z. I cant make you out at all. I am rather good at making out people as a rule; but I cant make head or tail of you.

a. I am not here to be made out. You are not here to make people out, but to revel in the enjoyments you have paid for. Deck tennis, deck quoits, shuffleboard, golf, squash rackets, the swimming pool, the gymnasium all invite you.

z. I am no good at games: besides, theyre silly. I'd rather sit and talk.

a. Then for heaven's sake talk to somebody else. I have no time for talk. I have to work my passage.

z. What do you mean: work your passage? You are not a sailor.

A. No. I make a precarious living on board ship by writing the Marco Polo Series of Chatty Guide Books. Unless I complete two thousand words a day I am bankrupt. I cannot complete them if you persist in talking to me.

Z. Do you mean you are writing a book about this cruise?

A. I am trying to—under great difficulties.

Z. Will I be in it?

A. [*grimly*] You will.

Z. How thrilling! I have never been put in a book before. You will read me what you have written about me, wont you?

A. When the book is published you can read it to your heart's content.

Z. But I should like you to get me right. After all, what do you know about me? I will tell you the whole of my life if you like.

A. Great heavens, NO. Please dont.

Z. Oh, I dont care who knows it.

A. Evidently. You would hardly offer to tell it to a perfect stranger if you cared, or if it was of the smallest interest.

Z. Oh, I'd never think of you as a stranger. Here we are on the same ship, arnt we? And most people would think my life quite a romance. Wouldnt you really like to hear it?

A. No, I tell you. When I want romances I invent them for myself.

Z. Oh, well, perhaps you wouldnt think it very wonderful. But it was a regular treat for me. You may think because I am well dressed and travelling de lucks and all that, that I am an educated lady. But I'm not.

A. I never supposed for a moment that you were.

Z. But how could you know? How did you find out?

A. I didnt find out. I knew.

Z. Who told you?

A. Nobody told me.

Z. Then how did you know?

A. [exasperated] How do I know that a parrot isnt a bird of paradise?

Z. Theyre different.

A. Precisely.

Z. There you are, you see. But what would you take me for if you met me in a third class carriage?

A. I should not notice you.

Z. I bet you would. I maynt be a beauty; but when I get into a railway carriage every man in it has a look at me.

A. I am not Everyman. Everyman thinks that every woman that steps into a railway carriage may be the right woman. But she is always a disappointment.

Z. Same with the women, isnt it? If you were a woman youd know.

A. I am a woman; and you are a man, with a slight difference that doesnt matter except on special occasions.

Z. Oh, what a thing to say! I never could bring myself to believe that. I know, of course, that men have their weaknesses and their tempers; but all the same there is something wonderful you can get from a man that you never could get from a woman. Dont you think so?

A. Inexperienced men think there is something wonderful you can get from a woman that you never could get from a man. Hence many unhappy marriages.

z. Are you married?

a. Widower. Are you?

z. Oh, thats the first time youve asked me a question. We're getting on, arnt we?

a. No. I am not getting on with my work.

z. Youre an intellectual, arnt you?

a. What do you think you mean by an intellectual?

z. Only that you consider me no better than an idiot, and that you were a bad husband, most likely.

a. You are quite right on both points.

z. I thought so.

a. And now, please, may I go on with my work?

z. Please yourself. I'm not hindering you.

a. Thank you [*he resumes his writing*].

A pause.

z. What books would you recommend me to read to improve my mind?

a. [*shouting furiously*] Steward.

z. Oh, you shouldnt trouble the steward now. He's busy getting the soup.

a. I want him to remove my chair to the very furthest extremity of this ship.

z. I always say it's fresher under the awning at the end. You dont mind if I move too, do you?

a. If you persecute me any more I shall go overboard. Dont you see that I want to be left alone to work, and that your chatter is preventing me from working?

z. [*sympathetically*] It is annoying to have somebody talking to you all the time when you dont want to. But it's just as bad when you want to talk, and the other person wont, isnt it?

a. There are three or four hundred persons on this ship. Cannot you find one of them with the same insatiable thirst for conversation as yourself?

z. Well; but we all have to make ourselves agreeable, havnt we?

a. Not at oneanother's expense. You are not making yourself agreeable to me at present: you are driving me mad.

z. My father used to say that men and women are always driving oneanother mad.

a. That sounds literary. Was your father a man of letters?

z. Yes: I should think he was. A postman.

a. A what?

z. A postman. A village postman.

a. Ha ha! Ha ha ha!

z. What is there funny in that?

a. I dont know. Ha ha! The postman's daughter hath ripe red lips: butter and eggs and a pound of cheese! Ha ha ha!

z. Well, I'm glad Ive amused you. But I don't think it's very polite of you to laugh at my father.

a. [*punctiliously—recovering himself*] You are right. I was rude. But a good laugh is worth a hundred pounds to me. I feel a different man. Forgive me. You see, you quoted a remark of your father's—almost an epigram—which suggested that he must have been a man of genius.

z. Well, so he was. He had a genius for walking.

a. For what?

z. For walking. When he was a child, he won a prize as The Infant Pedestrian. And would you believe it, my mother was that indoory that she grudged having to go out and do her marketing. After we had a telephone put in she never went out at all.

A. Thats strange. As she was never out and he was never in, the household should have been a quiet one; but that remark of his about men and women driving oneanother mad rather suggests the opposite.

Z. So it was the opposite. She was always complaining of being lonely; and he was always at her to take more exercise. When they were not quarrelling about that, they were quarrelling about me. You see, they had great ambitions for me. She wanted me to be a parlormaid in a great house. He wanted me to be a telephone operator. He said there is no future for the great houses and a great future for telephones.

A. And you? Had you no ambition for yourself?

Z. Oh, I wanted to be something romantic, like an acrobat in a circus.

A. And what actually happened?

Z. I became shop assistant and telephone operator in the village shop.

A. Do village shop assistants and telephone girls—

Z. Operators.

A. Pardon: operators. Do they earn enough to take cruises round the world in pleasure ships?

Z. Not they. I won the first prize in a newspaper competition. My mother wanted me to save it: she said it would help me to get a thrifty husband. My father told me to blue it all in a lump while I had the chance. "You will be poor all your life," he said; "but now you have the chance of living at the rate of five thousand a year for four months. Dont miss it," he said: "see what it's like. Have your fling" he said; "for they never can take that away from you once youve had it." His idea was a walking tour, spending the nights in the best hotels; but I chose the ship because it's more dressy and more people to look at. Besides, I can get all the walking I want round the deck. At the end of the cruise back I go to the village shop without a penny.

A. Have they found out here that you are not a lady?

Z. The Americans dont know the difference: they think my telephone talk is aristocratic; and the English wont speak to anyone anyhow. And lots of them are just like me.

A. Well, how do you like living at the rate of five thousand a year? Is it worth it?

Z. It is while the novelty lasts. You see, when youre at home you get tired of doing the same thing every day: the same places! the same faces! the same old round. When you get a holiday you go off in a crowded hot excursion train to the seaside and make yourself tired and miserable just because it's a change; and youd do anything for a change. But here it's change all the time until you begin to realize what it is to have a settled home and belong somewhere. I shant be sorry to get home to the shop and the telephone. I get such a dreadful lost dog feeling sometimes. Other times it seems such a foolish waste of money. And I hate wasting money.

A. Thats an extremely attractive point in your character. My wife used to waste my money. Stick to that and you will get married in no time.

Z. Oh, I have had plenty of offers. But you know it's a terrible thing to be a poor man's wife when you have been accustomed to a clean decent job. I have seen so many bright jolly girls turn into dirty old drudges through getting married.

A. Dont be afraid of dirt. Mine is a clean job; but I often wish I had a dirty one to exercise me and keep me in health. Women are so set on clean collars that they make their sons clerks when they would be stronger and earn more money as navvies. I wish I was a navvy instead of writing guide books.

z. Well, whats to prevent you?

A. I am not trained to manual work. Half an hour of it would make me wish myself dead. And five minutes of my work would produce a strike among the navvies. I am only a writing machine, just as a navvy is a digging machine.

z. I dont think the world is rightly arranged: do you?

A. We must take the world as we find it. It's we that are not rightly arranged.

z. Thats what I mean. Well, I suppose I mustnt interrupt your work.

A. You mean that the steward is coming round with the soup at last.

z. Well, it's half past eleven, isnt it?

The steward appears with the soup and offers it to z, who seizes it eagerly; then to A.

A. No, thank you. No soup.

He buries himself in his work, unmolested.

She buries herself in the soup.

SECOND CONVERSATION

In a village shop and post office on the Wiltshire Downs on a fine summer morning. The counter is for general shopping for most of its length; but one end is reserved and railed in for postal business. A couple of chairs are available for customers. The goods for sale include ginger beer in stone bottles, tablets of milk chocolate, glass jars of sweets containing (inter alia) sugared almonds, all on the counter; cheese, butter, and Hovis bread handy to the scales; and, in front of the counter, a sack of apples on the floor and some string bags hanging from the rafters.

z. [*invisible*] Th-reee ni-nnn. Sorry: no such number. Whoo-mmm do you want? Doctor Byles? One fi-fff. You are through.

A *comes in. He is in hiking costume, with stick and rucksack, but wears well cut breeches (not plus fours) instead of shorts. Seeing nobody to attend to him he raps loudly on the counter with his stick.* z *emerges.*

A. I want a packet of milk chocolate—

z. Thanks very much.

A. [*continuing*]—a couple of hard apples—

z. Thanks very much. [*She comes out through the counter to get them from the sack*].

A. [*continuing*]—quarter of a pound of Cheddar cheese—

z. Thanks very much.

A. Dont interrupt me. You can express your gratitude for the order when I have finished. Quarter of a

149

pound of your best butter, a small loaf of Hovis, and twopennyworth of sugared almonds.

z. Anything else?

a. No, thank you.

z. Thanks very much [*she goes back through the counter to cut and weigh the butter and cheese*].

He sits down watching her deft but leisurely proceedings.

a. Do you sell baskets?

z. We sell everything. Hadnt you better have a string bag? It's handier; and it packs away almost to nothing when it's empty.

a. What is a string bag? Shew me one.

z. [*coming out and taking one down*] This is the cheapest. Or would like you a better quality with a Zip fastening?

a. Certainly not. I should have the trouble of opening and shutting it, and the worry of wondering whether it would open or shut, with no compensatory advantage whatever.

z. Thats just like you. Youre not a bit changed.

a. What do you mean? I have been in this shop for less than two minutes. Why should I have changed in that time?

z. Excuse me: I shouldnt have mentioned it. Will you take a string bag?

a. Yes.

z. Thanks very much. Shall I put the rest of the order into it?

a. Of course. What else do you suppose I am buying it for? Have you any buttermilk?

z. Sorry. We dont stock it.

a. Any ginger beer?

z. Yes. We have a very good local brew.

a. Shove a bottle into the string bag.

z. Thanks very much.

a. How many times a day do you say thanks very much?

z. Depends on the number of orders.

a. Dont say it to me again, if you dont mind. It gets on my nerves.

z. It used to get on mine, at first. But I am used to it.

a. Have you a guide book of this village?

z. Sorry. Theres a leaflet in the church, written by the vicar. You are expected to put tuppence in the box for it. Excuse me; but the chocolates are tuppence, sixpence, and a shilling. Which size would you run to?

a. It is a poor heart that never rejoices. I will have a shilling one.

z. Thanks very much.

a. Dont.

z. Excuse me: I cant help it. I say it without thinking: same as if you touched a button.

The telephone rings.

a. Someone has touched the button.

z. [*vanishing into the post office section*] What number please? Whitehall on-n-n-e two on-n-n-e two. I will ring you. Whitehall one two one two. Yes. [*She reappears*]. Thats a police call.

a. You need not point the information at me. I am not the criminal.

z. Oh, it isnt a criminal. Somebody thats been broadcasted on the wireless as lost. You know the sort of thing. Missing from his home since January the first. Last seen in a deck chair on the Empress of Patagonia talking to a female. Suffering from loss of memory.

A. How extraor— [*the telephone rings again*].

z. Excuse me. [*She vanishes*]. You are through to Whitehall. [*She reappears*].

A. You have hit on an extraordinary coincidence. I wonder whether you will believe me when I tell you that in January last I was sitting on the deck of a ship named the Empress of Patagonia, and that I was talking to a female—or rather she was talking to me. How that woman did talk!

z. And are you suffering from loss of memory?

A. Certainly not. I never forget anything.

z. Oh, then it cant be you, can it?

A. There! Can it? That woman always finished up with can it? wont it? isnt it? so that you had to answer her out of common politeness. Take care never to pick up that trick or you will be murdered some day.

z. Some people are like that. It often goes with orange colored eyes [*or whatever color her eyes happen to be*]. Did you notice the color of her eyes?

A. No: I never notice things like that. I am not a detective. It is people's characters that impress me; I cant tell you the color of her hair or the shape of her nose; but I can tell you that she was a most fearful nuisance. How much does all that come to?

z. The string bag sixpence, chocolates a shilling: one and sixpence. The ginger beer is—

A. Spare me the details. Will ten shillings cover it?

z. Oh yes, of course. You shouldn't be so careless about money.

A. [*presenting a Treasury note*] Cease preaching. Take it; and give me the change.

z. Let me see. Eighteenpence, and fourpence for the

ginger beer is one and tenpence, isnt it?

A. Have I denied it?

z. Cheese threepence: two and a penny; butter six-pence: two and sevenpence; apples we sell by the pound. Hadnt you better have a pound?

A. How many to the pound?

z. Three.

A. I cannot eat more than two apples at a time. Charge me for a pound; and eat the odd one yourself.

z. Oh well, say threepence for two: thats two and tenpence, isnt it?

A. I dont know.

z. Hovis, tuppence halfpenny. Three shillings and a halfpenny. Do you happen to have a halfpenny to save having to take fippence halfpenny in coppers?

A. I hate halfpennies: I always throw them away. Stop. I have one. Here.

z. Thanks very much. [*Handing him his change coin by coin*]. Three, four, five, seven and six, ten. Thanks very much.

A. [*pocketing his change, but remaining comfortably seated*] Dont you find it rather dull in this village shop saying thanks very much all day?

z. Well, no matter where you are you are doing the same thing all day and every day, arnt you? The only way to get it off your mind is to live in the same place and stick at the same job. Then you never have to think about it. Thats the way the people live here; and they live for ever so long: eighty's no age here. Grandfather will be a hundred and two in August. Thats because he's never had to worry about what he'll do or where he'll go. He just imagines and imagines. It's the only way to be happy and longlived.

A. But if your imagination has only one village in it it must be pretty bare. How would you like to live in a room with only one chair in it.

z. Well, if you have only one seat what more do you want than one chair? Up at the castle there are thirtysix chairs of one sort or another in the big drawing room; but Lady Flopping cant flop on more than one, can she?

A. [*pointing to the vacant chair*] May I suggest that you flop on that one while we talk?

z. [*sitting down*] Thanks very much.

A. I am not interrupting your work, I hope. There is nothing so maddening as to be talked to when you want to work.

z. Talking is part of the work in a village shop.

A. Tell me: do you ever read?

z. I used to read travels and guide books. We used to stock the Marco Polo series. I was mad about travelling. I had daydreams about the glory that was Greece, the grandeur that was Rome, and all that flapdoodle.

A. Flapdoodle!

z. Well, I suppose I shouldnt call it that; but it ended in my going to Rome and Athens. They were all right; but the old parts were half knocked down; and I couldnt see any glory or grandeur different to Cheltenham. I was glad to be home again. And I had so wanted to meet the Marco Polo man and walk about with him in the ruins by moonlight and hear him go on about them!

A. The Marco Polo man! The milkman! the postman! the muffin man! the Marco Polo man! Some frustrated poet, earning his crust by quoting scraps of verse to bring the Call of the East to dreaming telephone girls.

z. Operators.

A. Operators dont dream. Girls! girls of the golden west. Did that poor devil never bring you the Call of the East?

z. I'd read about it in novels and seen it on the films. They were all about moony drunkards and sheeks and the sort of girls that go dotty about them. I went right round the world to see the reality. Pretty places, of course; but the heat! and the mosquitoes! and the smells!! Travelling just destroyed the world for me as I imagined it. Give me this village all the time.

A. Had you no thrill when you stood somewhere where a poet had said "Stop; for thy tread is on an empire's dust"?

z. A guide, you mean. Theyd take the poetry out of anything; and all the time youre thinking what you ought to give them. If you fancy empires' dusts and all that sort of thing you should meet our vicar and start him talking about our standing stones, and the barrows on the downs, and the Mound. Every grain of our dust, he says, is full of history. Same everywhere, I expect.

A. Are you married?

z. No. Why? Have you any intentions?

A. Dont be in a hurry. Weve known each other less than ten minutes.

z. How much better do you think you will know me when we have talked for twenty years?

A. That is profoundly true. Still, I must think it over.

z. Nobody would ever marry if they thought it over. Youve got to take your chance, no matter how long you think.

A. You are in a hurry.

z. Well, I am past the age at which girls marry here, though I'm the pick of this village. Thats because I thought all my offers over. So I have made up my mind to take the next man that asks me, provided he's reasonably suitable.

A. Do I strike you as being reasonably suitable?

z. Well, I think I have the sort of commonsense you need to keep you straight. And you being a widower know what to expect from a woman. An inexperienced man expects the earth.

A. How do you know that I am a widower?

z. You told me.

A. Did I? When did I tell you?

z. Never mind. You did. I have noticed you have a bad memory; but I have a very good one; so it wont matter.

A. Steady. Steady. I have not yet made myself liable to an action for breach of promise.

z. Dont be afraid. I'm not that sort. We dont consider it respectable here.

A. Should I get any money with you? Do you own the shop?

z. No. All the money I ever had I blued on a trip round the world. But Mrs Ward is getting too old for the business: she couldnt run it now without me. If you could afford to buy her an annuity she'd sell it.

A. I dont know how much annuities cost.

z. You will find it in Whitaker's almanac.

A. This is rather upsetting. Somehow I have always taken it for granted that when I married again I'd marry a woman with money.

z. Oh, that wouldnt suit you at all. She'd want to

spend it going into society and travelling about. How could you bear that sort of life? you that never spoke to anyone on the ship and wouldnt take any part in their games and dances! When it got about that you were the Marco Polo man—the man of all our dreams as you might say—I made a bet that I'd get you to talk to me; and I had all the trouble in the world to win it.

A. Do you mean to say that we have met before? That you were on that trip round the world?

z. Of course I do. But you never notice anything. Youre always reading or writing. The world doesnt exist for you. You never looked at me really. Youre shy with strangers, arnt you?

A. I am absolutely certain I never spoke to any woman on that ship. If I talk to women they always want to marry me.

z. Well, there you are, you see! The moment I set eyes on you I said to myself, "Now thats the sort of man that would suit me as a husband." I'd have said it even if you hadnt been the Marco Polo man.

A. Love at first sight: what?

z. Oh no. You know, if I fell in love with a man I'd never marry him: he could make me so miserable. But there was something about you: I dont exactly know what; but it made me feel that I could do with you in the house; and then I could fall in love with anyone I liked without any fear of making a fool of myself. I suppose it was because you are one of the quiet sort and dont run after women.

A. How do you know I dont run after women?

z. Well, if you want to know, it's because you didnt run after me. You mightnt believe it; but men do run after me.

A. Why?

z. Oh, how do I know? They dont know, themselves. But the lot of money they spend on things they dont want merely to come in and have a look at me and a word with me, you wouldnt believe. It's worth at least twenty pounds a year to the business.

A. [*putting on his glasses and looking at her attentively for the first time*] I shouldnt call you a pretty woman.

z. Oh, I'm not pretty. But what you might call desirable, dont you think?

A. [*alarmed*] No I dont think. May I explain? I am a man of letters and a gentleman. I am accustomed to associate with ladies. That means that I am accustomed to speak under certain well understood reserves which act as a necessary protection to both parties. You are not a lady: you are a villager; but somebody has educated you—probably the Church or the local authority—to a point at which you can impose on unobservant and unwary travellers. You have had finishing lessons on the telephone which give you a distinguished articulation: you can say Th-reee fiv-v-v-v-e ni-n-n-n instead of theree fauv nawn. But you have not acquired any of the reserves. You say what you think. You announce all the plans that wellbred women conceal. You play with your cards on the table instead of keeping them where a lady should keep them: up your sleeve.

z. Well, wheres the harm?

A. Oh, no harm. Quite the contrary. But I feel rushed.

z. What do you mean? rushed?

A. Rushed. Precipitated. Carried to lengths I had no intention of going to.

z. Well, it gets you somewhere: doesnt it?

a. Yes; but where?

z. Here. Theres no mystery about it. Here, in a good business in a village shop in a quiet place, with me to keep it straight and look after you.

a. May I ask how much that expression "looking after me" includes? Let me be clear on the point. As a matter of fact I possess a small property which I could sell for enough to purchase an annuity for old Mrs Williams—

z. Ward.

a. I believe I have enough to purchase annuities for both Mrs Ward and Mrs Williams, as they are presumably both centenarians. But why on earth should I complicate the transaction by marrying you? I could pay you your present wages—

z. Salary.

a. I beg your pardon: salary. You will retain your present position as my shopgirl.

z. Shop assistant.

a. I beg your pardon: shop assistant. You can then make your own matrimonial arrangements, and leave me to make mine.

z. Oh, I'll make my own matrimonial arrangements all right enough. You may depend on that.

a. Excuse me: I added "and leave me to make mine." Can I depend on you for that also?

z. Well, we'll see.

a. [angrily firm] No: you will not see.

z. Well, what?

a. I dont know what. I will not commit myself. We'll see.

z. Just so: we'll see. It's a bargain then?

A. No: it most certainly is not a bargain. When I entered this shop half an hour ago I had not the faintest notion of buying a village shop or marrying a village maiden or any of the things you have put into my head. Have you ever read the fable of the spider and the fly?

z. No; but I used to sing a song called the honeysuckle and the bee.

A. [*resolutely*] Good morning. [*He makes for the door*].

z. [*following him with the string bag*] You are forgetting your things.

A. [*taking it*] Thank you.

z. Thanks very much.

She tempts him to kiss her.

A. No!!! [*he strides out*].

THIRD CONVERSATION

A *is now the proprietor of the shop with* z *as his hired assistant. The counter has been fitted with a desk at the opposite end to the post-office section. At this* A *sits writing. He wears pepper-and-salt trousers of country cut, with an apron. He is in his shirtsleeves, and looks every inch a shopkeeper.* z *comes in through the post office, very fresh and matutinal.*

z. Morning, boss.

A. Good morning, slave.

z. I havnt begun slaving yet. You have been at it for half an hour. Whatever on earth are you working at so hard?

A. I am making out my balance sheet.

z. Oh, you neednt do that. The accountant's clerk from Salisbury does all that when he makes out the income tax return. Youre not expected to do figures in this village. Fancy old Mrs Ward doing such a thing!

A. When I bought this shop from Mrs Ward for an annuity I found she was much cleverer at figures than I was. She should have been a moneylender.

z. She was. She lent a shilling for a penny a week.

A. That must have been between four and five hundred per cent per annum. Shylock would have blushed.

z. Whats the good of it when you have to give credit at the shop, and then lend the customers the money to pay you?

A. Mrs Ward should have gone to Geneva. International finance would have come naturally to her.

z. Thats too clever for me. Anyhow, you neednt worry over a balance sheet. The accountant will do all that for you.

a. [*rising and waving the balance sheet proudly as he comes through the counter into the public part of the shop*] This is not an accountant's balance sheet. It is a Robinson Crusoe balance sheet.

z. [*following him*] Whatever's that?

a. Crusoe drew up a balance sheet of the advantages and disadvantages of being cast away on a desert island. I am cast away in a village on the Wiltshire Downs. I am drawing up a similar balance sheet. I propose to read it to you as far as I have got. [*He takes one of the customer's chairs*]. You can remind me of anything I have forgotten.

z. Lets have it. [*She takes the other chair*].

a. I begin with the credit entries.

z. Things to your own credit, you mean?

a. No, to the credit of village shopkeeping as a way of life.

z. Oh, you are silly, boss.

a. That is a disrespectful remark. As such, it should not be made to a boss by his slave. The understanding on which I raised your salary when I engaged you as my assistant was that our relations should be completely conventional and businesslike on your side, however I might occasionally forget myself.

z. [*rising*] Very well: you can keep your balance sheet to yourself: I will go on with the telephone call book.

a. You will do nothing of the sort. You will do what I tell you to do. That is what I pay you for. Sit down again. [*She does so*]. Now listen. [*He takes up his manuscript and reads*]. Item: I have sharpened my faculties, and greatly improved in observation and mathematics.

z. Couldnt you put it into shorter words? What does it mean?

a. It means that formerly I always took what money was given me without condescending to count it or attempting to calculate it. I can now both calculate and count quite rapidly. Formerly I made no distinctions between grades of butter and eggs. To me an egg was an egg: butter was butter. I now make critical distinctions of the greatest subtlety, and value them in terms of money. I am forced to admit that the shopkeeper is enormously superior to the Marco Polo man, and that I have learnt more in three months in this shop than I learnt in three years in Oxford.

z. I cant believe that about the learning. But see how your manners have improved!

a. My manners!!

z. Yes. Why, on that ship you hadnt a word to throw to a dog; and if anyone came near you you shrank up into yourself like a hedgehog, afraid that they didnt belong to your class and wanted to speak to you without an introduction. Now it's a pleasure to hear you say "Good morning; and what can I do for you today, Mrs Burrell?" and "Have you noticed the cauliflowers today, maam? Not a touch of frost on them!" and "Sparrowgrass very good today, my lady, if you would be wanting some."

a. I positively deny that I have ever in my life called asparagus sparrowgrass to an educated customer. Of course, when people are too ignorant to know the names of what they eat, that is another matter.

z. Well, anyhow, your manners have improved, havnt they?

a. I dont know. I know that they are no longer disinterested and sincere.

z. No more they never used to be. Never easy with anybody. Now you are hail fellow well met, as you might say, with everybody.

a. The world has become a world of customers. Let me write that down. [*He pencils on the back of his balance sheet*] "Manners will never be universally good until every person is every other person's customer."

z. Youre not a real shopkeeper yet, boss. All you want is to find something clever to write.

a. Well, why not? Find enough clever things to say, and you are a Prime Minister. Write them down, and you are a Shakespear.

z. Yes; but who wants to be a Prime Minister or a Shakespear? Youve got to make a living.

a. Well, am I not making a living? I am no poorer than when I bought the shop.

z. But if the money goes as fast as it comes you cant save anything.

a. I loathe saving. It turns human nature sour. "Cast your bread upon the waters; and it will return to you after many days."

z. And how are you to live for the many days with nothing to eat?

a. I dont know. One does, somehow. Stop asking questions; and let us get on with the balance sheet.

z. I speak for your good.

a. [*rising wrathfully*] The most offensive liberty one human being can possibly take with another. What business is it of yours?

z. [*rising and facing him*] If you wont think for yourself somebody else must think for you. It's my business as much as yours.

a. Oh, indeed! Who does this shop belong to? I mean to whom does this shop belong?

z. I get my living out of it, dont I? If it shuts up what becomes of me?

a. Well, if you come to that, what becomes of me? You can get another job. I very greatly doubt whether anyone would give me one. [*Calming down*]. Can you not be content with the fact that the shop is making enough to support two people? [*He resumes his seat*].

z. Aye; but suppose it had to support three people!

a. Why suppose? It hasnt: thats all.

z. It's not all. If you marry a stranger there will be three. And what about the children?

a. The remedy is simple. I shall not marry.

z. You dont know.

a. Neither do you.

z. Yes I do. You have married once; and you will marry twice. Somebody will snap you up. You are that sort of man.

a. If a woman snaps me up she must take the consequences. She must assist in the shop. And you will get the sack.

z. Oh, you are tiresome. [*She sits down, discouraged*]. But you see my point, at all events.

a. No. What point?

z. Well, that it's really cheaper to keep a wife than to pay an assistant. Let alone that you dont have to live a single life.

a. You can get rid of an assistant if she doesnt suit.

You cant get rid of a wife.

z. If people thought that way, theyd never get married.

A. Precisely.

z. In this life you have to take chances.

A. I have taken them, and escaped.

z. You wont escape here. We dont hold with bachelors here.

A. You cant do without a general shop here, nor a post office. While I command both I am in an impregnable strategic position.

z. Well, I dont like to say it; but people are beginning to talk.

A. Beginning! When did they ever stop?

z. Oh, theres no use talking to you.

A. Not the slightest.

z. Oh well then, take a month's notice. [*She rises*].

A. A month's notice!

z. Yes: a month's notice.

A. A month's notice because I refuse to marry some ridiculous village maiden or illiterate widow with whom I could not hold a moment's conversation!

z. Wives are not for conversation: thats for visitors. Youve had plenty of conversation with me.

A. Leave yourself out of this conversation, please.

z. Oh, very well. A month's notice.

A. Dont say that again. Utter nonsense. What have you to complain of? You are quite well off here. I purposely pay you ten pounds a year more than you could get anywhere else.

z. Why?

A. What do you mean, why?

z. Why do you pay me ten pounds more than you

could get another assistant for?

A. Heaven only knows!

Z. [*in a fury*] I'll go this very day. I'll go this very minute. You can keep my month. You dont know when youre well off. Youre selfish. I dont wonder your wife died. Did she die mad?

A. [*gravely*] As a matter of fact, she did. I am one of those unlucky men who draw the black chances in the lottery of marriage.

Z. [*remorsefully*] Oh, I didnt know: I didnt indeed. I was only joking. [*She sits again*]. I wouldnt have said it for the world if I'd known.

A. Never mind: I know you didnt mean it. By the way, I made an inconsiderate remark which hurt you. I did not intend that. I should have told you seriously that I pay you ten pounds more than the market rate because I value your services in the shop, and wish to offer you every inducement to stay here permanently.

Z. Ten pounds extra, to stay all my life here as a single woman!

A. Not necessarily. You can get married if you wish.

Z. Who to?

A. To whom? Oh, anyone.

Z. Anyone in the village is good enough for me; but nobody in the village is good enough for you: is that it?

A. Dont lose your temper again.

Z. I will if I like. And if you knew how near I was to putting a couple of extra words in, youd perhaps realize that a woman wants something more in life than a job and a salary.

A. I know that perfectly well. There is one thing we are all out for when we are young.

z. And what is that, pray?

a. Trouble, adventure, hardship, care, disappointment, doubt, misery, danger, and death.

z. Not me, thank you. All I want is a husband and
the usual consequences.

a. The same thing. Marriage is the village form of
all these adventures.

z. Oh, why dont you take a more cheerful view of
life?

a. I have learnt not to expect too much from life.
That is the secret of real cheerfulness, because I am
always getting agreeable surprises instead of desolating
disappointments.

z. Well, your second marriage may be an agreeable
surprise, maynt it?

a. What, exactly, do you mean by my second marriage? I have only been married once. I mean I have
been married only once.

z. Well, look here? Straight, now? Is there any man
in this village that would be suitable to me now that I
have got used to you?

a. My dear: men are all alike.

z. You mean it will make no difference to me who I
marry.

a. Very little, I am afraid.

z. And women are all alike too, arnt they?

a. [*suspicious*] What are you getting at?

z. If it doesnt matter who anybody marries, then it
doesnt matter who I marry and it doesnt matter who you
marry.

a. Whom, not who.

z. Oh, speak English: youre not on the telephone
now. What I mean is that if it doesnt matter to me it

doesnt matter to you either.

A. You admit, then, that it doesnt matter?

z. No I dont. It's a lie.

A. Oh!

z. Dont "oh" me. All men are not alike to me. There are men—and good nice men, too—that I wouldnt let touch me. But when I saw you on the ship I said to myself "I could put up with him."

A. Not at all. You told me just now that you said something quite different. I believe you really said something much more rapturous. Being rather a futile sort of person I attract vigorous women like you.

z. When you looked at me out of the corner of your eye—you looked at all the women out of the corner of your eye in spite of your keeping yourself so much to yourself—did you never say "I could put up with her"?

A. No. I said "Damn that woman: she wont stop talking to me and interrupting my work."

z. Well, I tell you we were made for oneanother. It maynt be as plain to you as to me yet; but if it's plain to me there must be something in it; for I'm never wrong when I see a thing quite plain. I dont believe youd ever have bought this shop and given up being a gentleman if I hadnt been here.

A. Now that you mention it I believe that is true. You were one of the amenities of the estate.

z. Well, I might be one of the amenities of the estate of holy matrimony, mightnt I?

A. Take care. You may find what you are trying to do easier than you think. About five per cent of the human race consists of positive masterful acquisitive people like you, obsessed with some passion which they must gratify at all hazards. The rest let them have their own way because they have neither the strength nor the courage to resist, or because the things the masterful ones want seem trifling beside the starry heavens and the destiny of Man. I am not one of the masterful ones. I am not worth marrying. Any woman could marry me if she took trouble enough.

z. Thats just what I'm afraid of. If I let you out of my sight for a month I might find you married to someone else at the end of it. Well, I'm taking no chances. I dont set up to be masterful: I dont like selfish uppish domineering people any more than you do; but I must and will have you; and thats all about it.

a. Well, you already have me—as an employer. And you are independent of me, and can leave me if you are not satisfied.

z. How can I be satisfied when I cant lay my hands on you? I work for you like a slave for a month on end; and I would have to work harder as your wife than I do now; but there come times when I want to get hold of you in my arms, every bit of you; and when I do I'll give you something better to think about than the starry heavens, as you call them. Youll find that you have senses to gratify as well as fine things to say.

a. Senses! You dont know what youre talking about. Look around you. Here in this shop I have everything that can gratify the senses: apples, onions, and acid drops; pepper and mustard; cosy comforters and hot water bottles. Through the window I delight my eyes with the old church and market place, built in the days when beauty came naturally from the hands of mediæval craftsmen. My ears are filled with delightful sounds, from the cooing of doves and the humming of bees to the wireless echoes of Beethoven and Elgar. My nose can gloat over our sack of fresh lavender or our special sixpenny Eau de Cologne when the smell of rain on dry earth is denied me. My senses are saturated with satisfactions of all sorts. But when I am full to the neck with onions and acid drops; when I am so fed up with mediæval architecture that I had rather die than look at another cathedral; when all I desire is rest from sensation, not more of it, what use will my senses be to me if the starry heavens still seem no more than a senseless avalanche of lumps of stone and wisps of gas— if the destiny of Man holds out no higher hope to him than the final extinction and annihilation of so mischievous and miserable a creature?

z. We dont bother about all that in the village.

A. Yes you do. Our best seller here is Old Moore's Almanack; and next to it comes Napoleon's Book of Fate. Old Mrs Ward would never have sold the shop to me if she had not become persuaded that the Day of Judgment is fixed for the seventh of August next.

z. I dont believe such nonsense. Whats it all got to do with you and me?

A. You are inexperienced. You dont know. You are the dupe of thoughtless words like sensuality, sensuousness, and all the rest of the twaddle of the Materialists. I am not a Materialist: I am a poet; and I know that to be in your arms will not gratify my senses at all. As a matter of mere physical sensation you will find the bodily contacts to which you are looking forward neither convenient nor decorous.

z. Oh, dont talk like that. You mustnt let yourself think about it like that.

A. You must always let yourself think about everything. And you must think about everything as it is, not as it is talked about. Your secondhand gabble about gratifying my senses is only your virgin innocence. We shall get quite away from the world of sense. We shall light up for oneanother a lamp in the holy of holies in the temple of life; and the lamp will make its veil transparent. Aimless lumps of stone blundering through space will become stars singing in their spheres. Our dull purposeless village existence will become one irresistible purpose and nothing else. An extraordinary delight and an intense love will seize us. It will last hardly longer than the lightning flash which turns the black night into infinite radiance. It will be dark again before you can clear the light out of your eyes; but you will have seen; and for ever after you will think about what you have seen and not gabble catchwords invented by the wasted virgins that walk in darkness. It is to give ourselves this magic moment that we feel that we must and shall hold oneanother in our arms; and when the moment comes, the world of the senses will vanish; and for us there will be nothing ridiculous, nothing uncomfortable, nothing unclean, nothing but pure paradise.

z. Well, I am glad you take a nice view of it; for now I come to think of it I never could bear to be nothing more to a man than a lollipop. But you mustnt expect too much.

a. I shall expect more than you have ever dreamt of giving, in spite of the boundless audacity of women. What great men would ever have been married if the female nobodies who snapped them up had known the enormity of their own presumption? I believe they all thought they were going to refine, to educate, to make real gentlemen of their husbands. What do you intend to make of me, I wonder?

z. Well, I have made a decent shopkeeper of you already, havnt I? But you neednt be afraid of my not appreciating you. I want a fancy sort of husband, not a common villager that any woman could pick up. I shall be proud of you. And now Ive nailed you, I wonder at my own nerve.

a. So do I.

z. I'm not a bit like that, you know, really. Something above me and beyond me drove me on. Thats why I know it will be all right. Dont be afraid. I cant make a fine speech about it like you; but it will be all right. I promise you that.

a. Very well. Go round to the rectory; and put up the banns. And tell the rector's wife that we got in some prime artichokes this morning. She's fond of artichokes.

z. You are sure you feel happy about it?

a. I dont know what I feel about it. Go and do as you are told; and dont ask ridiculous questions.

The telephone rings. She hastens to answer it.

z. Number, please? . . . Oh, an order. Thanks very much. . . . Yes: we have some very fine artichokes just in this morning. . . . Thanks very much: they shall be sent round directly. Oh; and theres something else—are you there? . . . Sorry to detain you: could I speak to the rector? . . . Yes: it's rather particular. It's about banns . . . banns . . . BANNS: b for beauty, a for audacity, two enns for nonsense, and s for singing. . . . Yes, banns: thats right. . . . Who are the what? . . . Oh, the parties! Of course. Well, it's—

The curtain falls

In the Sunda Strait,
 27th January 1933

ON THE ROCKS

A POLITICAL COMEDY

1933

PREFACE

EXTERMINATION

IN this play a reference is made by a Chief of Police to the political necessity for killing people: a necessity so distressing to the statesmen and so terrifying to the common citizen that nobody except myself (as far as I know) has ventured to examine it directly on its own merits, although every Government is obliged to practise it on a scale varying from the execution of a single murderer to the slaughter of millions of quite innocent persons. Whilst assenting to these proceedings, and even acclaiming and celebrating them, we dare not tell ourselves what we are doing or why we are doing it; and so we call it justice or capital punishment or our duty to king and country or any other convenient verbal whitewash for what we instinctively recoil from as from a dirty job. These childish evasions are revolting. We must strip off the whitewash and find out what is really beneath it. Extermination must be put on a scientific basis if it is ever to be carried out humanely and apologetically as well as thoroughly.

KILLING AS A POLITICAL FUNCTION

That killing is a necessity is beyond question by any thoughtful person. Unless rabbits and deer and rats and foxes are killed, or "kept down" as we put it, mankind must perish; and that section of mankind which lives in the country and is directly and personally engaged in the struggle with Nature for a living has no sentimental doubts that they must be killed. As to tigers and poisonous snakes, their incompatibility with human civilization is unquestioned. This does not excuse the use of cruel steel traps, agonizing poisons, or packs of hounds as methods of extermination. Killing can be cruelly or kindly done; and the deliberate choice of cruel ways, and their organization as popular pleasures, is sinful; but the sin is in the cruelty and the enjoyment of it, not in the killing.

The Sacredness of Human Life

In law we draw a line between the killing of human animals and non-human ones, setting the latter apart as brutes. This was founded on a general belief that humans have immortal souls and brutes none. Nowadays more and more people are refusing to make this distinction. They may believe in The Life Everlasting and The Life to Come; but they make no distinction between Man and Brute, because some of them believe that brutes have souls, whilst others refuse to believe that the physical materializations and personifications of The Life Everlasting are themselves everlasting. In either case the mystic distinction between Man and Brute vanishes; and the murderer pleading that though a rabbit should be killed for being mischievous he himself should be spared because he has an immortal soul and a rabbit has none is as hopelessly out of date as a gentleman duellist pleading his clergy. When the necessity for killing a dangerous human being arises, as it still does daily, the only distinction we make between a man and a snared rabbit is that we very quaintly provide the

man with a minister of religion to explain to him that
we are not killing him at all, but only expediting his
transfer to an eternity of bliss.

The political necessity for killing him is precisely like
that for killing the cobra or the tiger: he is so ferocious
or unscrupulous that if his neighbors do not kill him
he will kill or ruin his neighbors; so that there is nothing for it but to disable him once for all by making an
end of him, or else waste the lives of useful and harmless people in seeing that he does no mischief, and cag-
ing him cruelly like a lion in a show.

Here somebody is sure to interject that there is the
alternative of teaching him better manners; but I am
not here dealing with such cases: the real necessity arises
only in dealing with untameable persons who are constitutionally unable to restrain their violent or acquisitive impulses, and have no compunction about sacrific-
ing others to their own immediate convenience. To
punish such persons is ridiculous: we might as reasonably punish a tile for flying off a roof in a storm and
knocking a clergyman on the head. But to kill them is
quite reasonable and very necessary.

PRESENT EXTERMINATIONS

All this so far is mere elementary criminology, already dealt with very fully by me in my Essay on
Prisons, which I recommend to those readers who may
feel impelled to ramble away at this point into the pros-
ings about Deterrence beloved by our Prison commissioners and judges. It disposes of the dogma of the
unconditional sacredness of human life, or any other in-
carnation of life; but it covers only a corner of the field

opened up by modern powers of extermination. In Germany it is suggested that the Nordic race should exterminate the Latin race. As both these lingual stocks are hopelessly interbred by this time, such a sacrifice to ethnological sciolism is not practicable; but its discussion familiarizes the idea and clears the way for practicable suggestions. The extermination of whole races and classes has been not only advocated but actually attempted. The extirpation of the Jew as such figured for a few mad moments in the program of the Nazi party in Germany. The extermination of the peasant is in active progress in Russia, where the extermination of the class of ladies and gentlemen of so-called independent means has already been accomplished; and an attempt to exterminate the old Conservative professional class and the kulak or prosperous farmer class has been checked only by the discovery that they cannot as yet be done without. Outside Russia the extermination of Communists is widely advocated; and there is a movement in the British Empire and the United States for the extermination of Fascists. In India the impulse of Moslems and Hindus to exterminate one another is complicated by the impulse of the British Empire to exterminate both when they happen to be militant Nationalists.

Previous Attempts Miss the Point

The novelty and significance of these instances consist in the equal status of the parties. The extermination of what the exterminators call inferior races is as old as history. "Stone dead hath no fellow" said Cromwell when he tried to exterminate the Irish. "The only good

nigger is a dead nigger" say the Americans of the
Ku-Klux temperament. "Hates any man the thing he
would not kill?" said Shylock naïvely. But we white
men, as we absurdly call ourselves in spite of the testi-
mony of our looking glasses, regard all differently
colored folk as inferior species. Ladies and gentlemen
class rebellious laborers with vermin. The Dominicans,
the watchdogs of God, regarded the Albigenses as the
enemies of God, just as Torquemada regarded the Jews
as the murderers of God. All that is an old story: what
we are confronted with now is a growing perception
that if we desire a certain type of civilization and culture
we must exterminate the sort of people who do not fit
into it. There is a difference between the shooting at
sight of aboriginal natives in the back blocks of Australia
and the massacres of aristocrats in the terror which followed the foreign attacks on the French Revolution.
The Australian gunman pots the aboriginal natives to
satisfy his personal antipathy to a black man with uncut
hair. But nobody in the French Republic had this feeling
about Lavoisier, nor can any German Nazi have felt that
way about Einstein. Yet Lavoisier was guillotined; and
Einstein has had to fly for his life from Germany. It
was silly to say that the Republic had no use for chem-
ists; and no Nazi has stultified his party to the extent
of saying that the new National Socialist Fascist State
in Germany has no use for mathematician-physicists. The
proposition is that aristocrats (Lavoisier's class) and
Jews (Einstein's race) are unfit to enjoy the privilege
of living in a modern society founded on definite principles of social welfare as distinguished from the old
promiscuous aggregations crudely policed by chiefs who
had no notion of social criticism and no time to invent it.

King Charles's Head

It was, by the way, the English Revolution which introduced the category of Malignant or Man of Blood, and killed the King as an affirmation that even kings must not survive if they are malignant. This was much more advanced than the execution in the following century of Louis XV as an ordinary traitor, or of the Tsar in our own time to prevent his being captured by the Tchekoslovakian contingent and used as a standard to rally the royalist reaction. Charles affirmed a divine personal right to govern as against the parliament and would keep no bargain with it. Parliament denied his right, and set up against it a divine right of election winners to govern. They fought it out; and the victorious election winners exterminated the king, very logically. Finding that their authority still needed a royal disguise they drove a hard bargain for a crown with his son, and, after ejecting the next king who broke it, a still harder one with his Dutch grandson before they allowed the title of king, with nine tenths of the meaning knocked out of it, to be used as a matter of convenience again in England. Nobody had a word to say against Charles's private character. It was solely for incompatibility of politics that he was eliminated, or "liquidated" as we say now. There was a real novelty in the transaction. The Church had for centuries before compelled the secular State to liquidate heretics; and the slaughter of rebels who tried to substitute one dynasty for another, or to seize the throne for themselves, was common routine. But Charles was neither a heretic nor a rebel. He was the assertor of a divine right to govern without winning elections; and because that right could not co-exist with the supremacy of a much richer and more powerful plutocracy off went his head.

Charles was only the first victim. After Culloden the defeated Highland chiefs and their clansmen were butchered like sheep on the field. Had they been merely prisoners of war, this would have been murder. But as they were also Incompatibles with British civilization, it was only liquidation.

Right to Exterminate Conferred by Private Property

Having disposed of the divine right of kings the political liquidators turned their attention slowly to its derivatory the divine right of landlords, which had gradually disguised itself as private property in land. For when a tract of land becomes the private property of an individual who has to depend on it for his subsistence, the relation between him and the inhabitants of that tract becomes an economic one; and if they become economically superfluous or wasteful, he must exterminate them. This is continually happening wherever private property in land exists. If I possess land and find it profitable to grow wheat on it, I need many agricultural laborers to enable me to do it; and I tolerate their existence accordingly. If I presently find that it is more profitable to cover my land with sheep and sell their wool, I have to tolerate the existence of the sheep; but I no longer need tolerate the existence of the laborers; so I drive them off my land, which is my legal method of extermination, retaining only a few to act as shepherds. Later on I find that it is more profitable to cover my land with wild deer, and collect money from gentlemen and ladies who enjoy shooting them. I then exterminate my shepherds and keep only a few gamekeepers. But I may do much better by letting my land to industrialists for the erection of factories. They exterminate the sheep and the deer; but they need far more men than I needed even when I grew wheat. The driven-offs crowd into the factories and multiply like rabbits; and for the moment population grows instead of diminishing. But soon machines come along and make millions of proletarians economically superfluous. The factory owner accordingly sacks them, which is his legal method of extermination. During these developments the exterminated, or, as we call them, the evicted and sacked, try to avoid starvation partly by emigration, but mostly by offering themselves for all sorts of employment as soldiers, servants, prostitutes, police officers, scavengers, and operators of the immense machinery of amusement and protection for the idle rich classes created by the private property system. By organization in trade unions, municipal and parliamentary Labor Parties, and the like, and maintaining a sort of continual civil war consisting of strikes and riots, they extort from the proprietors enough to reduce the rate of extermination (shewn by the actuarial expectation of life of the unpropertied) for periods described as progressive, until the proprietors, by engaging in suicidal wars, are forced to intensify their economies, and the rate of extermination rises again.

DISGUISES UNDER WHICH PRIVATE EXTERMINATION OPERATES

Note that during all this the Registrar General's returns do not give us the deaths of the exterminated as

such, because the exterminated do not starve as lost
travellers starve in the desert. Their starvation is more
or less protracted; and when the final catastrophe arrives, it is disguised under an imposing array of doctors'
names for moribundity. The victims die mostly in their
first year, and subsequently at all ages short of the age
at which properly nourished people die. Sometimes
they are starved into attaining an age at which people
with well filled pockets eat themselves to death. Either
way and all ways the extermination is a real and permanent feature of private property civilization, though it
is never mentioned as such, and ladies and gentlemen
are carefully educated to be unconscious of its existence
and to talk nonsense about its facts when they are too
obvious or become too scandalous to be ignored, when
they often advocate emigration or Birth Control or war
as remedies. And against the facts there is a chronic
humanitarian revolt expressing itself either underground
or overground in revolutionary movements; making our
political constitutions very unstable; and imposing an
habitual disingenuousness on conservative statesmen.

Private Powers of Life and Death

Now the central fact of all these facts is that the
private proprietors have irresponsible powers of life and
death in the State. Such powers may be tolerated as
long as the Government is in effect a committee of
private proprietors; yet if such a committee be widened
into or superseded by a Government acting in the interest of the whole people, that Government will not
suffer any private class to hold the lives of the citizens
at its mercy and thereby become their real masters. A

popular Government, before it fully grasps the situation, usually begins by attempting to redistribute property in such a manner as to make everyone a petty proprietor, as in the French Revolution. But when the impossibility of doing this (except in the special case of agricultural land) becomes apparent, and the question is probed to the bottom by unpropertied political philosophers like Proudhon and Marx, private property is sooner or later excommunicated and abolished; and what was formerly called "real property" is replaced by ordinary personal property and common property administrated by the State.

All modern progressive and revolutionary movements are at bottom attacks on private property. A Chancellor of the Exchequer apologizing for an increase in the surtax, a Fascist dictator organizing a Corporate State, a Soviet Commissar ejecting a kulak and adding his acres to a collective farm, are all running the same race, though all of them except the Commissar may be extremely reluctant to win it. For in the long run the power to exterminate is too grave to be left in any hands but those of a thoroughly Communist Government responsible to the whole community. The landlord with his writ of ejectment and the employer with his sack, must finally go the way of the nobleman with his sword and his benefit of clergy, and of Hannibal Chollop with his bowie knife and pistol.

Let us then assume that private property, already maimed by factory legislation, surtax, and a good deal of petty persecution in England, and in Russia tolerated only provisionally as a disgraceful necessity pending its complete extirpation, is finally discarded by civilized communities, and the duty of maintaining it at all costs

replaced by the duty of giving effect to the dogma that
every ablebodied and ableminded and ablesouled person has an absolute right to an equal share in the national dividend. Would the practice of extermination
thereupon disappear? I suggest that, on the contrary,
it might continue much more openly and intelligently
and scientifically than at present, because the humanitarian revolt against it would probably become a humanitarian support of it; and there would be an end
of the hypocrisy, the venal special pleading, and the
concealment or ignoring of facts which are imposed on
us at present because extermination for the benefit of a
handful of private persons against the interests of the
race is permitted and practised. The old doctrine of the
sacredness of human life, which in our idiot asylums
at Darenth and elsewhere still terrifies us into wasting
the lives of capable people in preserving the lives of
monsters, was a crude expedient for beginning civilization. At present we discard it in dealing with murderers,
heretics, traitors, and (in Scotland) vitriol throwers,
who can be legally killed. A runaway convict can also
be summarily shot by a warder to save the trouble of
pursuing and recapturing him; and although the convict
is not under capital sentence and the case is therefore
clearly one of wilful murder, coroners' juries persist in
treating it as a harmless and necessary incident in prison
routine.

Unfortunately the whole question is bedevilled by our
anti-Christian vice of punishment, expiation, sacrifice,
and all the cognate tribal superstitions which are hammered into us in our childhood by barbarous scripturists,
irascible or sadist parents, and a hideous criminal code.
When the horrors of anarchy force us to set up laws that

forbid us to fight and torture one another for sport, we still snatch at every excuse for declaring individuals outside the protection of law and torturing them to our hearts content.

CRUELTY'S EXCUSES

There have been summits of civilization at which heretics like Socrates, who was killed because he was wiser than his neighbors, have not been tortured, but ordered to kill themselves in the most painless manner known to their judges. But from that summit there was a speedy relapse into our present savagery. For Wallace, whom the Scots adored as a patriot and the English executed as a traitor, the most cruel and obscene method of killing that the human imagination could conceive at its vilest was specially invented to punish him for being a traitor (or "larn him to be a toad"); and this sentence has been passed, though not carried out, within the memory of persons now living. John of Leyden, for being a Communist, was tortured so frightfully before being hung up in a cage on the church tower to starve to death in sight of all the citizens and their little children, that the bishop who was officially obliged to witness it died of horror. Joan of Arc, for wearing men's clothes and being a Protestant and a witch, was burnt alive, after a proposal to torture her had been barely defeated. The people who saw her burnt were quite accustomed to such spectacles, and regarded them as holiday attractions. A woman's sex was made an excuse for burning her instead of more mercifully hanging her. Male criminals were broken on the wheel: that is, battered to death with iron bars, until well into the nineteenth century. This was a public spectacle;

and the prolongation of the victim's suffering was so elaborately studied and arranged that Cartouche, one of the kings of scoundrelism, was bribed to betray his accomplices by the promise that he should be killed by the sixth blow of the bar. The wheel and the stake have lately gone out of use; but the Sadist mania for flogging seems ineradicable; for after a partially successful attempt to discard it in Victorian times it has revived again with redoubled ferocity: quite recently a criminal was sentenced to a flogging and ten years penal servitude; and although the victim escaped his punishment and gave a sensational advertisement to its savagery by committing suicide, nobody protested, though thirty years ago there would have been a strenuous outcry against it, raised by the old Humanitarian League, and voiced in Parliament by the Irish Nationalists. Alas! the first thing the Irish did when they at last enjoyed self-government was to get rid of these sentimental Nationalists and put flogging on their statute book in a series of Coercion Acts that would have horrified Dublin Castle. In a really civilized state flogging would cease because it would be impossible to induce any decent citizen to flog another. Among us a perfectly respectable official will do it for half a crown, and probably enjoy the job.

LEADING CASE OF JESUS CHRIST

I dislike cruelty, even cruelty to other people, and should therefore like to see all cruel people exterminated. But I should recoil with horror from a proposal to punish them. Let me illustrate my attitude by a very famous, indeed far too famous, example of the popular conception of criminal law as a means of delivering up victims to the normal popular lust for cruelty which has been mortified by the restraint imposed on it by civilization. Take the case of the extermination of Jesus Christ. No doubt there was a strong case for it. Jesus was from the point of view of the High Priest a heretic and an impostor. From the point of view of the merchants he was a rioter and a Communist. From the Roman Imperialist point of view he was a traitor. From the commonsense point of view he was a dangerous madman. From the nobbish point of view, always a very influential one, he was a penniless vagrant. From the police point of view he was an obstructor of thoroughfares, a beggar, an associate of prostitutes, an apologist of sinners, and a disparager of judges; and his daily companions were tramps whom he had seduced into vagabondage from their regular trades. From the point of view of the pious he was a Sabbath breaker, a denier of the efficacy of circumcision and the advocate of a strange rite of baptism, a gluttonous man and a winebibber. He was abhorrent to the medical profession as an unqualified practitioner who healed people by quackery and charged nothing for the treatment. He was not anti-Christ: nobody had heard of such a power of darkness then; but he was startlingly anti-Moses. He was against the priests, against the judiciary, against the military, against the city (he declared that it was impossible for a rich man to enter the kingdom of heaven), against all the interests, classes, principalities and powers, inviting everybody to abandon all these and follow him. By every argument, legal, political, religious, customary, and polite, he was the most complete enemy of the society of his time ever brought to the bar. He was guilty on every count of the indictment, and on many more that his accusers had not the wit to frame. If he was innocent then the whole world was guilty. To acquit him was to throw over civilization and all its institutions. History has borne out the case against him; for no State has ever constituted itself on his principles or made it possible to live according to his commandments: those States who have taken his name have taken it as an alias to enable them to persecute his followers more plausibly.

It is not surprising that under these circumstances, and in the absence of any defence, the Jerusalem community and the Roman government decided to exterminate Jesus. They had just as much right to do so as to exterminate the two thieves who perished with him. But there was neither right nor reason in torturing him. He was entitled to the painless death of Socrates. We may charitably suppose that if the death could have been arranged privately between Pilate and Caiaphas Jesus would have been dispatched as quickly and suddenly as John the Baptist. But the mob wanted the horrible fun of seeing somebody crucified: an abominably cruel method of execution. Pilate only made matters worse by trying to appease them by having Jesus flogged. The soldiers, too, had to have their bit of sport, to crown him with thorns and, when they buffeted him, challenge him ironically to guess which of them had struck the blow.

"Crosstianity"

All this was cruelty for its own sake, for the pleasure of it. And the fun did not stop there. Such was and is the attraction of these atrocities that the spectacle of them has been reproduced in pictures and waxworks and exhibited in churches ever since as an aid to piety. The chief instrument of torture is the subject of a special Adoration. Little models of it in gold and ivory are worn as personal ornaments; and big reproductions in wood and marble are set up in sacred places and on graves. Contrasting the case with that of Socrates, one is forced to the conclusion that if Jesus had been humanely exterminated his memory would have lost ninetynine per cent of its attraction for posterity. Those who were specially susceptible to his morbid attraction were not satisfied with symbolic crosses which hurt nobody. They soon got busy with "acts of faith" which consisted of great public shows at which Jews and Protestants or Catholics, and anyone else who could be caught out on a point of doctrine, were burnt alive. Cruelty is so infectious that the very compassion it rouses is infuriated to take revenge by still viler cruelties.

The tragedy of this—or, if you will, the comedy— is that it was his clearness of vision on this very point that set Jesus so high above his persecutors. He taught that two blacks do not make a white; that evil should not be countered by worse evil but by good; that revenge and punishment only duplicate wrong; that we should conceive God, not as an irascible and vindictive tyrant but as an affectionate father. No doubt many private amiabilities have been inspired by this teaching; but politically it has received no more quarter than Pilate gave it. To all Governments it has remained paradoxical and impracticable. A typical acknowledgment of it was the hanging of a crucifix above the seat of the judge who was sentencing evildoers to be broken on the wheel.

CHRISTIANITY AND THE SEVENTH COMMANDMENT

Now it is not enough to satirize this. We must examine why it occurred. It is not enough to protest that evildoers must not be paid in their own coin by treating them as cruelly as they have treated others. We still have to stop the mischief they do. What is to be done with them? It is easy to suggest that they should be reformed by gentleness and shamed by non-resistance. By all means, if they respond to that treatment. But if gentleness fails to reform them and non-resistance encourages them to further aggression, what then? A month spent in a Tolstoyan community will convince anybody of the soundness of the nearest police inspector's belief that every normal human group contains not only a percentage of saints but also a percentage of irreclaimable scoundrels and good-for-noughts who will wreck any community unless they are expensively restrained or cheaply exterminated. Our Mosaic system of vindictive punishment, politely called "retributory" by Prison Commissioners, disposes of them temporarily; but it wastes the lives of honest citizens in guarding them; sets a horrible example of cruelty and malicious injury; costs a good deal of money that might be better spent; and, after all, sooner or later lets the scoundrel loose again to recommence his depredations. It would be much more sensible and less cruel to treat him as we treat mad dogs or adders, without malice or cruelty, and without reference to catalogues of particular crimes. The notion that persons should be safe from extermination as long as they do not commit wilful murder, or levy war against the Crown, or kidnap, or throw vitriol, is not only to limit social responsibility unnecessarily, and to privilege the large range of intolerable misconduct that lies outside them, but to divert attention from the essential justification for extermination, which is always incorrigible social incompatibility and nothing else.

THE RUSSIAN EXPERIMENT

The only country which has yet awakened to this extension of social responsibility is Russia. When the Soviet Government undertook to change over from Capitalism to Communism it found itself without any instruments for the maintenance of order except a list of crimes and punishments administered through a ritual of criminal law. And in the list of crimes the very worst offences against Communist society had no place: on the contrary they were highly honored and rewarded. As our English doggerel runs, the courts could punish a man for stealing the goose from off the common, but not the man who stole the common from the goose. The idler, that common enemy of mankind who robs everybody all the time, though he is so carefully protected from having his own pocket picked, incurred no penalty, and had actually passed the most severe laws against any interference with his idling. It was the business of the Soviet to make all business public business and all persons public servants; but the view of the ordinary Russian citizen was that a post in a public service was an exceptional stroke of good luck for the holder because it was a sinecure carrying with it the privilege of treating the public insolently and extorting bribes from it. For example, when the Russian railways were communized, some of the local stationmasters interpreted the change as meaning that they might now be as lazy and careless as they pleased, whereas in fact it was of life-or-death importance that they should redouble their activity and strain every nerve to make the service efficient. The unfortunate Commissar who was Minister of Transport found himself obliged to put a pistol in his pocket and with his own hand shoot stationmasters who had thrown his telegrams into the dustbin instead of attending to them, so that he might the more impressively ask the rest of the staff whether they yet grasped the fact that orders are meant to be executed.

INADEQUACY OF PENAL CODES

Now being Minister of Transport, or Minister of any other public service, is a whole time job: it cannot be permanently combined with that of amateur executioner, carrying with it the reputation in all the capitalist papers of the west of being a ferocious and cold-blooded murderer. And no conceivable extension of the criminal code nor of the service disciplines, with their lists of specific offences and specific penalties, could have provided for instant exemplary exterminations of this kind, any more than for the growing urgency of how to dispose of people who would not or could not fit themselves into the new order of things by conforming to its new morality. It would have been easy to specify certain offences and certain penalties in the old fashion: as, for instance, if you hoard money you will be shot; if you speculate in the difference in purchasing power of the rouble in Moscow and Berlin you will be shot; if you buy at the Co-operative to sell at the private trader's shop you will be shot; if you take bribes you will be shot; if you falsify farm or factory balance sheets you will be shot; if you exploit labor you will be shot; and it will be useless to plead that you have been brought up to regard these as normal business activities, and that the whole of respectable society outside Russia agrees with you. But the most elaborate code of this sort would still have left unspecified a hundred ways in which wreckers of Communism could have sidetracked it without ever having to face the essential questions: are you pulling your weight in the social boat? are you giving more trouble than you are worth? have you earned the privilege of living in a civilized community? That is why the Russians were forced to set up an Inquisition or Star Chamber, called at first the Cheka and now the Gay Pay Oo (Ogpu), to go into these questions and "liquidate" persons who could not answer them satisfactorily. The security against the abuse of this power of life and death was that the Cheka had no interest in liquidating anybody who could be made publicly useful, all its interests being in the opposite direction.

LIMITED LIABILITY IN MORALS

Such a novelty is extremely terrifying to us, who are still working on a system of limited liability in morals. Our "free" British citizens can ascertain exactly what they may do and what they may not do if they are to keep out of the hands of the police. Our financiers know that they must not forge share certificates nor overstate their assets in the balance sheets they send to their shareholders. But provided they observe a few conditions of this kind they are free to enter upon a series of quite legitimate but not the less nefarious operations. For example, making a corner in wheat or copper or any other cornerable commodity and forcing up prices so as to make enormous private fortunes for themselves, or making mischief between nations through the Press to stimulate the private trade in armaments. Such limited liability no longer exists in Russia, and is not likely to exist in the future in any highly civilized state. It may be quite impossible to convict a forestaller or regrator under a criminal code of having taken a single illegal step, but quite easy to convince any reasonable body of judges that he is what the people call "a wrong one." In Russia such a conviction would lead to his disappearance and the receipt by his family of a letter to say that they need not wait up for him, as he would not return home any more.[1] In our country he would enjoy his gains in high honor and personal security, and thank his stars that he lived in a free country and not in Communist Russia.

But as the new tribunal has been forced on Russia by pressure of circumstances and not planned and thought out at leisure, the two institutions, the Ogpu and the ordinary police administering the criminal code, work side by side, with the odd result that the surest way to escape the Ogpu is to commit an ordinary crime and take refuge in the arms of the police and the magistrate, who cannot exterminate you because capital punishment has been abolished in Russia (liquidation by the Ogpu is not punishment: it is only "weeding the garden"); and the sentence of imprisonment, though it may seem severe to us in view of the cruelty of our

[1] Note, however, that a sentence of extermination should never be so certain as to make it worth the delinquent's while to avoid arrest by murdering his or her pursuers.

treatment of criminals, will be carried out with comparative leniency, and probably, if the culprit behaves well, be remitted after a while. As four years imprisonment is considered enough for any reasonable sort of murder, a cornerer who finds himself in imminent danger of detection and liquidation by the Ogpu would be well advised to lose his temper and murder his mother-in-law, thereby securing a lease of life for at least four years.

Sooner or later this situation will have to be thoroughly studied and thought out to its logical conclusion in all civilized countries. The lists of crimes and penalties will obsolesce like the doctors' lists of diseases and medicines; and it will become possible to be a judge without ceasing to be a Christian. And extermination, my present subject, will become a humane science instead of the miserable mixture of piracy, cruelty, vengeance, race conceit, and superstition it now is.

Natural Limit to Extermination

Fortunately the more frankly and realistically it is faced the more it detaches itself from the associations with crude slaughter which now make it terrible. When Charlemagne founded the Holy Roman Empire (as far as anyone can be said to have founded it) he postulated that all its subjects must be Catholic Christians, and made an amateurish attempt to secure this condition of social stability by killing everyone who fell into his power and refused to be baptized. But he cannot ever have got very far with it, because there is one sort of bird you must not kill on any pretext whatever: namely, the goose that lays the golden eggs. In Russia the Soviet Government began by a Charlemagnesque attempt to exterminate the bourgeoisie by classing them as intelligentsia, restricting their rations, and putting their children at the foot of the overcrowded educational list. They also proscribed the kulak, the able, hardheaded, hard-fisted farmer who was richer than his neighbors and liked to see them poorer than himself. Him they rudely took by the shoulders and threw destitute into the lane. There were plausible reasons for this beginning of selection in population; for the moral outlook of the bourgeoisie and the kulaks was dangerously anti-social. But the results were disastrous. The bourgeoisie contained the professional class and the organizing business class. Without professional men and business organizers nothing could be done in the industries; and the hope that picked members of the proletariat could take up professional and organizing work on the strength of their native talent in sufficient numbers was crushingly disappointed. When the kulak was thrown out of his farm, and his farming ability paralyzed, food ran short. Very soon the kulak had to be thrown back into his farm and told to carry on until his hour had come; and a pleasant convention was established whereby all educated persons, however obviously ladies or gentlemen, who were willing to assure the authorities that their fathers had "worked on the land with their hands" were accepted as genuine proletarians, and transferred from the infamous category of intelligentsia to the honorable one of "the intellectual proletariat." Even Lenin and his colleagues, all ultra-bourgeois (otherwise they would never have so absurdly overestimated the intellectual resources of the proletariat and been so contemptuous of the pretension of their own class to be indispensable), allowed their parents to be described as hornyhanded

cultivators of the soil. The pretence has now become a
standing joke; but you will still come up against it if
you accuse any Russian of being a lady or gentleman.

INCOMPATIBILITY OF PEASANTRY WITH MODERN CIVILIZATION

These, however, are merely expedients of transition.
The Russian proletariat is now growing its own professional and organizing class; and the ex-bourgeois is
dying out, after seeing his children receive a sound Communist education and being lectured by them on his old-
fashioned prejudices. And the planners of the Soviet
State have no time to bother about moribund questions;
for they are confronted with the new and overwhelming
necessity for exterminating the peasants, who still exist
in formidable numbers. The notion that a civilized State
can be made out of any sort of human material is one of
our old Radical delusions. As to building Communism
with such trash as the Capitalist system produces it is out
of the question. For a Communist Utopia we need a population of Utopians; and Utopians do not grow wild
on the bushes nor are they to be picked up in the slums:
they have to be cultivated very carefully and expensively. Peasants will not do; yet without the peasants
the Communists could never have captured the Russian
Revolution. Nominally it was the Soviets of peasants
and soldiers who backed Lenin and saved Communism
when all Western Europe set on him like a pack of
hounds on a fox. But as all the soldiers were peasants,
and all the peasants hungry for property, the military
element only added to the peasants' cry of Give us land,
the soldiers' cry of Give us peace. Lenin said, in effect,

Take the land; and if feudally minded persons obstruct you, exterminate them; but do not burn their houses, as you will need them to live in. And it was the resultant legions of petty landed proprietors that made Lenin's position impregnable, and provided Trotsky and Stalin with the Red soldiers who defeated the counter-revolutionists of 1918. For the counter-revolution, in which we, to our eternal shame, took part (England sets the example of revolution and then attacks all other countries which presume to follow it), meant bringing the old landlords back; and the peasant fought against that as the mercenaries and conscripts of the Capitalist armies would not fight in favor of it.

A Peasant Victory is a Victory for Private Property

So far so good for Lenin; but the war against the counter-revolutionists, when it ended in victory for the peasant proprietor, was really a victory for private property, and was therefore succeeded by a fiercer struggle between the fanatically Communist Government and the fiercely individualist peasant proprietor, who wanted the produce of his plot for himself, and had no notion of pooling it with anybody, least of all with the urban proletarians who seemed like another species to him. Left to themselves the moujiks would have reproduced Capitalist civilization at its American worst in ten years. Thus the most urgent task before the victorious Communist Government was the extermination of the moujik; and yet the moujik, being still the goose that laid the golden eggs, could not be exterminated summarily without incidentally exterminating the whole Russian nation.

The way out of this deadlock was obvious enough, though very expensive and tedious. You can exterminate any human class not only by summary violence but by bringing up its children to be different. In the case of the Russian peasantry the father lives in a lousy kennel, at no man's call but his own, and extracts a subsistence by primitive methods from a strip of land on which a tractor could hardly turn even if he could afford such a luxury, but which is his very own. His book is a book of Nature, from which all wisdom can be gathered by those who have been taught to read it by due practice on printed books; but he has not been so practised, and for cultural purposes has to be classed as ignorant, though he knows things that university professors do not know. He is brutalized by excessive muscular labor; he is dirty; his freedom from civilized control leaves him so unprotected from the tyranny of Nature that it becomes evident to his children that the highly regulated people in the nearest collectivist farm, where thousands of acres are cultivated by dozens of tractors, and nobody can put his foot on one of the acres or his hand on one of the tractors and say "This is my own to do what I like with," are better fed and housed, nicer, and much more leisured, and consequently free, than he ever is.

PREVENTIVE EXTERMINATION: ITS DIFFICULTIES

In short, you exterminate the peasant by bringing up his children to be scientifically mechanized farmers and to live a collegiate life in cultivated society. It sounds simple; but the process requires better planning than is always forthcoming (with local famines and revolts as the penalty); for while the grass grows the steed

starves; and when education means not only schools
and teachers, but giant collective farms equipped with
the most advanced agricultural machinery, which means
also gigantic engineering works for the production of
the machinery, you may easily find that you have spent
too much on these forms of capitalization and are running short of immediately consumable goods, presenting
the spectacle of the nation with the highest level of general culture running short of boots and tightening its
belt for lack of sufficient food.

I must not suggest that this has occurred all over
Russia; for I saw no underfed people there; and the
children were remarkably plump. And I cannot trust
the reports; for I have no sooner read in The Times a
letter from Mr Kerensky assuring me that in the Ukraine the starving people are eating one another, than
M. Herriot, the eminent French statesman, goes to
Russia and insists on visiting the Ukraine so that he
may have ocular proof of the alleged cannibalism, but
can find no trace of it. Still, between satiety and starvation mitigated by cannibalism there are many degrees
of shortage; and it is no secret that the struggle of the
Russian Government to provide more collective farms
and more giant factories to provide agricultural machinery for them has to be carried on against a constant
clamor from the workers for new boots and clothes, and
more varied food and more of it: in short, less sacrifice
of the present to the future. As Stalin said quaintly
"They will be demanding silver watches next." The
constant correction of the inevitable swerves towards one
extreme or the other, analogous to the control of the
Bank rate by the Bank of England (only enormously
more laborious), strains all the wit and industry of the

Russian rulers; and occasional sideslips must be inevitable during these years when the ablest and oldest Communists are still learners.

TEMPERAMENTAL DIFFICULTIES

Even when the extinction of the bourgeoisie and the kulaks and the old aristocracy is complete, and the Russian population consists of citizens educated as Communists, there will still be questions to settle which are at bottom questions as to the sort of civilization that is desirable; and this involves a decision as to the sort of people that are desirable and undesirable. Some of us, believing that a more primitive life than ours would be happier and better, advocate "a return to nature." Others dream of a much more mechanized, specialized, and complicated life. Some of us value machinery because it makes a shorter working day possible for us: others value it because it enriches us by increasing the product per hour. Some of us would like to take things easy and retire at 60: others would like to work their utmost and retire at 40. Some of us will say Let us be content with £200 a year: others No: let us live at the rate of £20,000 a year and strain every faculty to earn it. Some of us want a minimum of necessary work and a maximum of liberty to think and discover and experiment in the extension of science and art, philosophy and religion, sport and exploration: others, caring for none of these things, and desiring nothing more than to be saved the trouble of thinking and to be told what to do at every turn, would prefer thoughtless and comfortable tutelage and routine, not knowing what to do with themselves when at liberty. A life filled with scientific curiosity would be hell for the people who would not cross the street to find out whether the earth is flat or round; and a person with no ear for music would strenuously object to work for the support of municipal bands, whilst people of Shakespear's tastes would agitate for the extermination of the unmusical.

Importance of Laziness for Fallowing

Some of these differences could be settled on give-and-take lines. The division of society into classes with different tastes and capacities—different natures, as folks call it—would not shake social stability provided everyone had an equal share of the national dividend. It is not true that it takes all sorts to make a world; for there are some sorts that would destroy any world very soon if they were suffered to live and have their way; but it is true that in the generations of men continuous high cultivation is not expedient: there must be fallows, or at least light croppings, between the intense cultivations; for we cannot expect the very energetic and vital Napoleon to be the son of any equally energetic father or the father of an equally vital son. Nobody has yet calculated how many lazy ancestors it takes to produce an indefatigable prodigy; but it is certain that dynasties of geniuses do not occur, and that this is the decisive objection to hereditary rulers (though not, let me hasten to add, to hereditary figure heads). There is a large field for toleration here: the clever people must suffer fools gladly, and the easygoing ones find out how to keep the energetic ones busy. There may be as good biological reasons for the existence of the workshy as of the workmad. Even one and the same person may have spells of intense activity and slackness varying from weeks to years.

Nevertheless there will be conflicts to the death in the creation of artificial humanity. There is nothing that can be changed more completely than human nature when the job is taken in hand early enough. Such artificial products as our agricultural laborers and urban mechanics, our country gentlemen and city plutocrats, though they are from the same human stock, are so different that they cannot live together without great discomfort, and are practically not intermarriageable. It is possible to get rid of their social incompatibility by giving them all the same education and income, and ranking them all in the same class. For example, Lord Lonsdale is not in the least socially incompatible with Dean Inge, though a really critical naturalist would as soon class Shetland ponies with zebras as lump these two gentlemen under the same heading. But the question remains, what is this same education to be? The training of the scholar and the sportsman may split and diverge as they adolesce; but they must start from a common training and a common morality as children. And when the state has to prescribe a uniform moral curriculum the variety of our temperaments makes it impossible to please everybody. The Quaker and the Ritualist, the Fundamentalist and the Freethinker, the Vegetarian and the flesh eater, the missionary and the cannibal, the humanitarian and the sportsman-hunter, the military terrorist and the Christian, will not agree as to the faiths and habits to be inculcated upon the children of the community in order that they may be good citizens. Each temperament will demand the extermination of the other through the schools and nurseries, and the establishment of its temperamental faith and habits as standard in these factories of future citizens. All will agree to exterminate illiteracy by compulsory reading, writing, and arithmetic: indeed they have already done so. But all will not agree on a standard religion. Yet a standard religion is indispensable, however completely it may shed the old theologies. Every attempt to banish religion from the schools proves that in this respect Nature abhors a vacuum, and that the community must make up its mind, or have its mind made up for it by its official thinkers, as to what its children are to be taught to believe and how they should be trained to behave. Compromise is ruled out by the nature of the case. What compromise is possible between myself, for instance, who believe in the religion of Creative Evolution, the economics of Socialism, and a diet from which the dead bodies of men, fish, fowls, and animals are rigidly excluded, and my Fundamentalist neighbors who believe that all Evolutionists go to hell; that children languish and die without beefsteaks; and that without private property civilization must perish? We cannot exterminate one another at present; but the time cannot be very far off when the education authorities will have to consider which set of beliefs is the better qualification for citizenship in Utopia.

ECLECTIC RELIGIONS

They will probably pigeon-hole both, and proceed eclectically to compile several creeds suitable to the several capacities and ages of the children. For there is clearly no sense in offering the religion of a mature and scholarly philosopher to a child of five, nor attempting to bring the cosmogonies of Dante and Aquinas, Hegel and Marx, within the comprehension of a village dunce. Nurses rule their little charges by threatening them with bogies in whose existence no nurse believes, exactly as Mahomet ruled his Arabs by promises of a paradise and threats of a hell the details of which he must have known to be his own invention even if he did believe generally in a post mortem life of rewards and punishments for conduct in this world. Therefore I do not suggest that the education authorities in Utopia will seek for absolute truth in order to inculcate it though the heavens fall. Nor do I advise a return to Queen Elizabeth's plan of 39 Articles to please everybody by alternately affirming and denying all the disputed beliefs. The likeliest outcome is an elaborate creed of useful illusions, to be discarded bit by bit as the child is promoted from standard to standard or form to form, except such of them as adults may be allowed to comfort themselves with for the sake of the docility they produce.

There would be nothing new in this: it is what our authorities do at present, except that they do it unsystematically and unconsciously, being mostly more or less duped themselves by the illusions. Unfortunately they allow the illusions to fall behind the times and become incredible, at which point they become exceedingly dangerous; for when people are brought up on creeds which they cannot believe, they are left with no creeds at all, and are apt to buy pistols and take to banditry bag snatching and racketeering when employment fails and they find themselves short of money. It is the importance of keeping our inculcated illusions up to date that throws our higher professional classes into wild alarm when the individual liberty of thought, speech, and conscience which they think they possess (this is one of their inculcated illusions) is threatened by the dictatorships which are springing up all over the world as our pseudo-democratic parliamentary institutions reduce themselves more and more disastrously to absurdity.

IMPORTANCE OF FREE THOUGHT

Let me try to straighten this out for them. It was very generally believed as lately as in Victorian times that religious education consisted in imparting to children certain eternal, final, and absolute truths. I, for instance, being the son of an Irish Protestant gentleman, found myself, at the dawn of my infant conscience, absolutely convinced that all Roman Catholics go to hell when they die, a conviction which involved not only a belief in the existence of hell but a whole series of implications as to the nature and character of God. Now that I am older I cannot regard this as anything more than a provisional hypothesis which, on consideration, I must definitely reject. As the more pious of my uncles would have put it, I have lost my religious faith and am in peril of damnation as an Apostate. But I do not present my creed of Creative Evolution as anything more than another provisional hypothesis. It differs from the old Dublin brimstone creed solely in its greater credibility: that is, its more exact conformity to the facts alleged by our scientific workers, who have somehow won that faith in their infallibility formerly enjoyed by our priests. No future education authority, unless it is as badly educated as our present ones, will imagine that it has any final and eternal truths to inculcate: it can only select the most useful working hypotheses and inculcate them very much as it inculcates standard behavior throughout that vast field of civilized conduct in which it does not matter in the least how people act in particular situations provided they all act in the same way, as in the rule of the road. All the provisional hypotheses may be illusions; but if they conduce to beneficial conduct they must be inculcated and acted on by Governments until better ones arrive.

Toleration Mostly Illusory

But, cry the professors, are the hypotheses never to be questioned? Is disillusion to be punished as a crime? That will always depend a good deal on circumstances. One of the best religious brains in England has said that the war of 1914–18 was foolish and unnecessary; and nobody now dreams of prosecuting him; but he would not have been allowed to go through the trenches from platoon to platoon saying so just before zero hour, with or without the addition "Sirs, ye are brethren: why do ye wrong one to another?" I have no illusion of being free to say and write what I please. I went round the world lately preaching that if Russia were thrust back from Communism into competitive Capitalism, and China developed into a predatory Capitalist State, either independently or as part of a Japanese Asiatic hegemony, all the western States would have to quintuple their armies and lie awake at nights in continual dread of hostile aeroplanes, the obvious moral being that

whether we choose Communism for ourselves or not,
it is our clear interest, even from the point of view of
our crudest and oldest militarist diplomacy, to do everything in our power to sustain Communism in Russia and
extend it in China, where at present provinces containing
at the least of many conflicting estimates eighteen millions of people, have adopted it. Now I was not physically prevented from saying this, nor from writing and
printing it. But in a western world suffering badly from
Marxphobia, and frantically making itself worse like a
shrew in a bad temper, I could not get a single newspaper to take up my point or report my utterance. When
I say anything silly, or am reported as saying anything
reactionary, it runs like wildfire through the Press of
the whole world. When I say anything that could
break the carefully inculcated popular faith in Capitalism the silence is so profound as to be almost audible.
I do not complain, because I do not share the profes-
sorial illusion that there is any more freedom for dis-
illusionists in the British Empire and the United States
of North America than in Italy, Germany, and Russia.
I have seen too many newspapers suppressed and editors
swept away, not only in Ireland and India but in London in my time, to be taken in by Tennyson's notion
that we live in a land where a man can say the thing he
will. There is no such country. But this is no excuse
for the extravagances of censorship indulged in by
jejune governments of revolutionists, and by Churches
who imagine they possess the eternal truth about everything, to say nothing of hereditary autocrats who conceive that they are so by divine right. Our papers are
silent about the suppression of liberty in Imperialist
Japan, though in Japan it is a crime to have "dangerous

thoughts." In my native Ireland, now nominally a Free
State, one of my books is on the index; and I have no
doubt all the rest will follow as soon as the clerical censorship discovers their existence. In Austria my chronicle
play St Joan had to be altered to please Catholic authorities who know much less about Catholicism than I
do. In America books which can be bought anywhere
in Europe are forbidden. The concentration of British
and American attention on the intolerances of Fascism
and Communism creates an illusion that they do not
exist elsewhere; but they exist everywhere, and must be
met, not with ridiculous hotheaded attacks on Germany,
Italy, and Russia, but by a restatement of the case for
Toleration in general.

LEADING CASES: SOCRATES AND JESUS

It is a historical misfortune that the most world-
famous victims of persecution made no valid defence.
Socrates and Jesus are the most talked of in Christian
countries. Socrates at his trial was in full possession of
his faculties, and was allowed to say everything he had
to say in his defence; but instead of defending his right
to criticize he infuriated his accusers by launching at
them a damning contrast between their infamous corruption and mendacity and his own upright disinterest-
edness and blameless record as citizen and soldier. Jesus
made no defence at all. He did not regard himself as a
prisoner being tried for a vulgar offence and using all
his wit to escape condemnation. He believed that he
was going through a sacrificial rite in which he should be
slain, after which he should rise from the dead and come
again in glory to establish his kingdom on earth for ever.

It does not matter to our present purpose whether this was the delusion of a madman or a hard and holy fact: in either case the question of toleration was not at issue for him; therefore he did not raise it.

THE CASE OF GALILEO

In the epoch which Jesus inaugurated, or at least in which his name was habitually taken in vain, we have Joan of Arc and John of Leyden, Giordano Bruno and Galileo, Servetus and John Hus and the heroes of Foxe's Book of Martyrs standing out in our imagination from thousands of forgotten martyrdoms. Galileo is a favored subject with our scientists; but they miss the point because they think that the question at issue at his trial was whether the earth went round the sun or was the stationary centre round which the sun circled. Now that was not the issue. Taken by itself it was a mere question of physical fact without any moral significance, and therefore no concern of the Church. As Galileo was not burnt and certainly not abhorred, it is quite credible that both his immediate judges and the Pope believed with at least half their minds that he was right about the earth and the sun. But what they had to consider was whether the Christian religion, on which to the best of their belief not only the civilization of the world but its salvation depended, and which had accepted the Hebrew scriptures and the Greek testament as inspired revelations, could stand the shock of the discovery that many of its tales, from the tactics of Joshua in the battle of Gibeon to the Ascension, must have been written by somebody who did not know what the physical universe was really like. I am quite familiar with the pre-Galileo universe of the Bible and St Augustine. As a child I thought of the earth as being an immense ground floor with a star studded ceiling which was the floor of heaven, and a basement which was hell. That Jesus should be taken up into the clouds as the shortest way to heaven seemed as natural to me as that, at the Opera, Mephistopheles should come up from hell through a trap in the floor. But if instead of telling me that Jesus was taken up into the clouds and that the disciples saw him no more, which still makes me feel quite holy, you tell me that he went up like a balloon into the stratosphere, I do not feel holy: I laugh obstreperously. The exalting vision has suddenly become a ribald joke. That is what the Church feared; and that is what has actually happened. Is it any wonder that the Pope told Galileo that he really must keep his discoveries to himself, and that Galileo consented to deny them? Possibly it was the Pope who, to console him, whispered "E pur se muove."

FIGMENT OF THE SELFREGARDING ACTION

St Joan did not claim toleration: she was so far from believing in it that she wanted to lead a crusade of extermination against the Husites, though she was burnt for sharing their heresy. That is how all the martyrs have missed the point of their defence. They all claimed to possess absolute truth as against the error of their persecutors, and would have considered it their duty to persecute for its sake if they had had the power. Real toleration: the toleration of error and falsehood, never occurred to them as a principle possible for any sane government. And so they have left us no model defence.

And there is no modern treatise known to me which quite supplies this need. Stuart Mill's Essay on Liberty satisfied the nineteenth century, and was my own first textbook on the subject; but its conclusion that selfregarding actions should not be interfered with by the authorities carries very little weight for Socialists who perceive that in a complex modern civilization there are no purely selfregarding actions in the controversial sphere. The color of a man's braces or a woman's garters may concern the wearers alone; but people have never been burnt for wearing black underclothes instead of white; and the notion that preaching a sermon or publishing a pamphlet can be classed as a selfregarding action is manifestly absurd. All great Art and Literature is propaganda. Most certainly the heresies of Galileo were not selfregarding actions: his feat of setting the earth rolling was as startling as Joshua's feat of making the sun stand still. The Church's mistake was not in interfering with his liberty, but in imagining that the secret of the earth's motion could be kept, and fearing that religion could not stand the shock of its disclosure, or a thousand such. It was idiotic to try to adapt Nature to the Church instead of continually adapting the Church to Nature by changing its teaching on physical matters with every advance made in our knowledge of Nature. In treating the legend of Joshua's victory as a religious truth instead of insisting that it did not make the smallest difference to religion whether Joshua was any more real than Jack the Giant Killer, and that Galileo might play skittles with the whole solar system without moving the Eternal Throne and the Papal Chair which was its visible tangible symbol on earth a single inch, it lost a great opportunity, as it has since lost many others, leaving itself open to the reproach of stupidity in not understanding Galileo's argument, of pride in not having humility enough to admit that it had been wrong in its astronomy, and of feebleness of faith and confusion of the temporal with the spiritual as aforesaid, laying itself open to much damaging Protestant and scientific disparagement, both mostly open to precisely the same reproaches.

INCOMPLETENESS OF THE GREAT TRIALS

No doubt Galileo missed the real point at issue as completely as Socrates or Jesus. For this we need not blame him: he was a physicist and not a politician; and to him the only questions at issue were whether the earth moved or not, and whether a ten pound cannon ball would fall twice as fast as a five pound one or only just as fast and no faster. But Socrates was by vocation and habit a solver of problems of conduct, both personal and political; and Jesus, who had spent his life in propounding the most staggering paradoxes on the same subject, not by any means always in the abstract, but as personal directions to his followers, must, if he had any sense of moral responsibility, have been challenged by his own conscience again and again as to whether he had any right to set men on a path which was likely to lead the best of them to the cross and the worst of them to the moral destruction described by St Augustine. No man could expressly admit that his word would bring not peace but a sword without having satisfied himself that he was justified in doing so. He must have been told as frequently as I have been told that he was giving pain to many worthy people; and even with the

fullest allowance for the strain of impishness with which
the Life Force endows those of us who are destined by
it to *épater le bourgeois*, he cannot have believed that
the mere satisfaction of this Punchesque *Schadenfreude*
could justify him in hurting anyone's feelings. What,
then, would have been his defence if, at his trial, he
had been his old self, defending himself as an accused
man threatened with a horrible penalty, instead of a
god going through an inevitable ordeal as a prelude to
the establishment of his kingdom on earth?

A Modern Passion Play Impossible

The question is of such importance at the present
crisis, when the kingdoms are breaking up, and upstart
rulers are sowing their wild oats by such grotesque per-
secutions that Galileo's great successor Einstein is a
plundered fugitive from officially threatened extermination, that I must endeavor to dramatize the trial of
Jesus as it might have proceeded had it taken place
before Peter uttered his momentous exclamation "Thou
art the Christ." I have been asked repeatedly to dramatize the Gospel story, mostly by admirers of my drama-
tization of the trial of St Joan. But the trial of a dumb
prisoner, at which the judge who puts the crucial question to him remains unanswered, cannot be dramatized
unless the judge is to be the hero of the play. Now Pilate,
though perhaps a trifle above the average of colonial
governors, is not a heroic figure. Joan tackled her judges
valiantly and wittily: her trial was a drama ready made,
only needing to be brought within theatrical limits of
time and space to be a thrilling play. But Jesus would
not defend himself. It was not that he had not a word

to say for himself, nor that he was denied the opportunity of saying it. He was not only allowed but challenged to defend himself. He was an experienced public speaker, able to hold multitudes with his oratory, happy and ready in debate and repartee, full of the illustrative hypothetical cases beloved of lawyers (called parables in the Gospels), and never at a loss when plied with questions. If ever there was a full dress debate for the forensic championship to be looked forward to with excited confidence by the disciples of the challenged expert it was this trial of Christ. Yet their champion put up no fight: he went like a lamb to the slaughter, dumb. Such a spectacle is disappointing on the stage, which is the one thing that a drama must not be; and when the disappointment is followed by scourging and crucifixion it is unbearable: not even the genius of our Poet Laureate, with all the magic of Canterbury Cathedral for scenery, can redeem it except for people who enjoy horror and catastrophe for their own sake and have no intellectual expectations to be disappointed.

DIFFERENCE BETWEEN READER AND SPECTATOR

It may be asked why the incident of the trial and execution must fail on the stage, seeing that the gospel narrative is so pathetic, and so many of us have read it without disappointment. The answer is very simple: we have read it in childhood; and children go on from horror to horror breathlessly, knowing nothing of the constitutional questions at issue. Some of them remain in this condition of intellectual innocence to the end of their lives, whilst the cleverer ones seldom reconsider the impressions they have received as little children. Most Christians, I suspect, are afraid to think about it critically at all, having been taught to consider criticism blasphemous when applied to Bible stories. Besides, there are a thousand things that will pass in a well told story that will not bear being brought to actuality on the stage. The evangelists can switch off our attention from Jesus to Peter hearing the cock crow (or the bugle blow) or to Pilate chaffering with the crowd about Barabbas; but on the stage the dumb figure cannot be got rid of: it is to him that we look for a speech that will take us up to heaven, and not to the weeping of Peter and the bawling of the mob, which become unbearable interruptions instead of skilful diversions.

For my part, when I read the story over again as an adult and as a professional critic to boot, I felt the disappointment so keenly that I have been ever since in the condition of the musician who, when he had gone to bed, heard somebody play an unresolved discord, and could not go to sleep until he had risen to play the resolution on his piano. What follows is my attempt to resolve Pilate's discord. I begin with the narrative of St John, the only one of the four which represents Jesus as saying anything more than any crazy person might in the same circumstances.

PILATE. Are you the king of the Jews?

JESUS. Do you really want to know? or have those people outside put it into your head to ask me?

PILATE. Am I a Jew, that I should trouble myself about you? Your own people and their priests have brought you to me for judgment. What have you done?

JESUS. My kingdom is not of this world: if it were,

my followers would have fought the police and rescued me. But that sort of thing does not happen in my kingdom.

PILATE. Then you are a king?

JESUS. You say so. I came into this world and was born a common man for no other purpose than to reveal the truth. And everyone capable of receiving the truth recognizes it in my voice.

PILATE. What is truth?

JESUS. You are the first person I have met intelligent enough to ask me that question.

PILATE. Come on! no flattery. I am a Roman, and no doubt seem exceptionally intelligent to a Jew. You Jews are always talking about truth and righteousness and justice: you feed on words when you are tired of making money, or too poor to have anything else to feed on. They want me to nail you up on a cross; but as I do not yet see what particular harm you have done I prefer to nail you down to an argument. Fine words butter no parsnips in Rome. You say your vocation is to reveal the truth. I take your word for it; but I ask you what is truth?

JESUS. It is that which a man must tell even if he be stoned or crucified for telling it. I am not offering you the truth at a price for my own profit: I am offering it freely to you for your salvation at the peril of my own life. Would I do that if I were not driven by God to do it against all the protests of my shrinking flesh?

PILATE. You Jews are a simple folk. You have found only one god. We Romans have found many; and one of them is a God of Lies. Even you Jews have to admit a Father of Lies whom you call the devil, deceiving yourselves with words as usual. But he is a very potent god, is he not? And as he delights not only in lies but in all other mischief such as stonings and crucifixions of innocent men, how am I to judge whether it is he who is driving you to sacrifice yourself for a lie, or Minerva driving you to be sacrificed for the truth? I ask you again, what is truth?

JESUS. It is what you know by your experience to be true or feel in your soul must be true.

PILATE. You mean that truth is a correspondence between word and fact. It is true that I am sitting in this chair; but I am not the truth and the chair is not the truth: we are only the facts. My perception that I am sitting here may be only a dream; therefore my perception is not the truth.

JESUS. You say well. The truth is the truth and nothing else. That is your answer.

PILATE. Aye; but how far is it discoverable? We agree that it is true that I am sitting in this chair because our senses tell us so; and two men are not likely to be dreaming the same dream at the same moment. But when I rise from my chair this truth is no longer true. Truth is of the present, not of the future. Your hopes for the future are not the truth. Even in the present your opinions are not the truth. It is true that I sit in this chair. But it is true that it is better for your people that I should sit in this chair and impose on them the peace of Rome than that they should be left to slaughter oneanother in their own native savagery, as they are now clamoring to me to slaughter you?

JESUS. There is the peace of God that is beyond our understanding; and that peace shall prevail over the peace of Rome when God's hour strikes.

PILATE. Very pretty, my friend; but the hour of the

gods is now and always; and all the world knows what
the peace of your Jewish God means. Have I not read
it in the campaigns of Joshua? We Romans have purchased the *pax Romana* with our blood; and we prefer
it as a plain understandable thing which keeps men's
knives off oneanother's throats to your peace which is
beyond understanding because it slaughters man woman
and child in the name of your God. But that is only our
opinion. It is not yours. Therefore it is not necessarily
the truth. I must act on it, because a governor must act
on something: he cannot loaf round the roads and talk
beautifully as you do. If you were a responsible governor instead of a poetic vagrant, you would soon discover that my choice must lie, not between truth and
falsehood, neither of which I can ever ascertain, but
between reasonable and well informed opinion and sentimental and ill informed impulse.

JESUS. Nevertheless, opinion is a dead thing and impulse a live thing. You cannot impose on me with your
reasonable and well informed opinion. If it is your will
to crucify me, I can find you a dozen reasons for doing
so; and your police can supply you with a hundred facts
to support the reasons. If it is your will to spare me I
can find you just as many reasons for that; and my disciples will supply you with more facts than you will
have time or patience to listen to. That is why your lawyers can plead as well for one side as another, and can
therefore plead without dishonor for the side that pays
them, like the hackney charioteer who will drive you
north as readily as south for the same fare.

PILATE. You are cleverer than I thought; and you are
right. There is my will; and there is the will of Cæsar
to which my will must give way; and there is above

Cæsar the will of the gods. But these wills are in continual conflict with oneanother; therefore they are not truth; for truth is one, and cannot conflict with itself. There are conflicting opinions and conflicting wills; but there is no truth except the momentary truth that I am sitting in this chair. Yet you tell me that you are here to bear witness to the truth! You, a vagrant, a talker, who have never had to pass a sentence nor levy a tax nor issue an edict! What have you to say that I should not have the presumption scourged out of you by my executioners?

JESUS. Scourging is not a cure for presumption, nor is it justice, though you will perhaps call it so in your report to Cæsar: it is cruelty; and that cruelty is wicked and horrible because it is the weapon with which the sons of Satan slay the sons of God is part of the eternal truth you seek.

PILATE. Leave out cruelty: all government is cruel; for nothing is so cruel as impunity. A salutary severity—

JESUS. Oh please! You must excuse me, noble Governor; but I am so made by God that official phrases make me violently sick. Salutary severity is ipecacuanha to me. I have spoken to you as one man to another, in living words. Do not be so ungrateful as to answer me in dead ones.

PILATE. In the mouth of a Roman words mean something: in the mouth of a Jew they are a cheap substitute for strong drink. If we allowed you you would fill the whole world with your scriptures and psalms and talmuds; and the history of mankind would become a tale of fine words and villainous deeds.

JESUS. Yet the word came first, before it was made flesh. The word was the beginning. The word was with

God before he made us. Nay, the word was God.

PILATE. And what may all that mean, pray?

JESUS. The difference between man and Roman is but a word; but it makes all the difference. The difference between Roman and Jew is only a word.

PILATE. It is a fact.

JESUS. A fact that was first a thought; for a thought is the substance of a word. I am no mere chance pile of flesh and bone: if I were only that, I should fall into corruption and dust before your eyes. I am the embodiment of a thought of God: I am the Word made flesh: that is what holds me together standing before you in the image of God.

PILATE. That is well argued; but what is sauce for the goose is sauce for the gander; and it seems to me that if you are the Word made flesh so also am I.

JESUS. Have I not said so again and again? Have they not stoned me in the streets for saying it? Have I not sent my apostles to proclaim this great news to the Gentiles and to the very ends of the world? The Word is God. And God is within you. It was when I said this that the Jews—my own people—began picking up stones. But why should you, the Gentile, reproach me for it?

PILATE. I have not reproached you for it. I pointed it out to you.

JESUS. Forgive me. I am so accustomed to be contradicted—

PILATE. Just so. There are many sorts of words; and they are all made flesh soon or later. Go among my soldiers and you will hear many filthy words and witness many cruel and hateful deeds that began as thoughts. I do not allow those words to be spoken in my presence.

I punish those deeds as crimes. Your truth, as you call it, can be nothing but the thoughts for which you have found words which will take effect in deeds if I set you loose to scatter your words broadcast among the people. Your own people who bring you to me tell me that your thoughts are abominable and your words blasphemous. How am I to refute them? How am I to distinguish between the blasphemies of my soldiers reported to me by my centurions and your blasphemies reported to me by your High Priest?

JESUS. Woe betide you and the world if you do not distinguish!

PILATE. So you think. I am not frightened. Why do you think so?

JESUS. I do not think: I know. I have it from God.

PILATE. I have the same sort of knowledge from several gods.

JESUS. In so far as you know the truth you have it from my God, who is your heavenly father and mine. He has many names and his nature is manifold. Call him what you will: he is still Our Father. Does a father tell his children lies?

PILATE. Yes: many lies. You have an earthly father and an earthly mother. Did they tell you what you are preaching?

JESUS. Alas! no.

PILATE. Then you are defying your father and mother. You are defying your Church. You are breaking your God's commandments, and claiming a right to do so. You are pleading for the poor, and declaring that it is easier for a camel to pass through the eye of a needle than for a rich man to enter your God's paradise. Yet you have feasted at the tables of the rich, and encouraged harlots to spend on perfume for your feet money that might have been given to the poor, thereby so disgusting your treasurer that he has betrayed you to the High Priest for a handful of silver. Well, feast as much as you please: I do not blame you for refusing to play the fakir and make yourself a walking exhibition of silly austerities; but I must draw the line at your making a riot in the temple and throwing the gold of the moneychangers to be scrambled for by your partizans. I have a law to administer. The law forbids obscenity, sedition, and blasphemy. You are accused of sedition and blasphemy. You do not deny them: you only talk about the truth, which turns out to be nothing but what you like to believe. Your blasphemy is nothing to me: the whole Jewish religion is blasphemy from beginning to end from my Roman point of view; but it means a great deal to the High Priest; and I cannot keep order in Jewry except by dealing with Jewish fools according to Jewish folly. But sedition concerns me and my office very closely; and when you undertook to supersede the Roman Empire by a kingdom in which you and not Cæsar are to occupy the throne, you were guilty of the uttermost sedition. I am loth to have you crucified; for though you are only a Jew, and a half baked young one at that, yet I perceive that you are in your Jewish way a man of quality; and it makes me uneasy to throw a man of quality to the mob, even if his quality be only a Jewish quality. For I am a patrician and therefore myself a man of quality; and hawks should not pick out hawks' eyes. I am actually condescending to parley with you at this length in the merciful hope of finding an excuse for tolerating your blasphemy and sedition. In defence you offer me nothing but an empty phrase about the truth. I am sincere in wishing to spare you; for if I do not release you I shall have to release that blackguard Barabbas, who has gone further than you and killed somebody, whereas I understand that you have only raised a Jew from the dead. So for the last time set your wits to work, and find me a sound reason for letting a seditious blasphemer go free.

JESUS. I do not ask you to set me free; nor would I accept my life at the price of Barabbas's death even if I believed that you could countermand the ordeal to which I am predestined. Yet for the satisfaction of your longing for the truth I will tell you that the answer to your demand is your own argument that neither you nor the prisoner whom you judge can prove that he is in the right; therefore you must not judge me lest you be yourself judged. Without sedition and blasphemy the world would stand still and the Kingdom of God never be a stage nearer. The Roman Empire began with a wolf suckling two human infants. If these infants had not been wiser than their fostermother your empire would be a pack of wolves. It is by children who are wiser than their fathers, subjects who are wiser than their emperors, beggars and vagrants who are wiser than their priests, that men rise from being beasts of prey to believing in me and being saved.

PILATE. What do you mean by believing in you?

JESUS. Seeing the world as I do. What else could it mean?

PILATE. And you are the Christ, the Messiah, eh?

JESUS. Were I Satan, my argument would still hold.

PILATE. And I am to spare and encourage every heretic, every rebel, every lawbreaker, every rapscallion lest he should turn out to be wiser than all the generations who made the Roman law and built up the Roman Empire on it?

JESUS. By their fruits ye shall know them. Beware how you kill a thought that is new to you. For that thought may be the foundation of the kingdom of God on earth.

PILATE. It may also be the ruin of all kingdoms, all law, and all human society. It may be the thought of the beast of prey striving to return.

JESUS. The beast of prey is not striving to return: the kingdom of God is striving to come. The empire that looks back in terror shall give way to the kingdom that looks forward with hope. Terror drives men mad: hope and faith give them divine wisdom. The men whom you fill with fear will stick at no evil and perish in their sin: the men whom I fill with faith shall inherit the earth. I say to you Cast out fear. Speak no more vain things to me about the greatness of Rome. The greatness of Rome, as you call it, is nothing but fear: fear of the past and fear of the future, fear of the poor, fear of the rich, fear of the High Priests, fear of the Jews and Greeks who are learned, fear of the Gauls and Goths and Huns who are barbarians, fear of the Carthage you destroyed to save you from your fear of it and now fear worse than ever, fear of imperial Cæsar, the idol you have yourself created, and fear of me, the penniless vagrant, buffeted and mocked, fear of everything except the rule of God: faith in nothing but blood and iron and gold. You, standing for Rome, are the universal coward: I, standing for the kingdom of God, have braved everything, lost everything, and won an eternal crown.

PILATE. You have won a crown of thorns; and you

shall wear it on the cross. You are a more dangerous fellow than I thought. For your blasphemy against the god of the high priests I care nothing: you may trample their religion into hell for all I care; but you have blasphemed against Cæsar and against the Empire; and you mean it, and have the power to turn men's hearts against it as you have half turned mine. Therefore I must make an end of you whilst there is still some law left in the world.

JESUS. Law is blind without counsel. The counsel men agree with is vain: it is only the echo of their own voices. A million echoes will not help you to rule righteously. But he who does not fear you and shews you the other side is a pearl of the greatest price. Slay me and you go blind to your damnation. The greatest of God's names is Counsellor; and when your Empire is dust and your name a byword among the nations the temples of the living God shall still ring with his praise as Wonderful! Counsellor! the Everlasting Father, the Prince of Peace.

THE SACREDNESS OF CRITICISM

And so the last word remains with Christ and Handel; and this must stand as the best defence of Tolerance until a better man than I makes a better job of it.

Put shortly and undramatically the case is that a civilization cannot progress without criticism, and must therefore, to save itself from stagnation and putrefaction, declare impunity for criticism. This means impunity not only for propositions which, however novel, seem interesting, statesmanlike, and respectable, but for propositions that shock the uncritical as obscene, seditious, blasphemous, heretical, and revolutionary. That sound Catholic institution, the Devil's Advocate, must be privileged as possibly the Herald of the World to Come. The difficulty is to distinguish between the critic and the criminal or lunatic, between liberty of precept and liberty of example. It may be vitally necessary to allow a person to advocate Nudism; but it may not be expedient to allow that person to walk along Piccadilly stark naked. Karl Marx writing the death warrant of private property in the reading room of the British Museum was sacred; but if Karl Marx had sent the rent of his villa in Maitland Park to the Chancellor of the Exchequer, and shot the landlord's agents when they came to distrain on his furniture or execute a writ of ejectment, he could hardly have escaped hanging by pleading his right to criticize. Not until the criticism changes the law can the magistrate allow the critic to give effect to it. We are so dangerously uneducated in citizenship that most of us assume that we have an unlimited right to change our conduct the moment we have changed our minds. People who have a vague notion that Socialism is a state of society in which everyone gives away everything he possesses to everybody else occasionally reproach me because I, being a Socialist, do not immediately beggar myself in this fashion. People who imagined, more specifically, that a Socialist could not consistently keep a motor car, almost succeeded in making a public question of the possession of such a vehicle by a Prime Minister who at that time professed Socialism. But even if these idiots had really understood what they were talking about, they would have been wrong in supposing that a hostile critic of the existing social order either could or should behave as if he were living in his own particular Utopia. He may, at most, be a little eccentric at the cost of being indulged as slightly cracked.

On the other hand the Government, too, has not only a right but a duty of criticism. If it is to abandon once for all its savage superstition that whoever breaks the law is fair game for the torturers, and that the wrong wrought by the evildoer can be expiated and undone by a worse wrong done to him by judges and priests: if it is to substitute the doctrine of Jesus that punishment is only a senseless attempt to make a white out of two blacks, and to abolish the monstrous list of crimes and punishments by which these superstitions have been re-duced to practice for routine officials, then there must be a stupendous extension of governmental criticism; for every crime will raise the essential critical question whether the criminal is fit to live at all, and if so whether he is fit to live under more or less tutelage and discipline like a soldier, or at normal liberty under an obligation to make good the damage he has cost.

For such functions as these we shall need critics edu-cated otherwise than our judges of today; but the same may be said of all whose public functions transcend the application of a routine.

I have no doubt that the eradication of malice, vindic-tiveness, and Sadist libido on these terms from the per-sonal contacts of citizens with their rulers, far from hav-ing a reassuring effect, is likely to be rather terrifying at first, as all people with any tenderness of conscience will feel the deepest misgivings as to whether they are really worth keeping alive in a highly civilized community; but that will wear off as standards of worth get estab-lished and known by practice. In the meantime the terror will act as a sort of social conscience which is dangerously lacking at present, and which none of our model educational establishments ever dreams of inculcating.

Ayot St Lawrence,
22nd October, 1933.

ON THE ROCKS

ACT I

*The Cabinet Room in number ten Downing Street,
Westminster, the official residence of the British Prime
Minister. The illustrious holder of that office, Sir Arthur
Chavender, is reading The Times on the hearth under
the portrait of Walpole. The fireplace wall is covered
with bookshelves; but one bit of it, on Walpole's right,
is a masked door, painted with sham books and shelves,
leading to the Minister's private apartments; and in the
end of the same wall, on Walpole's left, is a door leading to the office of Sir Arthur's private secretary Miss
Hilda Hanways. The main door is in the side wall on
Walpole's right. In the opposite wall on his left are the
spacious windows. Everything is on an imposing scale,
including an oblong table across the middle of the room,
with fourteen leather upholstered chairs, six at each side
and one at each end, pushed in all along it. The presidential chair is the central one next the cold fireplace
(it is mid-July); and there is a telephone and a switch-
board on the table within reach of it. Sir Arthur has
pulled it round and is making himself comfortable in
it as he reads. At the end of the table nearest the window a silver tray, with coffee and milk for one person,
indicates Sir Arthur's unofficial seat. In the corner farthest from Walpole, on his right, is a writing bureau and
chair for the secretary. In the corresponding corner on
his left, an armchair. There is a bluebook lying, neglected and dusty, on a half empty shelf of the bookcase*

within reach of the Prime Minister's seat.

Sir Arthur can hardly be much less than fifty; but his natural buoyancy makes him look younger. He has an orator's voice of pleasant tone; and his manners are very genial. In oldish clothes he has the proper aristo-cratic air of being carelessly but well dressed, an easy feat for him, as he is so trimly built that any clothes would look well cut on him. On the whole, a very en-gaging personality.

He reads The Times until his secretary hurries in from her office, with her notebook and a sheaf of letters in her hand. Her age is unknown; but she is made up to pass as reasonably young and attractive. She looks capable; but she does not carry the burden of State af-fairs as easily as the Prime Minister. Both are worried; but with a difference. She is worried not only by an excess of business but a sense of responsibility. He is equally worried by the excess of business; but in him enjoyment of his position leaves no doubt in his mind as to his own entire adequacy to it.

HILDA. I hear you have been asking for me, Sir Arthur. I'm so sorry to be late; but really the streets are becoming quite impassable with the crowds of unem-ployed. I took a taxi; but it was no use: we were blocked by a procession; and I had to get out and push my way through. [*She goes to her bureau*].

SIR ARTHUR [*rising*] What on earth good do they think they can do themselves by crowding aimlessly about Westminster and the public offices?

HILDA. Thank Goodness the police wont let them into Downing Street. [*She sits down*]. They would be all over the doorstep.

SIR ARTHUR. It's all so foolish—so ignorant, poor chaps! [*He throws The Times on the table and moves to the end chair, where his coffee is*]. They think because I'm Prime Minister I'm Divine Providence and can find jobs for them before trade revives. [*He sits down and fidgets with his papers*].

HILDA. Trafalgar Square's full. The Horse Guards parade is full. The Mall is full all the way down to Marlborough House and Buckingham Palace.

SIR ARTHUR. They have no right to be there. Trafalgar Square is not a public place: it belongs to the Commissioner of Woods and Forests. The Horse Guards parade is reserved for the military. The Mall is a thoroughfare: anyone stopping there is guilty of obstruction. What are the police thinking of? Why dont they clear them out?

HILDA. I asked the policeman who got me through to the gates why they didnt. He said "We're only too glad to have them where they cant break any windows, and where the mounted men can have a fair whack at the Hooligan Fringe when they get too obstreperous."

SIR ARTHUR. Hooligan Fringe! He got that out of the papers. It only encourages them to write them up like that.

HILDA. Sir Broadfoot Basham has come over from Scotland Yard. He is talking to Lady Chavender.

SIR ARTHUR [*rising and making for the telephone*] Yes: I telephoned for him. He really must do something to stop these meetings. It was a mistake to make a man with a name like that Chief Commissioner of Police. People think him a trampling, bashing, brutal terrorist no matter how considerately the police behave. What we need is a thoroughly popular figure. [*He takes up the telephone*] Ask Sir Broadfoot Basham to come up.

HILDA. I dont think any chief of police could be popular at present. Every day they are bludgeoning deputations of the unemployed. [*She sits down and busies herself with letters*].

SIR ARTHUR. Poor devils! I hate that part of the business. But what are the police to do? We cant have the sittings of the local authorities threatened by deputations. Deputations are frightful nuisances even in the quietest times; but just now they are a public danger.

The Chief Commissioner of Police enters by the main door. A capable looking man from the military point of view. He is a gentleman: and his manners are fairly pleasant; but they are not in the least conciliatory.

Hilda rises and pulls out a chair for him at the end of the table nearest to her and farthest from Sir Arthur; then returns to her work at her desk. Sir Arthur comes round to his side of the table.

SIR ARTHUR. Morning, Basham. Sit down. I'm devilishly busy; but you are always welcome to your ten minutes.

BASHAM [*coolly, sitting down*] Thank you. You sent for me. [*Anxiously*] Anything new?

SIR ARTHUR. These street corner meetings are going beyond all bounds.

BASHAM [*relieved*] What harm do they do? Crowds are dangerous when theyve nothing to listen to or look at. The meetings keep them amused. They save us trouble.

SIR ARTHUR. Thats all very well for you, Basham; but think of the trouble they make for me! Remember: this is a National Government, not a party one. I am up against my Conservative colleagues all the time; and they cant swallow the rank sedition that goes on every day at these meetings. Sir Dexter Rightside—you know what a regular old Diehard he is—heard a speaker say that if the police used tear gas the unemployed would give old Dexy something to cry for without any tear gas. That has brought matters to a head in the Cabinet. We shall make an Order in Council to enable you to put a stop to all street meetings and speeches.

BASHAM [*unimpressed—slowly*] If you dont mind, P.M., I had rather you didnt do that.

SIR ARTHUR. Why not?

BASHAM. Crowd psychology.

SIR ARTHUR. Nonsense! Really, Basham, if you are going to come this metaphysical rot over me I shall begin to wonder whether your appointment wasnt a mistake.

BASHAM. Of course it was a mistake. Dealing with the unemployed is not a soldier's job; and I was a soldier. If you want these crowds settled on soldierly lines, say so; and give me half a dozen machine guns. The streets will be clear before twelve o'clock.

SIR ARTHUR. Man: have you considered the effect on the bye-elections?

BASHAM. A soldier has nothing to do with elections. You shew me a crowd and tell me to disperse it. All youll hear is a noise like a watchman's rattle. Quite simple.

SIR ARTHUR. Far too simple. You soldiers never understand the difficulties a statesman has to contend with.

BASHAM. Well, whats your alternative?

SIR ARTHUR. I have told you. Arrest the sedition mongers. That will shut old Dexy's mouth.

BASHAM. So that Satan may find mischief still for idle

hands to do. No, P.M.: the right alternative is mine:
keep the crowd amused. You ought to know that, I
think, better than most men.

SIR ARTHUR. I! What do you mean?

BASHAM. The point is to prevent the crowd doing
anything, isnt it?

SIR ARTHUR. Anything mischievous: I suppose so.
But—

BASHAM. An English crowd will never do anything,
mischievous or the reverse, while it is listening to
speeches. And the fellows who make the speeches can
be depended on never to do anything else. In the first
place, they dont know how. In the second, they are
afraid. I am instructing my agents to press all the talking societies, the Ethical Societies, the Socialist societies,
the Communists, the Fascists, the Anarchists, the Syn-
dicalists, the official Labor Party, the Independent Labor
Party, the Salvation Army, the Church Army and the
Atheists, to send their best tub-thumpers into the streets
to seize the opportunity.

SIR ARTHUR. What opportunity?

BASHAM. They dont know. Neither do I. It's only a
phrase that means nothing: just what they are sure to
rise at. I must keep Trafalgar Square going night and
day. A few Labor M.P.s would help. You have a rare
lot of gasbags under your thumb in the House. If you
could send half a dozen of them down to the Yard,
I could plant them where they would be really useful.

SIR ARTHUR [incensed] Basham: I must tell you that
we are quite determined to put a stop to this modern
fashion of speaking disrespectfully of the House of
Commons. If it goes too far we shall not hesitate to bring
prominent offenders to the bar of the House, no matter

what their position is.

BASHAM. Arthur: as responsible head of the police, I am up against the facts all day and every day; and one of the facts is that nowadays nobody outside the party cliques cares a brass button for the House of Commons. [*Rising*] You will do what I ask you as to letting the speaking go on, wont you?

SIR ARTHUR. Well, I—er—

BASHAM. Unless you are game to try the machine guns.

SIR ARTHUR. Oh do drop that, Basham [*he returns to his chair and sits moodily*].

BASHAM. Righto! We'll let them talk. Thanks ever so much. Sorry to have taken up so much of your time: I know it's priceless. [*He hurries to the door; then hesitates and adds*] By the way, I know it's asking a lot; but if you could give us a turn in Trafalgar Square yourself—some Sunday afternoon would be best—it—

SIR ARTHUR [*springing up, thoroughly roused*] I!!!!

BASHAM [*hurriedly*] No: of course you couldnt. Only it would do such a lot of good—keep the crowd quiet talking about it for a fortnight. However, of course it's impossible: say no more: so long. [*He goes out*].

SIR ARTHUR [*collapsing into his chair*] Well, really! Basham's losing his head. I wonder what he meant by saying that I ought to know better than most men. What ought I to know better than most men?

HILDA. I think he meant that you are such a wonderful speaker you ought to know what a magical effect a fine speech has on a crowd.

SIR ARTHUR [*musing*] Do you know, I am not at all sure that there is not something in his idea of my making a speech in Trafalgar Square. I have not done such a thing for many many years; but I have stood between the lions in my time; and I believe that if I were to tackle the unemployed face to face, and explain to them that I intend to call a conference in March next on the prospects of a revival of trade, it would have a wonderfully soothing effect.

HILDA. But it's impossible. You have a conference every month until November. And think of the time taken by the travelling! One in Paris! Two in Geneva! One in Japan! You cant possibly do it: you will break down.

SIR ARTHUR. And shall I be any better at home here leading the House? sitting up all night in bad air listening to fools insulting me? I tell you I should have been dead long ago but for the relief of these conferences: the journeys and the change. And I look forward to Japan. I shall be able to pick up some nice old bric-a-brac there.

HILDA. Oh well! You know best.

SIR ARTHUR [*energetically*] And now to work. Work! work! work! [*He rises and paces the floor in front of the table*]. I want you to take down some notes for my speech this afternoon at the Church House. The Archbishop tells me that the Anglo-Catholics are going mad on what they call Christian Communism, and that I must head them off.

HILDA. There are those old notes on the economic difficulties of Socialism that you used at the British Association last year.

SIR ARTHUR. No: these parsons know too much about that. Besides, this is not the time to talk about economic difficulties: we're up to the neck in them. The Archbishop says "Avoid figures; and stick to the fact that

Socialism would break up the family." I believe he is right: a bit of sentiment about the family always goes down well. Just jot this down for me. [*Dictating*] Family. Foundation of civilization. Foundation of the empire.

HILDA. Will there be any Hindus or Mahometans present?

SIR ARTHUR. No. No polygamists at the Church House. Besides, everybody knows that The Family means the British family. By the way, I can make a point of that. Put down in a separate line, in red capitals, "One man one wife." Let me see now: can I work that up? "One child one father." How would that do?

HILDA. I think it would be safer to say "One child one mother."

SIR ARTHUR. No: that might get a laugh—the wrong sort of laugh. I'd better not risk it. Strike it out. A laugh in the wrong place in the Church House would be the very devil. Where did you get that necklace? it's rather pretty. I havent seen it before.

HILDA. Ive worn it every day for two months. [*Striking out the "one child" note*] Yes?

SIR ARTHUR. Then—er—what subject are we on? [*Testily*] I wish you wouldnt interrupt me: I had the whole speech in my head beautifully; and now it's gone.

HILDA. Sorry. The family.

SIR ARTHUR. The family? Whose family? What family? The Holy Family? The Royal Family? The Swiss Family Robinson? Do be a little more explicit, Miss Hanways.

HILDA [*gently insistent*] Not any particular family. THE family. Socialism breaking up the family. For the

Church House speech this afternoon.

SIR ARTHUR. Yes yes yes, of course. I was in the House yesterday until three in the morning; and my brains are just so much tripe.

HILDA. Why did you sit up? The business didnt matter.

SIR ARTHUR [*scandalized*] Not matter! You really must not say these things, Miss Hanways. A full dress debate on whether Jameson or Thompson was right about what Johnson said in the Cabinet!

HILDA. Ten years ago.

SIR ARTHUR. What does that matter? The real question: the question whether Jameson or Thompson is a liar, is a vital question of the first importance.

HILDA. But theyre both liars.

SIR ARTHUR. Of course they are; but the division might have affected their inclusion in the next Cabinet. The whole House rose at it. Look at the papers this morning! Full of it.

HILDA. And three lines about the unemployed, though I was twenty minutes late trying to shove my way through them. Really, Sir Arthur, you should have come home to bed. You will kill yourself if you try to get through your work and attend so many debates as well: you will indeed.

SIR ARTHUR. Miss Hanways: I wish I could persuade you to remember occasionally that I happen to be the leader of the House of Commons.

HILDA. Oh, what is the use of leading the House if it never goes anywhere? It just breaks my heart to see the state you come home in. You are good for nothing next morning.

SIR ARTHUR [*yelling at her*] Dont remind me of it:

do you think I dont know? My brain is overworked: my mental grasp is stretched and strained to breaking point. I shall go mad. [*Pulling himself together*] However, it's no use grousing about it: I shall have a night off going to Geneva, and a week-end at Chequers. But it is hard to govern a country and do fifty thousand other things every day that might just as well be done by the Beadle of Burlington Arcade. Well, well, we mustnt waste time. Work! work! work! [*He returns to his chair and sits down resolutely*]. Get along with it. What were we talking about?

HILDA. The family.

SIR ARTHUR [*grasping his temples distractedly*] Oh dear! Has Lady Chavender's sister-in-law been making a fuss again?

HILDA. No, no. The family. Not any real family. THE family. Socialism breaking up the family. Your speech this afternoon at the Church House.

SIR ARTHUR. Ah, of course. I am going dotty. Thirty years in Parliament and ten on the Front Bench would drive any man dotty. I have only one set of brains and I need ten. I—

HILDA [*urgently*] We must get on with the notes for your speech, Sir Arthur. The morning has half gone already; and weve done nothing.

SIR ARTHUR [*again infuriated*] How can the busiest man in England find time to do anything? It is you who have wasted the morning interrupting me with your silly remarks about your necklace. What do I care about your necklace?

HILDA. You gave it to me, Sir Arthur.

SIR ARTHUR. Did I? Ha ha ha! Yes: I believe I did. I bought it in Venice. But come along now. What about that speech?

HILDA. Yes. The family. It was about the family.

SIR ARTHUR. Well, I know that: I have not yet become a complete idiot. You keep saying the family, the family, the family.

HILDA. Socialism and the family. How Socialism will break up the family.

SIR ARTHUR. Who says Socialism will break up the family? Dont be a fool.

HILDA. The Archbishop wants you to say it. At the Church House.

SIR ARTHUR. Decidedly I am going mad.

HILDA. No: you are only tired. You were getting along all right. One man one wife: that is where you stopped.

SIR ARTHUR. One man one wife is one wife too many, if she has a lot of brothers who cant get on with the women they marry. Has it occurred to you, Miss Hanways, that the prospect of Socialism destroying the family may not be altogether unattractive?

HILDA [*despairingly*] Oh, Sir Arthur, we must get on with the notes: we really must. I have all the letters to do yet. Do try to pick up the thread. The family the foundation of the empire. The foundation of Christianity. Of civilization. Of human society.

SIR ARTHUR. Thats enough about the foundation: it wont bear any more. I must have another word to work up. Let me see. I have it. Nationalization of women.

HILDA [*remonstrating*] Oh, Sir Arthur!

SIR ARTHUR. Whats the matter now?

HILDA. Such bunk!

SIR ARTHUR. Miss Hanways: when a statesman is not talking bunk he is making trouble for himself; and

Goodness knows I have trouble enough without making any more. Put this down. [*He rises and takes his platform attitude at the end of the table*]. "No, your Grace, my lords and gentlemen. Nationalize the land if you will; nationalize our industries if we must; nationalize education, housing, science, art, the theatre, the opera, even the cinema; but spare our women."

HILDA. [*having taken it down*] Is that the finish?

SIR ARTHUR. [*abandoning the attitude and pacing about*] No: write in red capitals under it "Rock of Ages."

HILDA. I think Rock of Ages will be rather a shock unless in connexion with something very sincere. May I suggest "The Church's One Foundation"?

SIR ARTHUR. Yes. Much better. Thank you. The family the Church's one foundation. Splendid.

Miss Flavia Chavender, 19, bursts violently into the room through the masked door and dashes to her father.

FLAVIA. Papa: I will not stand Mamma any longer. She interferes with me in every possible way out of sheer dislike of me. I refuse to live in this house with her a moment longer.

Lady Chavender follows her in, speaking as she enters, and comes between the Prime Minister and his assailant.

LADY CHAVENDER. I knew you were coming here to make a scene and disturb your father, though he has had hardly six hours sleep this week, and was up all night. I am so sorry, Arthur: she is uncontrollable.

David Chavender, 18, slight, refined, rather small for his age, charges in to the table.

DAVID [*in a childish falsetto*] Look here, Mamma. Cant you let Flavia alone? I wont stand by and see

her nagged at and treated like a child of six. Nag! nag!
nag! everything she does.

LADY CHAVENDER. Nag!! I control myself to the limit
of human endurance with you all. But Flavia makes a
study of annoying me.

FLAVIA. It's not true: I have considered you and given
up all the things I wanted for you until I have no in-
dividuality left. If I take up a book you want me to
read something else. If I want to see anybody you want
me to see somebody else. If I choose the color of my
own dress you want something different and dowdy. I
cant sit right nor stand right nor do my hair right nor
dress myself right: my life here is a hell.

LADY CHAVENDER. Flavia!!

FLAVIA [*passionately*] Yes, hell.

DAVID. Quite true. [*Fortissimo*] Hell.

LADY CHAVENDER [*quietly*] Miss Hanways: would
you mind—

HILDA. Yes, Lady Chavender [*she rises to go*].

FLAVIA. You neednt go, Hilda. You know what I
have to endure.

DAVID. Damn all this paralyzing delicacy! Damn it!

LADY CHAVENDER. Arthur—

SIR ARTHUR [*patting her*] Never mind, dear. They
must be let talk. [*He returns placidly to his chair*]. It's
just like the House of Commons, except that the speeches
are shorter.

FLAVIA Oh, it's no use trying to make papa listen to
anything. [*She throws herself despairingly into Basham's
chair and writhes*].

DAVID [*approaching Sir Arthur with dignity*] I really
think, father, you might for once in a way take some
slight interest in the family.

SIR ARTHUR. My dear boy, at this very moment I am making notes for a speech on the family. Ask Miss Hanways.

HILDA. Yes, Mr Chavender: Sir Arthur is to speak this afternoon on the disintegrating effect of Socialism on family life.

FLAVIA [*irresistible amusement struggling with hysterics and getting the better of them*] Ha ha! Ha ha ha!

DAVID [*retreating*] Ha ha! Haw! Thats the best— ha ha ha!

SIR ARTHUR. I dont see the joke. Why this hilarity?

DAVID. Treat the House to a brief description of this family; and you will get the laugh of your life.

FLAVIA. Damn the family!

LADY CHAVENDER. Flavia!

FLAVIA [*bouncing up*] Yes: there you go. I mustnt say damn. I mustnt say anything I feel and think, only what you feel and think. Thats family life. Scold, scold, scold!

DAVID. Squabble, squabble, squabble!

FLAVIA. Look at the unbearable way you treat me! Look at the unbearable way you treat Papa!

SIR ARTHUR [*rising in flaming wrath*] How dare you? Silence. Leave the room.

After a moment of awestruck silence Flavia, rather dazed by the avalanche she has brought down on herself, looks at her father in a lost way; then bursts into tears and runs out through the masked door.

SIR ARTHUR [*quietly*] Youd better go too, my boy.

David, also somewhat dazed, shrugs his shoulders and goes out. Sir Arthur looks at Hilda. She hurries out almost on tiptoe.

SIR ARTHUR [*taking his wife in his arms affectionately*]

Treat me badly! You!! I could have killed her, poor little devil.

He sits down; and she passes behind him and takes the nearest chair on his right.

She is a nice woman, and goodlooking; but she is bored; and her habitual manner is one of apology for being not only unable to take an interest in people, but even to pretend that she does.

LADY CHAVENDER. It serves us right, dear, for letting them bring themselves up in the post-war fashion instead of teaching them to be ladies and gentlemen. Besides, Flavia was right. I do treat you abominably. And you are so good!

SIR ARTHUR. Nonsense! Such a horrid wicked thing to say. Dont you know, my love, that you are the best of wives? the very best as well as the very dearest?

LADY CHAVENDER. You are certainly the best of husbands, Arthur. You are the best of everything. I dont wonder at the country adoring you. But Flavia was quite right. It is the first time I have ever known her to be right about anything. I am a bad wife and a bad mother. I dislike my daughter and treat her badly. I like you very much; and I treat you abominably.

SIR ARTHUR. No; no.

LADY CHAVENDER. Yes, yes. I suppose it's something wrong in my constitution. I was not born for wifing and mothering. And yet I am very very fond of you, as you know. But I have a grudge against your career.

SIR ARTHUR. My career! [*Complacently*] Well, theres not much wrong with that, is there? Of course I know it keeps me too much away from home. That gives you a sort of grudge against it. All the wives of successful men are a bit like that. But it's better to see too little of a husband than too much of him, isnt it?

LADY CHAVENDER. I am so glad that you really feel successful.

SIR ARTHUR. Well, it may sound conceited and all that; but after all a man cant be Prime Minister and go about with a modest cough pretending to be a nobody. Facts are facts; and the facts in my case are that I have climbed to the top of the tree; I am happy in my work; and—

LADY CHAVENDER. Your what?

SIR ARTHUR. You are getting frightfully deaf, dear. I said "my work."

LADY CHAVENDER. You call it work?

SIR ARTHUR. Brain work, dear, brain work. Do you really suppose that governing the country is not work, but a sort of gentlemanly diversion?

LADY CHAVENDER. But you dont govern the country, Arthur. The country isnt governed: it just slummocks along anyhow.

SIR ARTHUR. I have to govern within democratic limits. I cannot go faster than our voters will let me.

LADY CHAVENDER. Oh, your voters! What do they know about government? Football, prizefighting, war: that is what they like. And they like war because it isnt real to them: it's only a cinema show. War is real to me; and I hate it, as every woman to whom it is real hates it. But to you it is only part of your game: one of the regular moves of the Foreign Office and the War Office.

SIR ARTHUR. My dear, I hate war as much as you do. It makes a Prime Minister's job easy because it brings every dog to heel; but it produces coalitions; and I believe in party government.

LADY CHAVENDER [*rising*] Oh, it's no use talking to you, Arthur. [*She comes behind him and plants her hands on his shoulders*]. You are a dear and a duck and a darling; but you live in fairyland and I live in the hard wicked world. Thats why I cant be a good wife and take an interest in your career.

SIR ARTHUR. Stuff! Politics are not a woman's business: thats all it means. Thank God I have not a political wife. Look at Higginbotham! He was just ripe for the Cabinet when his wife went into Parliament and made money by journalism. That was the end of him.

LADY CHAVENDER. And I married a man with a hopelessly parliamentary mind; and that was the end of me.

SIR ARTHUR. Yes, yes, my pettums. I know that you have sacrificed yourself of keeping my house and sewing on my buttons; and I am not ungrateful. I am sometimes remorseful; but I love it. And now you must run away, I am very very very busy this morning.

LADY CHAVENDER. Yes, yes, very very busy doing nothing. And it wears you out far more than if your mind had something sensible to work on! Youll have a nervous breakdown if you go on like this. Promise me that you will see the lady I spoke to you about—if you wont see a proper doctor.

SIR ARTHUR. But you told me this woman is a doctor! [*He rises and breaks away from her*]. Once for all, I wont see any doctor. I'm old enough to do my own doctoring; and I'm not going to pay any doctor, male or female, three guineas to tell me what I know perfectly well already: that my brain's overworked and I must take a fortnight off on the links, or go for a sea voyage.

LADY CHAVENDER. She charges twenty guineas, Arthur.

SIR ARTHUR [*shaken*] Oh! Does she? What for?

ON THE ROCKS

LADY CHAVENDER. Twenty guineas for the diagnosis and twelve guineas a week at her sanatorium in the Welsh mountains, where she wants to keep you under observation for six weeks. That would really rest you; and I think you would find her a rather interesting and attractive woman.

SIR ARTHUR. Has she a good cook?

LADY CHAVENDER. I dont think that matters.

SIR ARTHUR. Not matter!

LADY CHAVENDER. No. She makes her patients fast.

SIR ARTHUR. Tell her I'm not a Mahatma. If I pay twelve guineas a week I shall expect three meals a day for it.

LADY CHAVENDER. Then you will see her?

SIR ARTHUR. Certainly not, if I have to pay twenty guineas for it.

LADY CHAVENDER. No, no. Only a social call, not a professional visit. Just to amuse you, and gratify her curiosity. She wants to meet you.

SIR ARTHUR. Very well, dear, very well, very well. This woman has got round you, I see. Well, she shant get round me; but to please you I'll have a look at her. And now you really must run away. I have a frightful mass of work to get through this morning.

LADY CHAVENDER. Thank you, darling. [*She kisses him*] May I tell Flavia she is forgiven?

SIR ARTHUR. Yes. But I havent really forgiven her. I'll never forgive her.

LADY CHAVENDER [*smiling*] Dearest. [*She kisses his fingers and goes out, giving him a parting smile as she goes through the masked door*].

Sir Arthur, left alone, looks inspired and triumphant. He addresses an imaginary assembly.

SIR ARTHUR. "My lords and gentlemen: you are not theorists. You are not rhapsodists. You are no longer young"—no, damn it, old Middlesex wont like that. "We have all been young. We have seen visions and dreamt dreams. We have cherished hopes and striven towards ideals. We have aspired to things that have not been realized. But we are now settled experienced men, family men. We are husbands and fathers. Yes, my lords and gentlemen: husbands and fathers. And I venture to claim your unanimous consent when I affirm that we have found something in these realities that was missing in the ideals. I thank you for that burst of applause: which I well know is no mere tribute to my poor eloquence, but the spontaneous and irresistible recognition of the great natural truth that our friends the Socialists have left out of their fancy pictures of a mass society in which regulation is to take the place of emotion and economics of honest human passion." Whew! that took a long breath. "They never will, gentlemen, I say they never will. They will NOT [*he smites the table and pauses, glaring round at his imaginary hearers*]. I see that we are of one mind, my lords and gentlemen. I need not labor the point." Then labor it for the next ten minutes. That will do. That will do. [*He sits down; rings the telephone bell; and seizes the milk jug, which he empties at a single draught*].

Hilda appears at the main door.

HILDA. Did you say you would receive a deputation from the Isle of Cats this morning? I have no note of it.

SIR ARTHUR. Oh, confound it, I believe I did. I totally forgot it.

HILDA. Theyve come.

SIR ARTHUR. Bother them!

HILDA. By all means. But how am I to get rid of them? What am I to say?

SIR ARTHUR [*resignedly*] Oh, I suppose I must see them. Why do I do these foolish things? Tell Burton to shew them in.

HILDA. Burton is in his shirt sleeves doing something to the refrigerator. I'd better introduce them.

SIR ARTHUR. Oh, bundle them in anyhow. And tell them I am frightfully busy.

She goes out, closing the door softly behind her. He pushes away the breakfast tray and covers it with The Times, which he opens out to its fullest extent for that purpose. Then he collects his papers into the vacant space, and takes up a big blue one, in the study of which he immerses himself profoundly.

HILDA. [*flinging the door open*] The worshipful the Mayor of the Isle of Cats.

The Mayor, thick and elderly, enters, a little shyly, followed by (a) an unladylike but brilliant and very confident young woman in smart factory-made clothes after the latest Parisian models, (b) a powerfully built loud voiced young man fresh from Oxford University, defying convention in corduroys, pullover, and unshaven black beard, (c) a thin, undersized lower middle class young man in an alderman's gown, evidently with a good conceit of himself, and (d) a sunny comfortable old chap in his Sunday best, who might be anything from a working man with a very sedentary job (say a watchman) to a city missionary of humble extraction. He is aggressively modest, or pretends to be, and comes in last with a disarming smile rather as a poor follower of the deputation than as presuming to form part of it.

They group themselves at the door behind the Mayor, who is wearing his chain of office.

SIR ARTHUR [*starting from his preoccupation with important State documents, and advancing past the fireplace to greet the Mayor with charming affability*] What! My old friend Tom Humphries! How have you been all these years? Sit down. [*They shake hands, whilst Hilda deftly pulls out a chair from the end of the table nearest the door*].

The Mayor sits down, rather overwhelmed by the cordiality of his reception.

SIR ARTHUR. [*continuing*] Well, well! fancy your being Mayor of—of—

HILDA [*prompting*] The Isle of Cats.

THE YOUNG WOMAN [*brightly, helping her out*] Down the river, Sir Arthur. Twenty minutes from your door by Underground.

THE OXFORD YOUTH [*discordantly*] Oh, he knows as well as you do, Aloysia. [*He advances offensively on Sir Arthur, who declines the proximity by retreating a step or two somewhat haughtily*]. Stow all this fo bunnum business, Chavender.

SIR ARTHUR. This what?

OXFORD YOUTH Oh, chuck it. You know French as well as I do.

SIR ARTHUR. Oh, faux bonhomme, of course, yes. [*Looking him up and down*]. I see by your costume that you represent the upper classes in the Isle of Cats.

OXFORD YOUTH. There are no upper classes in the Isle of Cats.

SIR ARTHUR. In that case, since it is agreed that there is to be no fo bunnum nonsense between us, may I ask what the dickens you are doing here?

OXFORD YOUTH. I am not here to bandy personalities. Whatever the accident of birth and the humbug of rank may have made me I am here as a delegate from the Borough Council and an elected representative of the riverside proletariat.

SIR ARTHUR [*suddenly pulling out a chair from the middle of the table—peremptorily*] Sit down. Dont break the chair. [*The Youth scowls at him and flings himself into the chair like a falling tree*]. You are all most welcome. Perhaps, Tom, you will introduce your young friends.

THE MAYOR [*introducing*] Alderwoman Aloysia Brollikins.

SIR ARTHUR [*effusively shaking her hand*] How do you do, Miss Brollikins? [*He pulls out a chair for her on the Oxford Youth's right*].

ALOYSIA. Nicely, thank you. Pleased to meet you, Sir Arthur. [*She sits*].

THE MAYOR. Alderman Blee.

SIR ARTHUR [*with flattering gravity, pressing his hand*] Ah, we have all heard of you, Mr Blee. Will you sit here? [*He indicates the presidential chair on the Oxford Youth's left*].

BLEE. Thank you. I do my best. [*He sits*].

THE MAYOR. Viscount Barking.

SIR ARTHUR [*triumphantly*] Ah! I thought so. A red Communist: what!

OXFORD YOUTH. Red as blood. Same red as the people's.

SIR ARTHUR. How did you get the blue out of it? The Barkings came over with the Conqueror.

OXFORD YOUTH [*rising*] Look here. The unemployed are starving. Is this a time for persiflage?

SIR ARTHUR. Camouflage, my lad, camouflage. Do you expect me to take you seriously in that get-up?

OXFORD YOUTH [*hotly*] I shall wear what I damn well please. I—

ALOYSIA. Shut up, Toffy. You promised to behave yourself. Sit down; and lets get to business.

BARKING [*subsides into his chair with a grunt of disgust*]!

SIR ARTHUR [*looking rather doubtfully at the old man, who is still standing*] Is this gentleman a member of your deputation?

THE MAYOR. Mr Hipney. Old and tried friend of the working class.

OXFORD YOUTH. Old Hipney. Why dont you call him by the name the East End knows him by? Old Hipney. Good old Hipney.

OLD HIPNEY. [*slipping noiselessly into the secretary's chair at the bureau*] Dont mind me, Sir Arthur. I dont matter.

SIR ARTHUR. At such a crisis as the present, Mr Hipney, every public-spirited man matters. Delighted to meet you. [*He returns to his own chair and surveys them now that they are all seated, whilst Hilda slips discreetly out into her office*]. And now, what can I do for you, Miss Brollikins? What can I do for you, gentlemen?

THE MAYOR [*slowly*] Well, Sir Arthur, as far as I can make it out the difficulty seems to be that you cant do anything. But something's got to be done.

SIR ARTHUR [*stiffening suddenly*] May I ask why, if everything that is possible has already been done?

THE MAYOR. Well, the unemployed are—well, unemployed, you know.

SIR ARTHUR. We have provided for the unemployed. That provision has cost us great sacrifices; but we have made the sacrifices without complaining.

THE OXFORD YOUTH [*scornfully*] Sacrifices! What sacrifices? Are you starving? Have you pawned your overcoat? Are you sleeping ten in a room?

SIR ARTHUR. The noble lord enquires—

OXFORD YOUTH [*furiously*] Dont noble lord me: you are only doing it to rattle me. Well, you cant rattle me. But it makes me sick to see you rolling in luxury and think of what these poor chaps and their women folk are suffering.

SIR ARTHUR. I am not rolling, Toffy—I think that is what Miss Brollikins called you. [*To Aloysia*] Toffy is a diminutive of Toff, is it not, Miss Brollikins?

OXFORD YOUTH. Yah! Now you have something silly to talk about, youre happy. But I know what would make you sit up and do something.

SIR ARTHUR. Indeed? Thats interesting. May I ask what?

OXFORD YOUTH. Break your bloody windows.

THE MAYOR. Order! order!

ALOYSIA. Come, Toffy! you promised not to use any of your West End language here. You know we dont like it.

SIR ARTHUR. Thats right, Miss Brollikins: snub him. He is disgracing his class. As a humble representative of that class I apologize for him to the Isle of Cats. I apologize for his dress, for his manners, for his language. He must shock you every time he opens his mouth.

BLEE. We working folks know too much of bad language and bad manners to see any fun in them or think they can do any good.

THE MAYOR. Thats right.

ALOYSIA. We are as tired of bad manners as Toffy is tired of good manners. We brought Toffy here, Sir Arthur, because we knew he'd speak to you as a dock laborer would speak to you if his good manners would let him. And he's right, you know. He's rude; but he's right.

OXFORD YOUTH. Yours devotedly, Brolly. And what has his Right Honorable nibs to say to that?

SIR ARTHUR [*concentrating himself on his adversary in the House of Commons manner*] I will tell the noble lord what I have to say. He may marshal his friends the unemployed and break every window in the West End, beginning with every pane of glass in this house. What will he gain by it? Next day a score or so of his followers will be in prison with their heads broken. A few ignorant and cowardly people who have still any money to spare will send it to the funds for the relief of distress, imagining that they are ransoming their riches. You, ladies and gentlemen, will have to put your hands in your pockets to support the wives and children of the men in prison, and to pay cheap lawyers to put up perfectly useless defences for them in the police courts. And then, I suppose, the noble lord will boast that he has made me do something at last. What can I do? Do you suppose that I care less about the sufferings of the poor than you? Do you suppose I would not revive trade and put an end to it all tomorrow if I could? But I am like yourself: I am in the grip of economic forces that are beyond human control. What mortal men could do this Government has done. We have saved the people from starvation by stretching unemployment benefit to the utmost limit of our national resources. We—

OXFORD YOUTH. You have cut it down to fifteen bob a week and shoved every man you could off it with your beastly means test.

SIR ARTHUR [*fiercely*] What do you propose? Will you take my place and put the dole up to five pounds a week without any means test?

THE MAYOR. Order! order! Why are we here? We are here because we are all sick of arguing and talking, and we want something doing. And here we are arguing and talking just as if it was an all night sitting of the Borough Council about an item of three-and-six for refreshments. If you, Sir Arthur, tell us that you cant find work for our people we are only wasting your time and our own, sitting here.

He rises. The rest, except Hipney, follow his example. Sir Arthur is only too glad to rise too.

SIR ARTHUR. At least I hope I have convinced you about the windows, Mr Mayor.

THE MAYOR. We needed no convincing. More crockery than windows will have to be broken if you gentlemen can do nothing to get us out of our present mess. But some people will say that a few thousands more to the relief funds is better than nothing. And some of the unemployed are glaziers.

SIR ARTHUR. Let us close our little talk on a more hopeful note. I assure you it has been intensely interesting to me; and I may tell you that signs of a revival of trade are not wholly wanting. Some of the best informed city authorities are of opinion that this year will see the end of the crisis. Some of them even hold that trade is already reviving. By the last returns the export of

Spanish onions has again reached the 1913 level.

OXFORD YOUTH. Holy Jerusalem! Spanish onions! Come on, Brolly. [*He goes out*].

THE MAYOR. Weve got nothing out of this. We dont run to Spanish in the Isle. [*Resignedly*] Good morning. [*He goes out*].

SIR ARTHUR [*winningly*] And do you, Miss Brollikins, feel that you have got nothing?

ALOYSIA. I feel what they feel. And I dont believe you feel anything at all. [*She goes out, followed by Blee*].

BLEE [*turning at the door*] The Mayor's wrong. Weve got something all right.

SIR ARTHUR [*brightening*] Indeed? What is it?

BLEE [*with intense contempt*] Your measure. [*He goes out*].

The Prime Minister, nettled by this gibe, resumes his seat angrily and pushes the bluebook out of his way. Then he notices that old Hipney has not budged from his seat at the secretary's bureau.

SIR ARTHUR. The deputation has withdrawn, Mr Hipney.

HIPNEY [*rising and coming to a chair at Sir Arthur's elbow, in which he makes himself comfortable with a disarmingly pleasant air of beginning the business instead of ending it*] Yes: now we can talk a bit. I been at this game now for fifty year.

SIR ARTHUR [*interested in spite of himself*] What game? Deputations?

HIPNEY. Unemployed deputations. This is my twelfth.

SIR ARTHUR. As many as that! But these crises dont come oftener than every ten years, do they?

HIPNEY. Not what you would call a crisis, perhaps.

But unemployment is chronic.

SIR ARTHUR. It always blows over, doesnt it? Trade revives.

HIPNEY. It used to. We was the workshop of the world then. But you gentlemen went out of the work-shop business to make a war. And while that was going on our customers had to find out how to make things for themselves. Now we shall have to be their customers when weve any money to buy with.

SIR ARTHUR. No doubt that has occurred to some extent; but there is still an immense fringe of the human race growing up to a sense of the necessity for British goods.

HIPNEY. All goods is alike to that lot provided theyre the cheapest. They tell me the Italians are tapping their volcanoes for cheap power. We dont seem able to tap nothing. The east is chock full of volcanoes; they think no more of an earthquake there than you would of a deputation. A Chinese coolie can live on a penny a day. What can we do against labor at a penny a day and power for next to nothing out of the burning bowels of the earth?

SIR ARTHUR. Too true, Mr Hipney. Our workers must make sacrifices.

HIPNEY. They will if you drive em to it, Srarthur. But it's you theyll sacrifice.

SIR ARTHUR. Oh come, Mr Hipney! you are a man of sense and experience. What good would it do them to sacrifice me?

HIPNEY. Not a bit in the world, sir. But that wont stop them. Look at yourself. Look at your conferences! Look at your debaters! They dont do no good. But you keep on holding them. It's a sort of satisfaction to you when you feel helpless. Well, sir, if you come to help-lessness there isnt on God's earth a creature more help-less than what our factories and machines have made of an English working man when nobody will give him a job and pay him to do it. And when he gets it what does he understand of it? Just nothing. Where did the material that he does his little bit of a job on come from? He dont know. What will happen to it when it goes out of the factory after he and his like have all done their little bits of jobs on it? He dont know. Where could he buy it if it stopped coming to him? He dont know. Where could he sell it if it was left on his hands? He dont know. He dont know nothing of the business that his life depends on. Turn a cat loose and itll feed itself. Turn an English working man loose and he'll starve. You have to buy him off with a scrap of dole to prevent his saying "Well, if I'm to die I may as well have the satisfaction of seeing you die first."

SIR ARTHUR. But—I really must press the point—what good will that do him?

HIPNEY. What good does backing horses do him? What good does drinking do him? What good does going to political meetings do him? What good does going to church do him? Not a scrap. But he keeps on doing them all the same.

SIR ARTHUR. But surely you recognize, Mr Hipney, that all this is thoroughly wrong—wrong in feeling—contrary to English instincts—out of character, if I may put it that way.

HIPNEY. Well, Srarthur, whatever's wrong you and your like have taken on yourselves the job of setting it right. I havnt: I'm only a poor man: a nobody, as you might say.

SIR ARTHUR. I have not taken anything on myself, Mr Hipney. I have chosen a parliamentary career, and found it, let me tell you, a very arduous and trying one: I might almost say a heartbreaking one. I have just had to promise my wife to see a doctor for brain fag. But that does not mean that I have taken it on myself to bring about the millennium.

HIPNEY [*soothingly*] Just so, Srarthur: just so. It tries you and worries you, and breaks your heart and does no good; but you keep on doing it. Theyve often wanted me to go into Parliament. And I could win the seat. Put up old Hipney for the Isle of Cats and your best man wouldnt have a chance against him. But not me: I know too much. It would be the end of me, as it's been the end of all the Labor men that have done it. The Cabinet is full of Labor men that started as red-hot Socialists; and what change has it made except that theyre in and out at Bucknam Palace like peers of the realm?

SIR ARTHUR. You ought to be in Parliament, Mr Hipney. You have the making of a first-rate debater in you.

HIPNEY. Psha! An old street corner speaker like me can debate the heads off you parliamentary gentlemen. You stick your thumbs in your waistcoat holes and wait half an hour between every sentence to think of what to say next; and you call that debating. If I did that in the Isle not a man would stop to listen to me. Mind you, I know you mean it as a compliment that I'd make a good parliamentary debater. I appreciate it. But people dont look to Parliament for talk nowadays: that game is up. Not like it was in old Gladstone's time, eh?

SIR ARTHUR. Parliament, Mr Hipney, is what the

people of England have made it. For good or evil we have committed ourselves to democracy. I am here because the people have sent me here.

HIPNEY. Just so. Thats all the use they could make of the vote when they got it. Their hopes was in you; and your hopes is in Spanish onions. What a world it is, aint it, Srarthur?

SIR ARTHUR. We must educate our voters, Mr Hipney. Education will teach them to understand.

HIPNEY. Dont deceive yourself, Srarthur: you cant teach people anything they dont want to know. Old Dr Marx—Karl Marx they call him now—my father knew him well—thought that when he'd explained the Capitalist System to the working classes of Europe theyd unite and overthrow it. Fifty years after he founded his Red International the working classes of Europe rose up and shot one another down and blew one another to bits, and turned millions and millions of their infant children out to starve in the snow or steal and beg in the sunshine, as if Dr Marx had never been born. And theyd do it again tomorrow if they was set on to do it. Why did you set them on? All they wanted was to be given their job, and fed and made comfortable according to their notion of comfort. If youd done that for them you wouldnt be having all this trouble. But you werent equal to it; and now the fat's in the fire.

SIR ARTHUR. But the Government is not responsible for that. The Government cannot compel traders to buy goods that they cannot sell. The Government cannot compel manufacturers to produce goods that the traders will not buy. Without demand there can be no supply.

HIPNEY. Theres a powerful demand just now, if demand is what you are looking for.

SIR ARTHUR. Can you point out exactly where, Mr Hipney?

HIPNEY. In our children's bellies, Srarthur. And in our own.

SIR ARTHUR. That is not an effective demand, Mr Hipney. I wish I had time to explain to you the inexorable laws of political economy. I—

HIPNEY [*interrupting him confidentially*] No use, Srarthur. That game is up. That stuff you learnt at college, that gave you such confidence in yourself, wont go down with my lot.

SIR ARTHUR [*smiling*] What is the use of saying that economic science and natural laws wont go down, Mr Hipney? You might as well say that the cold of winter wont go down.

HIPNEY. You see, you havnt read Karl Marx, have you?

SIR ARTHUR. Mr Hipney, when the Astronomer Royal tells me that it is twelve o'clock by Greenwich time I do not ask him whether he has read the nonsense of the latest flat earth man. I have something better to do with my time than to read the ravings of a half-educated German Communist. I am sorry you have wasted your own time reading such stuff.

HIPNEY. Me read Marx! Bless you, Srarthur, I am like you: I talk about the old doctor without ever having read a word of him. But I know what that man did for them as did read him.

SIR ARTHUR. Turned their heads, eh?

HIPNEY. Just that, Srarthur. Turned their heads. Turned them right round the other way to yours. I dont know whether what Marx said was right or wrong, because I dont know what he said. But I know that he puts into every man and woman that does read him a conceit that they know all about political economy and can look down on the stuff you were taught at college as ignorant old-fashioned trash. Look at that girl Aloysia Brollikins! Her father was a basket maker in Spitalfields. She's full of Marx. And as to examinations and scholarships and certificates and gold medals and the like, she's won enough of them to last your whole family for two generations. She can win them in her sleep. Look at Blee! His father was a cooper. But he managed to go through Ruskin College. You start him paying out Marx, and proving by the materialist theory of history that Capitalism is bound to develop into Communism, and that whoever doesnt know it is an ignorant nobody or a half-educated college fool; and youll realize that your college conceit is up against a Marxist conceit that beats anything you ever felt for cocksureness and despising the people that havnt got it. Look across Europe if you dont believe me. It was that conceit, sir, that nerved them Russians to go through with their Communism in 1917.

SIR ARTHUR. I must read Marx, Mr Hipney. I knew I had to deal with a sentimental revolt against unemployment. I had no idea that it had academic pretensions.

HIPNEY. Lord bless you, Srarthur, the Labor movement is rotten with book learning; and your people dont seem ever to read anything. When did an undersecretary ever sit up half the night after a hard day's work to read Karl Marx or anyone else? No fear. Your hearts are not in your education; but our young people lift themselves out of the gutter with it. Thats how you can shoot and you can ride and you can play golf; and some of you can talk the hind leg off a donkey; but when it comes to book learning Aloysia and Blee can wipe the floor with you.

SIR ARTHUR. I find it hard to believe that the Mayor ever burnt the midnight oil reading Marx.

HIPNEY. No more he didnt. But he has to pretend to, same as your people have to pretend to understand the gold standard.

SIR ARTHUR [laughing frankly] You have us there, Mr Hipney. I can make neither head nor tail of it; and I dont pretend to.

HIPNEY. Did you know the Mayor well, Srarthur? You called him your old friend Tom.

SIR ARTHUR. He took the chair for me once at an election meeting. He has an artificial tooth that looks as if it were made of zinc. I remembered him by that. [Genially—rising]. What humbugs we Prime Ministers have to be, Mr Hipney! You know: dont you? [He offers his hand to signify that the conversation is over].

MR HIPNEY [rising and taking it rather pityingly] Bless your innocence, Srarthur, you dont know what humbug is yet. Wait til youre a Labor leader. [He winks at his host and makes for the door].

SIR ARTHUR. Ha ha! Ha ha ha! Goodbye, Mr Hipney: goodbye. Very good of you to have given me so much of your time.

HIPNEY. Youre welcome to it, Srarthur. Goodbye. [He goes out].

Sir Arthur presses a button to summon Hilda. Then he looks at his watch, and whistles, startled to find how late it is. Hilda comes in quickly through the masked door.

SIR ARTHUR. Do you know how late it is? To work! Work! work! work! Come along.

HILDA. I am afraid you cant do any work before you start for the Church House lunch. The whole morning is gone with those people from the Isle of Cats.

SIR ARTHUR. But I have mountains of work to get through. With one thing and another I havnt been able to do a thing for the last three weeks; and it accumulates and accumulates. It will crush me if I dont clear it off before it becomes impossible.

HILDA. But I keep telling you, Sir Arthur, that if you will talk to everybody for half an hour instead of letting me get rid of them for you in two minutes, what can you expect? You say you havnt attended to anything for three weeks; but really you havnt attended to anything since the session began. I hate to say anything; but really, when those Isle of Cats people took themselves off your hands almost providentially, to let that ridiculous old man talk to you for an hour—! [*She sits down angrily*].

SIR ARTHUR. Nonsense! he didnt stay two minutes; and I got a lot out of him. What about the letters this morning?

HILDA. I have dealt with them: you neednt bother. There are two or three important ones that you ought to answer: I have put them aside for you when you have time.

Flavia and David dash into the room through the masked door even more excited and obstreperous than before, Flavia to her father's right, David to his left.

FLAVIA. Papa: weve been to a meeting of the unemployed with Aloysia and Toffy.

DAVID. Such a lark!

FLAVIA. We saw a police charge. David was arrested.

SIR ARTHUR. Do you mean to say that you went with

those people who were here?

FLAVIA. Yes: theyve come back to lunch with us.

SIR ARTHUR. To lunch!!!

DAVID. Yes. I say: Aloysia's a marvellous girl.

SIR ARTHUR [*determinedly*] I dont mind the girl; but if that young whelp is coming to lunch here he must and shall change his clothes.

DAVID. He's gone home to change and shave: he's dotty on Flavia.

SIR ARTHUR. Why am I afflicted with such children? Tell me at once what you have been doing. What happened?

DAVID. The police brought the Chancellor of the Exchequer to make a speech to the unemployed to quiet them. The first thing we heard him say was "Gentlemen: be patient. I promise you you will soon see the one thing that can revive our industries and save our beloved country: a rise in prices." The mob just gave one howl and went for him. Then the police drew their batons and charged.

FLAVIA. Davy couldnt stand the way the people were knocked about. He screamed to them to stand. The inspector collared him.

SIR ARTHUR. Of course he did. Quite right. Such folly! [*To David*] How do you come to be here if you were arrested? Who bailed you?

DAVID. I asked the inspector who in hell he thought he was talking to. Then Flavia cut in and told him who we were and that old Basham was like a father to us. All he said was "You go home, sir; and take your sister with you. This is no place for you." So as I was rather in a funk by that time we collected Aloysia and Toffy and bunked for home.

SIR ARTHUR. I have a great mind to have that inspector severely reprimanded for letting you go. Three months would have done you a lot of good. Go back to the drawing room, both of you, and entertain your new friends. You know you are not allowed to come in here when I am at work. Be off with you. [*He goes back to his seat*].

FLAVIA. Well, what are we to do? Mamma sends us in on purpose to interrupt you when she thinks you have done enough.

DAVID. She says it's all we're good for.

SIR ARTHUR. A Prime Minister should have no children. Will you get out, both of you; or must I ring for Burton to throw you out?

FLAVIA. Mamma says you are to lunch, Hilda. She wants another woman to make up the party.

HILDA. Oh dear! [*rising*] You must excuse me, Sir Arthur: I must telephone to put off some people who were coming to lunch with me at The Apple Cart. And I must change my frock.

FLAVIA [*squabbling*] You neednt dress up for Brollikins, need you?

DAVID. You let Aloysia alone. You dont want Hilda to dress up for Barking, I suppose.

SIR ARTHUR [*out of patience*] Get out. Do you hear? Get out, the lot of you.

HILDA. Do come, Miss Chavender. Your father is very busy.

SIR ARTHUR [*furious*] Get OUT.

They retreat precipitately through the masked door. Sir Arthur, left alone, rests his wearied head on the table between his arms.

SIR ARTHUR. At last, a moment's peace.

The word rouses the orator in him. He raises his head and repeats it interrogatively; then tries its effect sweetly and solemnly again and again.

SIR ARTHUR. Peace? . . . Peace. Peace. Peace. Peace. Peace. [*Now perfectly in tune*] "Yes, your Grace, my lords and gentlemen, my clerical friends. We need peace. We English are still what we were when time-honored Lancaster described us as 'This happy breed of men.' We are above all a domestic nation. On occasion we can be as terrible in war as we have always been wise and moderate in counsel. But here, in this Church House, under the banner of the Prince of Peace, we know that the heart of England is the English home. Not the battlefield but the fireside—yes, your Grace, yes, my lords and gentlemen, yes, my clerical friends, the fire—"

He starts violently as his eye, sweeping round the imaginary assembly, lights on a woman in grey robes contemplating him gravely and pityingly. She has stolen in noiselessly through the masked door.

SIR ARTHUR. Ffffff!!! Who is that? Who are you? Oh, I beg your pardon. You gave me such a— Whew!! [*He sinks back into his chair*] I didnt know there was anyone in the room.

The lady neither moves nor speaks. She looks at him with deepening pity. He looks at her, still badly scared. He rubs his eyes; shakes himself; looks again.

SIR ARTHUR. Excuse me; but are you real?

THE LADY. Yes.

SIR ARTHUR. I wish youd do something real. Wont you sit down?

THE LADY. Thank you. [*She sits down, very uncannily as it seems to him, in Basham's chair*].

SIR ARTHUR. Will you be so good as to introduce yourself? Who are you?

THE LADY. A messenger.

SIR ARTHUR. Please do not be enigmatic. My nerves are all in rags. I did not see you come in. You appeared there suddenly looking like a messenger of death. And now you tell me you are a messenger.

THE LADY. Yes: a messenger of death.

SIR ARTHUR. I thought so. [*With sudden misgiving*] You mean my death, I hope. Not my wife nor any of the children?

THE LADY [*smiling kindly*] No. Your death.

SIR ARTHUR [*relieved*] Well, thats all right.

THE LADY. You are going to die.

SIR ARTHUR. So are we all. The only question is, how soon?

THE LADY. Too soon. You are half dead already. You have been dying a long time.

SIR ARTHUR. Well, I knew I was overworking: burning the candle at both ends: killing myself. It doesnt matter. I have made my will. Everything is provided for: my wife will be comfortably off; and the children will have as much as is good for them.

THE LADY. You are resigned?

SIR ARTHUR. No; but I cannot help myself.

THE LADY. Perhaps I can help you. I am not only a messenger. I am a healer.

SIR ARTHUR. A what?

THE LADY. A healer. One who heals the sick. One who holds off death until he is welcome in his proper time.

SIR ARTHUR. You cannot help me. I am caught in the wheels of a merciless political machine. The political machine will not stop for you. It has ground many men to pieces before their time; and it will grind me.

THE LADY. My business is with life and death, not with political machinery.

SIR ARTHUR. In that case I am afraid you can be of no use to me; so will you think it very uncivil of me if I go on with my work?

THE LADY. Shall I vanish?

SIR ARTHUR. Not unless you have something else to do. As you are a ghost, and therefore not in time but in eternity, another ten minutes or so wont cost you anything. Somehow, your presence is helping me. A presence is a wonderful thing. Would you mind sitting there and reading The Times while I work?

THE LADY. I never read the newspapers. I read men and women. I will sit here and read you. Or will that make you self-conscious?

SIR ARTHUR. My dear ghost, a public man is so accustomed to people staring at him that he very soon has no self to be conscious of. You wont upset me in the least. You may even throw in a round of applause occasionally; so that I may find out the effective bits to work up.

THE LADY. Go on. I will wait as long as you like.

SIR ARTHUR. Thank you. Now let me me see where I was when you appeared. [*He takes up a scrap of paper on which he has made a memorandum*]. Ah yes: Ive got it. Peace. Yes: peace. [*Trying to make out a word*] Ence—ence—what? Oh, ensue! Of course: a good word. "My friends, lay and clerical, we must ensue peace. Yes, ensue peace. Peace. Disarmament." A burst of Pacifist applause there, perhaps. "Who says that we need a hundred battleships, gentlemen? Christian brotherhood is a safer defence than a thousand battleships. You have my pledge that the Government will be quite content with—with—" oh, well, my secretary will fill that in with whatever number of ships the Japanese are standing out for. By the way, do you think battleships are any real use now? Kenworthy says theyre not: and he was in the navy. It would be such a tremendous score for us at Geneva if we offered to scrap all our battleships. We could make up for them in aeroplanes and submarines. I should like to have the opinion of an impartial and disinterested ghost.

THE LADY. As I listen to you I seem to hear a ghost preparing a speech for his fellow ghosts, ghosts from a long dead past. To me it means nothing, because I am a ghost from the future.

SIR ARTHUR. Thats a curious idea. Of course if there are ghosts from the past there must be ghosts from the future.

THE LADY. Yes: women and men who are ahead of their time. They alone can lead the present into the future. They are ghosts from the future. The ghosts from the past are those who are behind the times, and can only drag the present back.

SIR ARTHUR. What an excellent definition of a Conservative! Thank Heaven I am a Liberal!

THE LADY. You mean that you make speeches about Progress and Liberty instead of about King and Country.

SIR ARTHUR. Of course I make speeches: that is the business of a politician. Dont you like speeches?

THE LADY. On the Great Day of Judgment the speechmakers will stand with the seducers and the ravishers, with the traffickers in maddening drugs, with those who make men drunk and rob them, who entice children and violate them.

SIR ARTHUR. What nonsense! Our sermons and speeches are the glories of our literature, and the inspired voices of our religion, our patriotism, and—of course—our politics.

THE LADY. Sermons and speeches are not religion, not patriotism, not politics: they are only the gibbering of ghosts from the past. You are a ghost from a very dead past. Why do you not die your bodily death? Is it fair for a ghost to go about with a live body?

SIR ARTHUR. This is too personal. I am afraid I cannot get on with my speech while you are there ordering my funeral. Oblige me by vanishing. Go. Disappear. Shoo!

THE LADY. I cannot vanish. [*Merrily changing her attitude*]. Shall we stop playing at ghosts, and accept one another for convenience sake as real people?

SIR ARTHUR. [*shaking off his dreaminess*] Yes, lets. [*He rises and comes to her*]. We have been talking nonsense. [*He pulls out a chair. They sit close together*]. You had me half hypnotized. But first, shake hands. I want to feel that you are real.

He offers his right hand. She seizes both his hands and holds them vigorously, looking straight into his eyes.

SIR ARTHUR [*brightening*] Well, I dont know whether this is real or not; but it's electric, and very soothing and jolly. Ah-a-a-ah! [*a deep sighing breath*]. And now, my dear lady, will you be good enough to tell me who the devil you are?

THE LADY [*releasing him*] Only your wife's lady doctor. Did she not tell you to expect me?

SIR ARTHUR. Of course, of course. How stupid of me! Yes, yes, yes, yes, yes, to be sure. And now I am going to be frank with you. I dont believe in doctors. Neither does my wife; but her faith in quacks is unlimited. And as I am on the verge of a nervous breakdown, she is planting every possible variety of quack on me—you will excuse the expression?—

THE LADY. I excuse everything from my patients. Go on.

SIR ARTHUR. Well, I receive them all as I am receiving you, just to gratify her, or rather to prevent her from making my life miserable. They all say the same obvious thing; and they are none of them of the slightest use. You are going to say it all over again. Can you forgive me for saying flatly that I will not pay you twenty guineas for saying it: not if you said it twenty times over?

THE LADY. Not even if I shew you how to cure yourself? The twenty guineas is an important part of the cure. It will make you take it seriously.

SIR ARTHUR. I know perfectly well how to cure myself. The cure is as simple as a b c. I am Prime Minister of Great Britain. That is, I am an overworked, overworried, overstrained, overburdened, overdriven man, suffering from late hours, irregular snatched meals, no time for digestion nor for enough sleep, and having to keep my mind at full stretch all the time struggling with problems that are no longer national problems but world problems. In short, I am suffering acutely from brain fag.

THE LADY. And the cure?

SIR ARTHUR. A fortnight's golf: thats the cure. I know it all by heart. So suppose we drop it, and part friends. You see, I am really frightfully busy.

THE LADY. That is not my diagnosis. [*She rises*]. Goodbye.

SIR ARTHUR [*alarmed*] Diagnosis! Have you been diagnosing me? Do you mean that there is something else the matter with me?

THE LADY. Not something else. Something different.

SIR ARTHUR. Sit down, pray: I can spare another two minutes. Whats wrong?

THE LADY [*resuming her seat*] You are dying of an acute want of mental exercise.

SIR ARTHUR [*unable to believe his ears*] Of—of—of WHAT, did you say?

THE LADY. You are suffering from that very common English complaint, an underworked brain. To put it in one word, a bad case of frivolity, possibly incurable.

SIR ARTHUR. *Frivolity!* Did I understand you to say that frivolity is a common English failing?

THE LADY. Yes. Terribly common. Almost a national characteristic.

SIR ARTHUR. Do you realize that you are utterly mad?

THE LADY. Is it you or I who have piloted England on to the rocks?

SIR ARTHUR. Come come! No politics. What do you prescribe for me?

THE LADY. I take my patients into my retreat in the Welsh mountains, formerly a monastery, now much stricter and perfectly sanitary. No newspapers, no letters, no idle ladies. No books except in the afternoon as a rest from thinking.

SIR ARTHUR. How can you think without books?

THE LADY. How can you have thoughts of your own when you are reading other people's thoughts?

SIR ARTHUR [*groaning*] Oh, do talk sense. What about golf?

THE LADY. Games are for people who can neither read nor think. Men trifle with their business and their politics; but they never trifle with their games. Golf gives them at least a week-end of earnest concentration. It brings truth home to them. They cannot pretend that they have won when they have lost, nor that they made a magnificent drive when they foozled it. The Englishman is at his best on the links, and at his worst in the Cabinet. But what your country needs is not your body but your mind. And I solemnly warn you that unless you exercise your mind you will lose it. A brain underexercised is far more injurious to health than an underexercised body. You know how men become bone lazy for want of bodily exercise. Well, they become brain lazy for want of mental exercise; and if nature meant them to be thinkers the results are disastrous. All sorts of bodily diseases are produced by half used minds; for it is the mind that makes the body: that is my secret, and the secret of all the true healers. I am sorry you will not allow me to take you a little on the way back to health with me. Good morning. [*She rises*].

SIR ARTHUR. Must you go?

THE LADY. Well, you are so busy—

SIR ARTHUR [*rising*] Ah yes: I forgot. I am frightfully busy. Still, if you could spare another minute—

THE LADY. If you wish. [*She sits down*].

SIR ARTHUR [*sitting down*] You see, what makes your diagnosis so pricelessly funny to me is that as a matter of fact my life has been a completely intellectual life, and my training the finest intellectual training in the world. First rate preparatory school. Harrow. Oxford.

Parliament. An Undersecretaryship. The Cabinet. Finally the Leadership of the House as Prime Minister. Intellect, intellect, all the time.

THE LADY. At Harrow you wrote Latin verses, did you not?

SIR ARTHUR. Yes, of course.

THE LADY. Do you write any now?

SIR ARTHUR. No, of course not. You dont understand. We learnt to write Latin verses not because the verses are any good—after all, it's only a trick of stringing old tags together—but because it's such a splendid training for the mind.

THE LADY. Have all the boys who made Latin verses at Harrow splendidly trained minds?

SIR ARTHUR. Yes. I unhesitatingly say yes. I dont mean, of course, that they are all geniuses; but if you go into the best society you will see that their minds are far superior to those of persons who have had no classical training.

THE LADY. You mean that they can all be trusted to say the same thing in the same way when they discuss public affairs.

SIR ARTHUR. Precisely. They are an educated class, you see.

THE LADY [coldly, rising] Yes: I see. I have really nothing more to say, Sir Arthur. [She takes a card from her bag and puts it on the table] That is the address of my retreat in Wales.

SIR ARTHUR [rising, rather disappointed at having produced no effect] But surely you cannot deny that a man is the better for having been put through the mill of our great educational system.

THE LADY. If a man is born with a hopelessly bad set

of teeth I think it is better for him, and kinder to him, to pull them all out and replace them with a good set of artificial teeth. If some of your political colleagues had not been provided with artificial political minds in the manner you describe they would have been left without any political minds at all. But in that case they would not have meddled in politics; and that, I think, would have been a public advantage. May I reserve a bedroom and a private study for you?

SIR ARTHUR. Pooh! I am not going to your retreat.

THE LADY [*steadfastly*] I think you are.

SIR ARTHUR. I give you up. You are factproof. I am lazy; I am idle; and I am breaking down from overwork. How logical!

THE LADY. All the idlest and laziest of my patients slave from morning to midnight trifling and tittle-tattling about great things. To a retreat, Sir Arthur: get thee to a retreat. I am never mistaken in my diagnosis. I shall telephone to ask whether my number one suite, with private bath and meditation parlor, is vacant.

SIR ARTHUR. No: I wont be rushed. Do you hear? I wont be rushed. [*She is quite unshaken; and he proceeds, much less resolutely*] Of course I shall have to go somewhere for a rest; and if you could really recommend it as a bracing place—

THE LADY. Bracing? What for?

SIR ARTHUR. Well, bracing, you know. Bracing.

THE LADY. Curious, how idle people are always clamoring to be braced! Like trousers.

SIR ARTHUR. Idle people! How you stick to your point! And what a humbug you are! Dont think you can impose on me with your meditation parlor and your dignified airs: I do that sort of thing myself occasionally;

and you know it's no use giving tracts to a missionary. But I feel somehow that you are good for me. You are a dear delightful bighearted wrongheaded half-educated crazyboots; but a woman may be all that and yet have the right instinct as to how to flirt intellectually with a tired thinker. Will you promise to talk to me if I come?

THE LADY. I will even let you talk to me. I guarantee that in a fortnight you will begin to think before you talk. Your dead mind will come to life. I shall make a man of you. Goodbye. [*She goes out quickly through the main door*].

SIR ARTHUR [*calling after her gaily*] Ha ha! Incorrible, incorrigible. [*He takes her card from the table, and contemplates it*]. Oh! I forgot to ask her how much a week she wants for that meditation parlor. [*He looks tragic*].

HILDA [*emerging from her office*] Anything the matter, Sir Arthur?

SIR ARTHUR. I am going into a retreat. Because my brain is underworked. Do you grasp that idea? Have you ever heard of a retreat for the mentally underworked?

HILDA. There is a very nice one at Sevenoaks that my aunt was sent to. But that is for inebriates.

SIR ARTHUR. The one I'm going to is for the mentally underworked, the thoughtless and brainless, the inveterately lazy and frivolous. Yes: the frivolous: your ears do not deceive you.

HILDA [*going to her desk*] Oh, well, theyll amuse you: you always get on well with people of that sort. Shall I pack your usual holiday books? some detective stories and Wordsworth?

SIR ARTHUR. No. You will procure all the books you

can find by a revolutionary German Jew named Harry
Marks—

HILDA. Dont you mean Karl Marx?

SIR ARTHUR. Thats the man. Karl Marx. Get me every
blessed book by Karl Marx that you can find translated
into English; and have them packed for the retreat.

HILDA. There are much newer books by Marxists:
Lenin and Trotsky and Stalin and people like that.

SIR ARTHUR. Get them all. Pack the lot. By George,
I'll teach Alderwoman Aloysia Brollikins to give herself
airs. I'll teach her and her rabble of half-baked half-
educated intellectual beggars-on-horseback that any Oxford man can beat them at their own silly game. I'll
just turn Karl Marx inside-out for them. [*The household
gong sounds*]. Lunch! Come on: that woman's given me
an appetite. [*He goes out impetuously through the
masked door*].

HILDA [*rushing after him*] No, no, Sir Arthur: the
Church House! the Church House! youve forgotten
that you have to lunch at [*her voice is lost in the distance*].

ACT II

The same scene on the 10*th November at* 9.30 *in the morning. There is a generous fire in the grate; and the visitors wear winter clothes. Basham is on the hearthrug, warming his back and reading The Daily Herald.*

BASHAM [*amazed by what he reads*] Gosh! [*He reads further*] Wh-e-e-ew!! [*He reads still further*] Well I'll be dashed!!!

Hilda enters through the main door, and announces an explosive elderly gentleman, evidently a person of consequence, who follows her.

HILDA. Sir Dexter Rightside.

SIR DEXTER [*joining Basham on the hearth*] Ah! That you, Basham? Have you come to arrest him?

BASHAM. You may well ask. He isnt up yet. Miss Hanways: is there any sign of his getting a move on?

HILDA [*much worried*] Lady Chavender wont allow him to be disturbed. She says his speech last night at the Guildhall banquet quite tired him out. People have been ringing up and calling all the morning; but she just puts her back to his door and says that anyone who makes noise enough to waken him leaves her service that minute.

SIR DEXTER. Nonsense! He must see me. Does Lady Chavender suppose that a Prime Minister can stand the country on its head without a word of warning to his colleagues and then go to bed as if he was tired out by a day's fishing?

HILDA [*desperate*] Well, what can *I* do, Sir Dexter?

[*She goes to her bureau*].

SIR DEXTER. Basham: go and break open his bedroom door.

BASHAM. I cant. I'm a policeman: I mustnt do it without a warrant. Go and do it yourself.

SIR DEXTER. I have a devilish good mind to. Can you conceive anything more monstrous, Basham? [*He sits down in the chair next the end chair*]. But I said that this would happen. I said so. When we made this damned coalition that they call a National Government I was entitled to the Prime Ministership. I was the Leader of the Conservative Party. I had an enormous majority in the country: the election proved that we could have done quite well without Chavender. But I had to give way. He humbugged us. He pretended that without his old guard of Liberals and his ragtag and bobtail of Labor men and Socialists and lawyers and journalists-on-the-make and used-up trade union secretaries, and all the rest of the democratic dregs of human society, we couldnt be sure of a majority. His golden voice was to do the trick. He was the popular man, the safe man: I was the unpopular Die Hard who couldnt be trusted to keep my temper. So I stood down. I sacrificed myself. I took the Foreign Secretaryship. Well, what price your safe man now? How do you like your Bolshy Premier? Who was right? the funkers and compromisers or the old Die Hard?

BASHAM. It's amazing. I could have sworn that if there was a safe man in England that could be trusted to talk and say nothing, to thump the table and do nothing, Arthur Chavender was that man. Whats happened to him? What does it mean? Did he go mad at the sanatorium, do you think? Or was he mad before that woman took him there?

SIR DEXTER. Mad! Not a bit of it. But you had better look up that woman's record: there may be money from Moscow behind this.

BASHAM. Arthur take money! Thats going too far.

SIR DEXTER. The woman took the money. It would be waste of money to bribe Chavender: you could always trust him to say whatever he thought would please his audience without being paid for it: damned mountebank.

BASHAM. But he didnt try to please his audience at the Guildhall. They wanted some of his best soothing syrup about law and order after the attack on the Lord Mayor's Show in the afternoon by the unemployed; but according to The Daily Herald here he gave them a dose of boiling Socialism instead.

SIR DEXTER [*nervously*] By the way, Basham, I hope you have the unemployed well in hand today.

BASHAM. Quiet as lambs. Theyre all reading the papers. New editions every half-hour. Like 1914 over again.

Sir Arthur's voice is heard, singing scales. Hilda looks in.

HILDA. I think I hear Sir Arthur singing. He must have got up.

SIR DEXTER. Singing! Is this a moment for minstrelsy?

HILDA. He always sings scales after his bath [*she vanishes*].

After a final burst of solfeggi the masked door is opened vigorously and Chavender enters beaming.

SIR ARTHUR. Ah, here you are, Dexy [*he proffers his hand*].

SIR DEXTER [*like a baited bull*] Dont attempt to shake hands with me. Dont dare call me Dexy.

SIR ARTHUR. What on earth's the matter? Got out at the wrong side of the bed this morning, eh? Frightfully sorry to have kept you waiting, Basham. Whats wrong with the Foreign Secretary this time?

SIR DEXTER. This time! What do you mean by this time?

SIR ARTHUR. Well theres nothing very novel about your turning up before breakfast in a blazing rage, is there? What is it, Basham?

BASHAM. Oh come, P.M.! If you were too drunk last night at the Guildhall to know what you were saying, youd better read the papers [*he offers his paper*].

SIR ARTHUR [*keeping his hands behind his back to warm them*] I remember perfectly well what I said last night. And I drank nothing but barley water.

BASHAM [*insisting*] But look at it, man. [*Quoting the headlines*] New program for winter session. Nationalization of ground rents. Nationalization of banks. Nationalization of collieries. Nationalization of transport.

SIR DEXTER [*moaning*] Nationalization of women. Why omit it? Why omit it?

BASHAM. No: nothing about women. Municipalization of urban land and the building trade, and consequent extinction of rates.

SIR DEXTER. Apostate!

BASHAM. No: nothing about the Church. Abolition of tariffs and substitution of total prohibition of private foreign trade in protected industries. State imports only, to be sold at State regulated prices.

SIR DEXTER. Rot! Incomprehensible and unheard-of rot.

BASHAM. Compulsory public service for all, irrespective of income, as in war time.

SIR DEXTER. Slavery. Call it by its proper name Slavery.

BASHAM. Restoration of agriculture. Collective farming. Nationalization of fertilizer industries. Nitrogen from the air. Power from the tides. Britain self-supporting and blockade proof.

SIR DEXTER. Madness. Ruin to our foreign trade.

BASHAM. Ruthless extinction of parasitism.

SIR DEXTER. You dont even know the present law. You have the Verminous Persons Act. What more do you want ?

BASHAM. Doubling of the surtax on unearned incomes.

SIR DEXTER. Yes: take our last penny! And when the little that the present ruinous taxation has left us is gone; when we have closed our accounts with the last tradesman and turned the last servant into the streets, where are they to find employment? Who is to pay their wages? What is to become of religion when nobody can afford pewrents or a penny to put in the plate? Even sport will not be safe: our breed of horses will be doomed; our packs of hounds sold or slaughtered; and our masters of hounds will be caddies on motor bicycles. That is to be England's future!

SIR ARTHUR. But is that all the papers have reported?

SIR DEXTER. All!!!

BASHAM. Oh come! All! Isnt that about enough?

SIR ARTHUR. But have they said nothing about our promise to restore the cuts made in the pay of the army and navy and police?

SIR DEXTER. Our promise! Whose promise?

BASHAM [interested] What was that you said? Are you going to put my men's wages up to the old figure?

SIR ARTHUR. We shall give you another five thousand

men; pay the old wages with a rise of ten per cent; and double your salary.

BASHAM. Whew! That alters the case a bit.

SIR DEXTER [*rising*] Basham: you are not going to allow yourself to be corrupted like this! Are you such a dupe as to imagine that free Englishmen will tolerate such a monstrous waste of public money?

BASHAM. If I have another five thousand men and a rise on the old wages, I'll answer for the free Englishmen. If they dont like it they can lump it.

SIR DEXTER. You really believe he can keep all the monstrous promises he has made?

BASHAM. No: of course he cant. But he can keep this one. He can raise the pay of the ranks and double my salary; and that is all that concerns me. I'm a policeman, not a politician.

SIR DEXTER. Youre a mercenary gangster and a damned fool: thats what you are. [*He flings himself into the end chair*].

BASHAM [*calmly*] You seem ruffled, Sir Dexter.

Before Sir Dexter can reply, Hilda returns and announces a new visitor.

HILDA. Admiral Sir Bemrose Hotspot. [*She goes out*].

Sir Bemrose is a halfwitted admiral; but the half that has not been sacrificed to his profession is sound and vigorous.

SIR BEMROSE [*in the breeziest spirits*] Morning, Dexy. Morning, Basham. [*Slapping Sir Arthur on the back*] Splendid, Arthur! Never heard you in better form. Thats the stuff to give em. [*They shake hands cordially*].

SIR DEXTER [*sobered by his astonishment*] Rosy: have you gone mad too? Have you forgotten that you are a Conservative and that it was as a Conservative that you were made First Lord of the Admiralty, at my personal suggestion and insistence, in this so-called National Government, which now, thank Heaven, wont last one day after the next meeting of Parliament?

SIR BEMROSE. Wont it, by Jove! It's safe for the next five years. What the country wants is straight orders, discipline, character, pluck, a big navy, justice for the British sailor, no sham disarmaments, and absolute command of the sea. If that isnt Conservatism what is Conservatism? But mind, Arthur, I must have twelve new aeroplane-carrying battleships. I have my eye on Japan. And theres America. And, of course, Russia.

SIR ARTHUR. You shall have them, Rosy. Twentyfour if you say the word.

SIR BEMROSE. Good! Then I'll answer for the House of Commons.

SIR DEXTER. Dont be silly. What can you do with the House of Commons, except empty it whenever you get up to speak?

SIR BEMROSE. I leave the speaking to Arthur: it's his job, not mine. But if there is any further attempt to starve the navy it can give you a little surprise at Westminster. How will you feel when you see a submarine come to the surface off the terrace, and the commander sends in word that he gives you just five minutes before he torpedoes the whole damned Front Bench?

SIR DEXTER. You are talking ridiculous nonsense. Do you suppose for a moment that the navy would be allowed to interfere in politics?

SIR BEMROSE. Who's to stop it? Where would Lenin and Stalin and Trotsky and all that Bolshy lot have been without the Baltic fleet and the Kronstadt sailors? Do you suppose the British navy, with its discipline and its respectable Conservative commanders, couldnt do what these Communist scoundrels did?

SIR DEXTER. How long would the British navy survive the abolition of property in this country? tell me that.

SIR BEMROSE. Dont talk to the navy about property. We dont live by property: we live by service. [*He takes the chair next to the presidential one, and pursues his personal grievance angrily*]. You and your confounded property owners grudge us a clerk's salary for commanding a battleship, and then dock a quarter off it for income tax. We cant set foot on shore without being rented and rated until we can hardly afford to educate our children. Thanks to Arthur, you are pledged now to give us our pay honestly free of income tax and make these lazy idle lubbers of landlords sweat for it. I call that the essence of Conservatism. Thats the way to dish these Labor chaps and Red flaggers and all the rest of the scum you have been pandering to ever since you gave them the vote. Give them whats good for them; and put their ballot papers behind the fire: thats what this country needs.

SIR ARTHUR. You see, Dexy: we have the navy and the police on our side.

SIR DEXTER. May I ask who are "we"?

SIR ARTHUR. Why, the National Government, of course. You and I, Dexy: you and I.

SIR DEXTER. It makes me sick to hear you couple my name with yours. It always did.

HILDA [*announcing*] The President of the Board of Trade. Mr Glenmorison.

Glenmorison is an easy mannered Scottish gentleman, distinctly the youngest of the party.

SIR ARTHUR. Hallo, Sandy. Sit down. Lets all sit down

and have it out.

They settle themselves at the table with their backs to the fire, Sir Arthur in the middle, Glenmorison on his left, Sir Bemrose on his right, and Sir Dexter and Basham right and left respectively.

GLENMORISON. Well, Sir Arthur, when you were letting yourself go so recklessly you might have said a word about Home Rule for Scotland. We may as well be hanged for a sheep as for a lamb.

SIR DEXTER. We! we! we! Who are we? If you mean the Cabinet, it is not responsible for the Prime Minister's frantic proceedings. He acted without consulting us. Do you suppose that if I had heard a word of this outburst of Bolshevism I should have consented to it?

SIR ARTHUR. That was why I didnt consult you.

SIR DEXTER. Psha!

SIR ARTHUR. The responsibility is mine and mine alone.

SIR BEMROSE. Not at all. I claim my share, Arthur. You got the part about the navy from me.

GLENMORISON. Same here, Sir Dexter. I claim at least two items.

SIR DEXTER. Much good may they do you. Arthur's seat is safe: anybody named Chavender can get in unopposed in his constituency because his cunning old father-in-law has every voter in the place bribed up to the neck. But your majority at the last election was seventeen: there were three recounts. Your seat's gone, anyhow.

GLENMORISON. On the contrary, Sir Dexter, it's safe for the first time in the history of Scotland.

SIR DEXTER. Safe! How? You will get the boot as a crazy Bolshevik unless you come out with me and repudiate Chavender promptly and decisively.

GLENMORISON. Oh, I'm afraid I cant do that, Sir Dexter. You see, the balance is held in my constituency by the tradesmen and shopkeepers. Their great grievance is the heavy rates. And though they are all doing middling well they think they could do better if they could raise enough capital to extend their businesses a bit. But the financiers and promoters wont look at small businesses. They are thinking in millions while my people are thinking in thousands, and mostly in only four figures at that. It's easy enough to get a couple of hundred thousand pounds if you are willing to call it a quarter of a million and pay interest on that sum. But what good is that to a man in the High Street in my constituency who wants from five to twenty thousand to extend his little business?

SIR DEXTER. Nonsense! The bank will give him an overdraft if his credit is good.

GLENMORISON. Yes; and call it in at the next slump and panic on the Stock Exchange. I can shew you half a dozen men who were forced into bankruptcy in the last panic, though they were as solvent as you or I. But Sir Arthur's proposal of panic-proof national and municipal banks, as ready and eager to find five thousand for the five thousand man as the financiers are to find a million on condition that enough of it sticks to their own fingers, is just the thing for my people. I darent say a word against it. It's an inspiration as far as my constituents are concerned. Theyre a canny lot, my people: theyd vote for the devil if he'd promise to abolish the rates and open a municipal bank. My majority fell to seventeen last time because I went to them with empty hands and a bellyful of advice to economize and make sacrifices. This bank nationalization is good business for them: theyll just jump at it.

SIR DEXTER. In short, you will make Utopian promises that you know very well will never be carried out.

GLENMORISON. You made a lot of Utopian promises, Sir Dexter, when you formed this National Government. Instead of carrying them out you told the voters to tighten their belts and save the Bank of England. They tightened their belts; and now the Bank of England is paying twelve and sixpence in the pound. Still, I admit, you pulled down my Liberal majority over my Conservative opponent from four thousand to seventeen. Ive got to pull that up again. I say nothing about the rest of the program; but I represent the small man; and on this bank business I am with Sir Arthur all the time.

HILDA [*announcing*] Sir Jafna Pandranath. [*She withdraws*].

This announcement creates a marked sensation. All five gentlemen rise as if to receive a royal personage. Sir Jafna is an elderly Cingalese plutocrat, small and slender to the verge of emaciation, elegantly dressed, but otherwise evidently too much occupied and worried by making money to get any fun out of spending it. One guesses that he must make a great deal of it; for the reverence with which he is received by the five Britons, compared with their unceremonious handling of one another, is almost sycophantic.

SIR JAFNA. Hallo! Am I breaking into a Cabinet meeting?

SIR ARTHUR. No: not a bit. Only a few friendly callers. Pray sit down.

SIR DEXTER [*offering the end chair to the visitor*] You are welcome, Sir Jafna: most welcome. You represent money; and money brings fools to their senses.

SIR JAFNA. Money! Not at all. I am a poor man. I never know from one moment to another whether I am worth thirteen millions or only three. [*He sits down. They all sit down*].

SIR BEMROSE. I happen to know, Sir Jafna, that your enterprises stand at twenty millions today at the very least.

GLENMORISON. Fifty.

SIR JAFNA. How do you know? How do you know? The way I am plundered at every turn! [*To Sir Dexter*] Your people take the shirt off my back.

SIR DEXTER. My people! What on earth do you mean?

SIR JAFNA. Your land monopolists. Your blackmailers. Your robber barons. Look at my Blayport Docks reconstruction scheme! Am I a public benefactor or am I not? Have I not enough to live on and die on without troubling myself about Blayport? Shall I be any the happier when it has ten square miles of docks instead of a tuppeny-hapeny fishing harbor? What have I to gain except the satisfaction of seeing a big publicly useful thing well done, and the knowledge that without me it could not be done? Shall I not be half ruined if it fails?

SIR BEMROSE. Well, whats wrong with it, old chap?

SIR JAFNA. Rosy: you make me puke. What is wrong with it is that the owners of all the miles of land that are indispensable to my scheme, and that without it would not be worth fifteen pounds an acre, are opening their mouths so wide that they will grab sixty per cent of the profit without lifting a finger except to pocket the wealth that I shall create. I live, I work, I plan, I shatter my health and risk all I possess only to enrich these parasites, these vampires, these vermin in the commonwealth. [*Shrieking*] Yes: vermin! [*Subsiding*]You were quite

right at the Guildhall last night, Arthur: you must nationalize the land and put a stop to this shameless ex-
ploitation of the financiers and entrepreneurs by a useless, idle, and predatory landed class.

SIR ARTHUR [*chuckling*] Magnificent! I have the
support of the City.

SIR JAFNA. To the last vote, to the last penny. These
pirates think nothing of extorting a million an acre for
land in the city. A man cannot have an address in London for his letters until he has agreed to pay them from
five hundred to a thousand a year. He cant even die
without paying them for a grave to lie in. Make them
disgorge, Arthur. Skin them alive. Tax them twenty
shillings in the pound. Make them earn their own living,
damn them. [*He wipes his brow and adds, rather hys-
terically*] Excuse me, boys; but if you saw the Blayport
estimates—! [*he can say no more*].

SIR DEXTER. May I ask you to address yourself to this
question not as an emotional oriental [*Sir Jafna chokes
convulsively*] but as a sane man of business. If you
destroy the incomes of our landed gentry where will you
find the capital that exists solely through their prudent
saving—their abstinence?

SIR JAFNA. Bah pooh! Pooh bah! I will find it where
they find it, in the product of the labor I employ. At
present I have to pay exorbitant and unnecessary wages.
Why? Because out of those wages the laborer has to pay
half or quarter as rent to the landlord. The laborer is
ignorant: he thinks he is robbed by the landlord; but
the robbed victim is me—ME! Get rid of the landlord
and I shall have all the capital he now steals. In addition
I shall have cheap labor. That is not oriental emotion: it
is British common-sense. I am with you, Arthur, to the

last drop of my oriental blood. Nationalized land: compulsory labor: abolition of rates: strikes made criminal: I heartily endorse them all in the name of Capital and private enterprise. I say nothing about the rest of your program, Arthur; but on these points no true Liberal can question your magnificent statesmanship.

SIR ARTHUR [*delighted*] You hear that, Dexy. Put that in your pipe and smoke it.

HILDA [*announcing*] His Grace the Duke of Domesday. [*She goes out*].

An elderly delicately built aristocrat comes in. Well preserved, but nearer 70 than 60.

THE DUKE [*surprised to see so many people*] Do I intrude, Arthur? I thought you were disengaged.

SIR ARTHUR. Not at all. Only a talk over last night. Make yourself at home.

SIR DEXTER. You come in the nick of time. Sir Jafna here has just been qualifying you as a bloodsucker, a pirate, a parasite, a robber baron and finally as vermin. Vermin! How do you like it?

THE DUKE [*calmly taking the end chair nearest the window, on Basham's left*] I wonder why the epithet robber is applied only to barons. You never hear of robber dukes; yet my people have done plenty of robbery in their time. [*With a sigh of regret*] Ah, thats all over now. The robbers have become the robbed. I wish you would create some intermediate class of honest folk. I dislike your calling me vermin, Arthur.

SIR ARTHUR. I didnt. It was Jafna.

THE DUKE. Ungrateful Jafna! He is buying up my Blayport estate for next to nothing.

SIR JAFNA. Next to nothing! Holy Brahma!

THE DUKE [*continuing*] He will make millions out of

it. After paying off the mortgages I shall get three and a half per cent on what is left to me out of the beggarly price he offers; and on that three and a half I shall be income-taxed and surtaxed. Jafna's grandsons will go to Eton. Mine will go to a Polytechnic.

SIR BEMROSE. Send them to Dartmouth, old chap. Theres a career for them in the navy now that Arthur is at the helm.

SIR DEXTER. A lieutenant's pay and pension for the future Duke of Domesday! Thats the proposition, is it?

THE DUKE. He will be lucky to have any pay at all. But I shall support you in any case, Arthur. You have at last publicly admitted that the death duties are unsound in principle, and promised to abolish them. That will save us from utter extinction in three generations; and the landed classes are with you to the last man for it. Accept the humble gratitude of a pauperized duke.

SIR DEXTER. And the rest of the program. Do you swallow that too?

THE DUKE. I doubt if the rest of the program will come off. Besides, I dont pretend to understand it. By the way, Sir Jafna, I wish you would take Domesday Towers off my hands for a while. I cant afford to live in it. I cant afford even to keep it dusted. You can have it for a hundred a year.

SIR JAFNA. Too far from town.

THE DUKE. Not by aeroplane. Do think it over.

Sir Jafna shrugs his shoulders and intimates that it is hopeless. The Duke resigns himself to the expected.

SIR ARTHUR. Dexy: you are in a minority of one. The landlords are on my side. The capitalists, big and little, are on my side. The fighting services are on my side. The police are on my side. If you leave us you go out into the wilderness alone. What have you to say?

SIR DEXTER. I have to say that you are a parcel of blind fools. You are trying to scuttle the ship on the chance of each of you grabbing a share of the insurance money. But the Country will deal with you. The Country does not want change. The Country never has wanted change. The Country never will want change. And because I will resist change while I have breath in my body I shall not be alone in England. You have all deserted me and betrayed your party; but I warn you that though I am utterly alone in this room . . .

HILDA [*reappearing*] The deputation, Sir Arthur. Theyve come back. [*She vanishes*].

The deputation enters. Hipney is not with them. Barking, shaved, brilliantly dressed, and quite transfigured, is jubilant. Aloysia glows indignation. Blee and the Mayor, doggedly wearing their hats and overcoats, are gloomy, angry, and resolute. They group themselves just inside the door, glowering at the Prime Minister and his colleagues.

SIR ARTHUR [*beaming*] Gentlemen: a Labor deputation from the Isle of Cats. The one element that was lacking in our councils. You have heard the voice of the peerage, of the city, of the King's forces. You will now hear the voice of the proletariat. Sit down, ladies and gentlemen.

THE MAYOR [*rudely*] Who are you calling the proletariat? Do you take us for Communists? [*He remains standing*].

ALOYSIA. What you are going to hear, Sir Arthur, is the voice of Labor. [*She remains standing*].

BLEE. The verdict of democracy. [*He remains standing*].

EARL OF BARKING. The bleating of a bloody lot of fools. I am with you, Chavender. [*He detaches himself from the group and flings himself into Hilda's chair with intense disgust*].

SIR ARTHUR [*surprised*] Am I to understand that your colleagues are against me?

THE MAYOR. Of course we're against you. Do you expect me to go back to my people and tell them they should vote for compulsory labor and doing away with strikes?

BLEE. Arent the workers enslaved enough already without your depriving them of that last scrap of their liberty? the only weapon they have against the capitalists?

SIR ARTHUR. My dear Mr Mayor, what is the right to strike? The right to starve on your enemy's doorstep and set the whole public against you. Which of you starves first when it comes to the point?

THE MAYOR. I am not going to argue. You can beat me at that. But if you think that the British workingman will listen to compulsory labor and putting down strikes you dont know the world youre living in; and thats all about it.

SIR ARTHUR. But we need not compel the workers to work: they are working already. We shall compel the idlers. Not only your idlers but our idlers: all the idle young gentlemen who do nothing but waste their own time and your labor.

BLEE. We know. Keep all the soft jobs for your lot and the hard ones for us. Do you take us for fools?

BARKING. He does. And you are fools.

SIR ARTHUR. I am glad to have your lordship's support.

ALOYSIA. Support your grandparents! He wants to

marry your daughter.

BARKING [*springing up*] Oh! You can hit below the belt, Aloysia. But as a matter of fact, I do want to marry your daughter, Chavender.

SIR ARTHUR. Hardly the moment to go into that now, is it?

BARKING. It was Aloysia and not I who let the cat out of the bag. Being a cat herself she had a fellow-feeling for the animal. [*He resumes his seat*].

BLEE. Youre an aristocrat, young-fellow-me-lad. I always said that when things got serious youd turn on us and side with your own.

BARKING. Rot! Youre always bragging that you are descended from the Blee of Blayport, whoever he may have been. I shouldnt have tuppence in my pocket if my grandfather hadnt made a fortune in pork pies and bought my father's Norman title for his daughter with it. The blue blood is in your skimpy little veins: the proletarian red's in mine.

ALOYSIA. Youve too much money, Toffy.

BARKING. I havnt had all the pluck taken out of me by poverty, like you chaps. And what good will it do me to have a lot of money when I have to work like anyone else?

SIR DEXTER. Why should a man work like anyone else if he has money?

BARKING. My brother had heaps of money; but he had to go into the trenches and fight like anyone else in the war. Thats how I came into the property.

BLEE. So we're all to be slaves for the sake of setting a few loafers to work. The workers will die sooner than put up with it. I want my liberty—

BARKING. Liberty to work fourteen hours a day and bring up three children on thirtyfour shillings a week, like your brother the shopman. To hell with your filthy liberty!

BLEE [*hotly*] I—

THE MAYOR. Order! order! Dont argue with him, Blee. No good ever comes of arguing with college men. I'm not arguing with Sir Arthur: I'm telling him. The long and the short of it is that if he dont withdraw that silly new program he'll lose every vote in the Isle of Cats. And what the Isle of Cats thinks today, all England thinks tomorrow.

SIR JAFNA. May I speak to this gentleman? Will you introduce me, Arthur?

SIR ARTHUR [*introducing*] Sir Jafna Pandranath. The Mayor of the Isle of Cats.

SIR JAFNA. You have heard of me, Mr Mayor. You know that I am a man who knows what he is talking about. Well, I tell you that the fundamental question is not the Labor question but the Land Question.

THE MAYOR. Yes: we all know that.

SIR JAFNA. Then you will vote for Sir Arthur because he will nationalize the land for you.

BLEE [*scornfully*] Yes, with compensation! Take the land with one hand and give back its cash value to the landlords with the other! Not likely, I ask again, do you take us for fools?

SIR ARTHUR [*introducing*] Mr Alderman Blee.

THE DUKE. Enchanted. I happen to be a landlord—a duke, in fact—and I can assure you, Mr Alderman, that as the compensation will come out of my own pocket and that of my unfortunate fellow landlords in the form of income tax, surtax, and estate duties—what you call death duties—you will get all your cash back and the land as well.

THE MAYOR. Blee: I tell you, dont argue. Stick to your point. No compensation.

BLEE. Not a penny, by God.

THE DUKE. You believe in God, Mr Alderman. I am charmed to hear it.

Here the Duke is astonished to find Aloysia towering over him and pointing an accusing finger at him. At the moment of his introduction of himself as a duke, her eyes lighted up; and she has moved menacingly across the hearth towards him until she is now standing behind the vacant chair between him and Basham.

ALOYSIA. Have you ever heard of the Domesday clearances?

THE DUKE. Clearances? Which clearances do you refer to? The latest cleared me out of Domesday Towers. I can no longer afford to live there.

ALOYSIA. Dont prevaricate. You know very well what I mean. It is written in blood and tears on the pages of working class history.

SIR ARTHUR [*introducing*] Alderwoman Aloysia Brollikins. The Duke of Domesday.

THE DUKE [*rising courteously*] Wont you sit down?

ALOYSIA [*sternly*] You shall not put me out by these tricks and ceremonies. My Lord Duke: I would rather touch the hand of the most degraded criminal in London than touch yours.

THE DUKE [*collapsing into his chair*] Great heavens! Why?

ALOYSIA. Do you forget how your family drove a whole countryside of honest hardworking Scotch crofters into the sea, and turned their little farms into deer forests because you could get more shooting rents out of them in that way? Do you forget that women in childbirth were carried out by your bailiffs to die by the road-side because they clung to their ancient homesteads and ignored your infamous notices to quit? Would it surprise you to learn that I am only one of thousands of young women who have read the hideous story of this monstrous orgy of house-breaking and murder, and sworn to our-selves that never, if we can help it, will it again be possible for one wicked rich man to say to a whole population "Get off the earth."

SIR JAFNA. Admirable! What did I tell you? Hear hear!

ALOYSIA. I thank you, Sir Jafna, for shewing this man that even hardened capitalist millionaires shudder when that story is told. You will not find it in your school histories; but in the new histories, the histories of the proletariat, it has been written, not by the venal academic triflers you call historians, but by the prophets of the new order: the men in whom the word is like a burning fire shut up in their bones so that they are weary of forbearing and must speak.

THE MAYOR. Aye: in the Bible, that is.

ALOYSIA. The Domesday Clearances filled your pockets with gold to console you for the horror and remorse of your dreams; but the vengeance they cried to God for in vain is upon you now that Labor is coming to its own; and it is your turn now to get off the earth.

BLEE. And in the face of all this, you come whining for compensation! Compensation!! Compensation from us to you! From the oppressed to the oppressor! What a mockery!

ALOYSIA. It is from you that we shall exact compensa-tion: aye, to the uttermost farthing. You are conspiring here with these capitalist bloodsuckers to rob us again of the value of what you have already stolen—to make us give you gilt edged securities in exchange for the land that no longer brings you in shooting rents; and you think we cannot see through the plot. But in vain is the net spread in sight of the bird. We shall expose you. We shall tell the story of the Domesday Clearances until the country rings with it if you dare to lift your dishonored head again in English politics. Your demand for compensation is dismissed, turned down: we spit it back in your face. The crofters whom you drove from their country to perish in a foreign land would turn in their graves at the chink of a single penny of public money in your hungry pocket. [*She tears out a chair from under the table and flops into it, panting with oratorical emotion*].

BLEE   Good for you, Brolly!

SIR JAFNA   [*enthused*] Hear hear! [*They hammer on the table with their kunckles*].

SIR BEMROSE

GLENMORISON

THE DUKE [*very appreciative*] What a magnificent speech, Miss Brollikins! I really must insist on your shaking hands with me before we part.

ALOYSIA. Never. How dare you ask me? [*She sweeps away from him and sits down in the opposite chair at the other side of the table*].

THE DUKE [*taking the armchair*] May I not have the privilege of telling my grandchildren how I once met and shook hands with the greatest orator of my time? I assure you all these shocking things happened before I was born.

BLEE [*bawling at him*] Yes; but you still pocket the shooting rents.

THE DUKE [*brusquely*] Of course I do; and so would

you too if you were in my place. [*Tenderly, to Aloysia*]
I assure you, Miss Brollikins, the people make much
more money out of my shooting tenants than they could
as crofters: they would not go back to croftering for
worlds. Wont you let bygones be bygones—except when
you are exercising your wonderful gift of eloquence on
the platform? Think of what your ancestors were doing
in those ruthless old days!

BARKING. Grabbing all they could get, like yours or
mine. Whats the good of tubthumping at these johnnies,
Brolly? Theyve been doing it themselves all their lives.
Cant you see that compensation makes them share the
loss fairly between them?

SIR BEMROSE. It's no use. These damned Liberals
cant understand anything but virtuous indignation.

THE MAYOR. Who are you calling a Liberal? I represent the Labor Party.

SIR BEMROSE. Youre a No Compensation man, arnt
you?

THE MAYOR. Of course I am.

SIR BEMROSE. Then youre a Liberal.

THE MAYOR. Call me what you like. I'm not arguing.
I'm telling you that the Labor Party of the Isle of
Cats puts down its foot and says No Compensation. Is
that plain?

SIR DEXTER. I am glad we have arrived at the same
conclusion from our opposite points of view, Mr Mayor.
The Party I represent, the Conservative Party, will
withdraw from the Coalition if there is the slightest
wobbling on this point. We shall defend our property
—and yours: yours, Mr Mayor, to the last drop of
our blood.

BASHAM [*incisively re-entering the conversation; they*

*had forgotten him, and now turn to him in some sur-
prise*] Our blood, you mean, dont you?

SIR DEXTER [*puzzled*] Whose blood?

BASHAM. The police's blood. You landed gentlemen
never do a thing yourselves: you only call us in. I have
twenty thousand constables, all full of blood, to shed it
in defence of whatever the Government may decide to
be your property. If Sir Arthur carries his point theyll
shed it for land nationalization. If you carry yours
theyll stand by your rent collectors as usual.

BLEE. The police come from the ranks of labor: dont
forget that.

BASHAM. Thats not how they look at it, Blee. They
feel that theyve escaped from the ranks of labor; and
theyre proud of it. They have a status which they feel
to be a part of the status of the Duke here.

THE DUKE. I suppose that is why they are always so
civil to me.

BASHAM. In short, Mister Blee, the police are what
you Socialists call class-conscious. You will find that out
if you are foolish enough to fall out with them.

BLEE. Who cut their pay? Tell me that.

SIR ARTHUR. I shall restore the cuts, Mr Alderman,
with a premium.

THE MAYOR. There! Now you see what comes of
arguing, Blee. It only gives him his chance.

ALOYSIA. You need not warn us, Sir Broadfoot Basham, D.S.O., K.C.M.G., O.B.E. In the Class War
your myrmidons will be well paid.

THE DUKE. Myrmidons!

ALOYSIA. We know too well what we have to expect
from your Janissaries.

BLEE. Your bludgeoning Bashi-Bazouks.

ALOYSIA. The Class War is a fact. We face it. What we want we shall have to take; and we know it. The good of the community is nothing to you: you care only for surplus value. You will never give up your privileges voluntarily. History teaches us that: the history you never read.

THE DUKE. I assure you, my dear Héloïse—

ALOYSIA. Héloïse! Who are you calling Héloïse?

THE DUKE. Pardon. I could not resist the French form of your charming name.

ALOYSIA [*interjects*] The cheek!

THE DUKE [*continuing*] I was merely going to point out, as between one student of history and another, that in the French Revolution it was the nobility who voluntarily abolished all their own privileges at a single sitting, on the sentimental principles they had acquired from reading the work of Karl Marx's revolutionary predecessor Rousseau. That bit of history is repeating itself today. Here is Sir Arthur offering us a program of what seems to me to be first rate Platonic Communism. I, a Conservative Duke, embrace it. Sir Jafna Pandranath here, a Liberal capitalist whose billions shame my poverty, embraces it. The Navy embraces it with the sturdy arms of Sir Bemrose Hotspot. The police are enthusiastic. The Army will be with Sir Arthur to the last man. He has the whole propertied class on his side. But the proletariat rises against him and spews out his Socialism through the eloquent lips of its Aloysia. I recall the warning my dear old father gave me when I was five years old. Chained dogs are the fiercest guardians of property; and those who attempt to unchain them are the first to be bitten.

ALOYSIA. Your Grace calls us dogs. We shall not forget that.

THE DUKE. I have found no friends better than faithful dogs, Miss Brollikins. But of course I spoke figuratively. I should not dream of calling you a dog.

ALOYSIA. No. As I am a female dog I suppose you will call me something shorter when my back is turned.

THE DUKE. Oh! Think of the names you have called me!

THE MAYOR. Well, if you will argue, Alderwoman Brollikins, there's no use my staying here. I wish I could stop your mouth as easy as I can stop my ears. Sir Arthur: youve planked down your program and weve planked down our answers. Either you drop compulsory labor and drop compensation or never shew your face in the Isle of Cats again. [*He goes out resolutely*].

BLEE. Take this from me. I am no Communist: I am a respectable Labor man, as law abiding as any man here. I am what none of you has mentioned yet: a democrat. I am just as much against Cabinet dictatorship as individual dictatorship. What I want done is the will of the people. I am for the referendum. I am for the initiative. When a majority of the people are in favor of a measure then I am for that measure.

SIR BEMROSE. Rot! The majority is never in favor of any measure. They dont know what a measure is. What they want is their orders, and as much comfort as they are accustomed to. The lower deck doesnt want to give orders, it looks to the bridge for them. If I asked my men to do my job theyd chuck me overboard; and serve me jolly well right! You just know nothing about it, because youve never had to command; and you havnt sense enough to obey and be thankful to those who have saved you the trouble of thinking for yourself and keeping you off the rocks.

BLEE. You havnt kept us off the rocks. We're on the rocks, the whole lot of us. So long, Rosy. [*He goes out*].

BARKING. Silly swine! When they are offered what they want they wont have it just because you fellows want it too. They think there must be a catch in it somewhere.

THE DUKE. There generally is. That is how you feel, Miss Brollikins, isn't it?

ALOYSIA. You dont know how I feel; and you never will. We are going to save ourselves and not be saved by you and your class. And I prefer Sir Dexter Rightside's downright outspoken opposition to your silly-clever cynicism and your sickening compliments.

THE DUKE. It is only in middle class books, Miss Brollikins, that noblemen are always cynical and insincere. I find you a most brilliant and delightful woman. May I not tell you so? And WHAT a speaker! Will you spend a quiet week-end with me in some out-of-the-way place in the country, and let me try to convince you that a duke is a human being like yourself?

ALOYSIA [*rearing*] Are you trying to seduce me?

THE DUKE. That would be exquisite, Miss Brollikins; but I am an old and very poor man. You are young, beautiful, and probably opulent. Can you find anything seductive about me?

ALOYSIA. Yes. Youre a duke. And you have the charm of a majestic ruin, if you understand me.

BARKING [*rising*] Come on out of this, Brolly: youre only making a fool of yourself listening to that old bird buttering you up. You just dont know when to go.

ALOYSIA [*moving to the hearthrug, behind Sir Arthur*] You can go if you like. I have some business with Sir Arthur that doesnt concern you. Get out.

SIR ARTHUR. Some business with me! Public business?

ALOYSIA. Not exactly.

SIR ARTHUR. Oh! Private business?

ALOYSIA. I dont care who knows it. But perhaps you would.

BARKING. She means to marry your son David. One below the belt for you, Brolly. Ha ha! Ha ha ha ha ha! [*He goes out roaring with laughter*].

SIR ARTHUR [*after a moment of shock*] I congratulate David, Miss Brollikins. Have you arranged the date?

ALOYSIA. I havnt mentioned it to him yet. I hope all you gentlemen will remember that I was not the one that blurted this out: it was your noble viscount. However, now it's out, I stand by it: David is a good boy; and his class is not his fault. Goodbye all. [*She goes to the door*].

THE DUKE [*rising*] And that week-end, Miss Brollikins? Or has David cut me out?

ALOYSIA. Right you are, Your Grace! I will call for you at Domesday House on Friday at half past four. As I shall bring a few friends we shall hire an omnibus from the London Transport; so you neednt trouble about a car. You wont mind my publishing an account of what happens as a special interview: you know that we Labor intelligentsia have to live by our brains. Au revoir. [*She goes out*].

THE DUKE. There is a frightful unexpectedness about these people. Where on earth shall I borrow the money to pay for the omnibus and entertain them all? [*He goes back to his chair at the end of the table and sits down*].

BASHAM. Your share will only be a few shillings, Duke; and she will reckon on having to pay for you. What girl in her class wouldnt foot the bill if she had a duke to walk out with?

THE DUKE. You reassure me, Sir Broadfoot. Thank you.

SIR DEXTER [*triumphant*] Well, Chavender? What have you to say now? When these people came in I was saying that though I was alone in this room, the people of England were on my side and always would be when it came to the point. Was I right or wrong?

SIR BEMROSE. We never meant to desert you, Dexy. You mustnt think that.

SIR ARTHUR. As you have no more intention of consulting the people of England than I have, the situation is unaltered.

SIR DEXTER. Than you have! What do you mean? Do you think you can govern in this country without the consent of the English people?

SIR ARTHUR. No country has ever been governed by the consent of the people, because the people object to be governed at all. Even you, who ought to know better, are always complaining of the income tax.

THE DUKE. But five shillings in the pound, Arthur! Five shillings in the pound!!

SIR DEXTER. Never mind my income tax. If what you said just now means anything it means that you are going to play fast and loose with democracy: that is, you think you are going to do something that both the people and the governing class of this country are determined you shall not do. The Conservative Party, which is ten times more really democratic than you Liberals have ever been, will carry the people with it against you. How do you propose to get over that? What are you banking on? Put your cards on the table if you really have any.

SIR ARTHUR. Well, here is my ace of trumps. The people of this country, and of all the European countries, and of America, are at present sick of being told that, thanks to democracy, they are the real government of the country. They know very well that they dont govern and cant govern and know nothing about Government except that it always supports profiteering, and doesn't really respect anything else, no matter what party flag it waves. They are sick of twaddle about liberty when they have no liberty. They are sick of idling and loafing about on doles when they are not drudging for wages too beggarly to pay the rents of anything better than overcrowded one-room tenements. They are sick of me and sick of you and sick of the whole lot of us. They want to see something done that will give them decent employment. They want to eat and drink the wheat and coffee that the profiteers are burning because they cant sell it at a profit. They want to hang people who burn good food when people are going hungry. They cant set matters right themselves; so they want rulers who will discipline them and make them do it instead of making them do the other thing. They are ready to go mad with enthusiasm for any man strong enough to make them do anything, even if it is only Jew baiting, provided it's something tyrannical, something coercive, something that we all pretend no Englishman would submit to, though weve known ever since we gave them the vote that theyd submit to anything.

SIR DEXTER [*impatiently*] Yes, yes: we know the cant of all the tuppeny-hapeny dictators who think themselves Mussolinis. Come down to tin tacks. How are you going to get it through Parliament?

SIR ARTHUR. I am not going to get it through Parliament: I am going to prorogue Parliament and then do it. When it is done I shall call a meeting of Parliament to pass an Act of Indemnity for all my proceedings.

SIR DEXTER. You cannot prorogue Parliament. Only the King can prorogue Parliament.

SIR ARTHUR. Precisely. Kings always have prorogued Parliament and governed without them until money ran short.

GLENMORISON. But, man alive, it is not His Majesty alone that you have to consider. The law courts will not enforce your decisions if they are illegal. The civil servants will sabotage you even if they dont flatly disobey you.

SIR ARTHUR. We shall sidetrack them quite easily by setting up new tribunals and special commissions manned by officials we can depend on.

SIR DEXTER. That was how Cromwell cut off King Charles's head. His commissioners found out afterwards that they were doing it with ropes round their rascally necks.

SIR ARTHUR. A rope round a statesman's neck is the only constitutional safeguard that really safeguards. But never fear the rope. As long as we give the people an honest good time we can do just what seems good to us. The proof of the pudding will be in the eating. That will be really responsible government at last.

SIR DEXTER. So that is your game, is it? Has it occurred to you that two can play at it? What can you do that I cannot do if you drive me to it: tell me that.

SIR ARTHUR. Nothing, if you are willing to take on my job. Are you?

SIR DEXTER. The job of ruining the country and destroying the empire? My job is to prevent you from doing that. And I will prevent you.

SIR ARTHUR. Your job is to prevent me or anybody else from doing anything. Your job is to prevent the world from moving. Well, it is moving; and if you dont get out of the way something will break; and it wont be the world.

SIR DEXTER. Nothing has broken so far except the heads of the unemployed when they are encouraged by your seditious rot to rebel against the laws of nature. England is not breaking. She stands foursquare where she always stood and always will stand: the strongest and greatest land, and the birthplace of the noblest imperial race, that ever God created.

SIR ARTHUR. Loud and prolonged cheering. Come! let us both stop tubthumping and talk business. The real master of the situation is Basham here, with his fifteen thousand police.

BASHAM. Twenty thousand.

SIR ARTHUR. Well, twenty thousand. They dont stop functioning when Parliament is prorogued, do they?

BASHAM. No. At Scotland Yard we look to the Home Secretary as far as we look to anybody.

SIR ARTHUR. I can make myself Home Secretary. So that will be all right.

SIR DEXTER. Will it, by George? If you and Basham dare to try your twenty thousand police on me, do you know what I will do?

SIR ARTHUR. What?

SIR DEXTER. I will put fifty thousand patriotic young Londoners into Union Jack shirts. You say they want discipline and action. They shall have them. They shall have machine guns and automatic pistols and tear gas bombs. My Party has the money. My Party has the newspapers. My Party has the flag, the traditions, the glory that is England, the pluck, the breed, the fighting spirit. One of us is worth ten of your half starved gutter-snipes and their leaders that never could afford more than a shilling for a dinner until they voted themselves four hundred a year out of our pockets.

SIR BEMROSE [*carried away*] Thats the stuff, Dexy. Now you are talking, by Jiminy.

BASHAM [*taking command of the discussion coolly*] You are all talking through your hats. The police can do nothing unless the people are on the side of the police. The police cant be everywhere: there arnt enough of them. As long as the people will call the police when anything goes wrong, and stop the runaway criminal and give evidence against him, then twenty thousand constables can keep eight million citizens in order. But if the citizens regard the policeman as their enemy—if the man who snipes a policeman in the back is not given in charge by the bystanders—if he is helped to get away—if the police cannot get a single citizen to go into the box and witness against him, where are you then? You have to double your force because the police must patrol in pairs: otherwise the men will be afraid to patrol at all. Your twenty thousand have to be rein-forced up to forty thousand for their own protection; but that doesn't protect you. You would have to put two policemen standing over every able-bodied man and woman in the town to see that they behaved themselves as you want them to behave. You would need not thousands of constables but millions.

SIR DEXTER. My Union Jack men would keep order, or theyd know the reason why.

BASHAM. And who would keep them in order, I should like to know: silly amateurs. And let me remind you of one thing. It seems easy to buy a lot of black shirts, or brown shirts, or red shirts, and give one to every hooligan who is out for any sort of mischief and every suburban out-of-work who fancies himself a patroit. But dont forget that the colored shirt is a uniform.

GLENMORISON. What harm is there in that? It enables a man to recognize his friends.

BASHAM. Yes; but it marks him out as an enemy in uniform; and to kill an enemy in uniform at sight is not murder: it's legitimate warfare.

SIR DEXTER. Monstrous! I should give no quarter to such an outrageous piece of sophistry.

BASHAM. In war you have to give quarter because you have to ask for it as often as to give it. It's easy to sit here and think of exterminating your opponents. But a war of extermination is a massacre. How long do you think a massacre would last in England today? Just as long as it takes a drunken man to get sick and sober.

GLENMORISON. Easy, Sir Broadfoot, easy, easy. Who is talking of extermination? I dont think you will ever induce respectable Britons to wear red-white-and-blue shirts; but surely you can have volunteers, special constables, auxiliary forces—

BASHAM [*flinching violently*] Auxiliary forces! I was

in command of them in Ireland when you tried that
game on the Irish, who were only a little handful of
peasants in their cabbage patch. I have seen these things.
I have done them. I know all about it: you know nothing about it. It means extermination; and when it comes
to the point you cant go through with it. I couldnt. I
resigned. You couldnt: you had to back down. And I
tell you, Dexy, if you try any colored shirt hooliganism
on me, I'll back the P.M. and shew you what Scotland
Yard can do when it's put to it.

SIR DEXTER. Traitor!

BASHAM. Liar! Now weve called one another names
how much farther has it got us?

GLENMORISON. Easy, easy: dont let us quarrel. I must
support the Prime Minister, Sir Dexter, to secure my
seat in Parliament. But I am a Liberal, and, as such,
bound by Liberal principles. Whatever we do must be
done through Parliament if I am to be a party to it.
I am all for the new program; but we must draw up a
parliamentary timetable for it. To carry out the program
will involve the introduction of at least twelve bills.
They are highly controversial bills: every one of them
will be resisted and obstructed to the very last clause.
You may have to go to the country on several of them.
The committees stages will last for weeks and weeks,
no matter how hard you work the guillotine: there will
be thousands of amendments. Then, when you have got
through what is left of your Bill and carried it, the
House of Lords will turn it down; and you will have
to wait two years and go through the whole job again
before you can get your Bill on the statute book as an
Act of Parliament. This program is not a matter of
today or tomorrow. I calculate that at the very least it

will take fifty years to get it through.

SIR ARTHUR. And you think the world will wait for that, Sandy?

GLENMORISON [*naïvely*] What else can it do?

SIR ARTHUR. It wont wait. Unless we can find a shorter way, the program will be fought out in the streets.

SIR DEXTER. And you think that in the streets you will win? You think the mob will be on your side? "Ye are many: they are few" eh? The Class War! Well, you will find out your mistake.

SIR ARTHUR. I dont believe in the Class War any more than you do, Dexy. I know that half the working class is slaving away to pile up riches, only to be smoked out like a hive of bees and plundered of everything but a bare living by our class. But what is the other half doing? Living on the plunder at second hand. Plundering the plunderers. As fast as we fill our pockets with rent and interest and profits theyre emptied again by West End tradesmen and hotel keepers, fashionable doctors and lawyers and parsons and fiddlers and portrait painters and all sorts, to say nothing of huntsmen and stablemen and gardeners. valets and gamekeepers and jockeys, butlers and housekeepers and ladies' maids and scullery maids and deuce knows who not.

THE DUKE. How true, Arthur! how profoundly true! I am with you there to the last drop of my blood.

SIR ARTHUR. Well, these parasites will fight for the rights of property as they would fight for their own skins. Can you get a Labor member into Parliament in the places where they are in a majority? No: there is no class war: the working class is hopelessly divided against itself. But I will tell you what there is. There is the gulf between Dexy's view of the world and mine.

There is the eternal war between those who are in the world for what they can get out of it and those who are in the world to make it a better place for everybody to live in.

SIR DEXTER [*rising*] I will not sit here listening to this disgusting ungentlemanly nonsense. Chavender: the coalition is dissolved. I resign. I shall take with me three quarters of the Cabinet. I shall expose the shamelessly corrupt motives of those who have supported you here today. Basham: you will get the sack the day after the King sends for me. Domesday: you have gone gaga: go home to bed and drivel where your dotage can do no harm. Rosy: you are a damned fool; and you ought to know it by this time. Pandranath: you are only a silly nigger pretending to be an English gentleman: you are found out. Good afternoon, gentlemen.

He goes out, leaving an atmosphere of awe behind him, in which the Indian is choking with indignation, and for the moment inarticulate.

SIR BEMROSE. This is awful. We cannot do without him.

SIR JAFNA [*finding his tongue*] I am despised. I am called nigger by this dirty faced barbarian whose forefathers were naked savages worshipping acorns and mistletoe in the woods whilst my people were spreading the highest enlightenment yet reached by the human race from the temples of Brahma the thousandfold who is all the gods in one. This primitive savage dares to accuse me of imitating him: me, with the blood in my veins of conquerors who have swept through continents vaster than a million dogholes like this island of yours. They founded a civilization compared to which your little kingdom is no better than a concentration camp.

What you have of religion came from the east; yet no Hindu, no Parsee, no Jain, would stoop to its crudities. Is there a mirror here? Look at your faces and look at the faces of my people in Ceylon, the cradle of the human race. There you see Man as he came from the hand of God, who has left on every feature the unmistakeable stamp of the great original creative artist. There you see Woman with eyes in her head that mirror the universe instead of little peepholes filled with faded pebbles. Set those features, those eyes, those burning colors beside the miserable smudged lumps of half baked dough, the cheap commercial copies of a far away gallery of masterpieces that you call western humanity, and tell me, if you dare, that you are the original and I the imitation. Do you not fear the lightning? the earthquake? the vengeance of Vishnu? You call me nigger, sneering at my color because you have none. The jackdaw has lost his tail and would persuade the world that his defect is a quality. You have all cringed to me, not for my greater nearness to God, but for my money and my power of making money and ever more money. But today your hatred, your envy, your insolence has betrayed itself. I am nigger. I am bad imitation of that eater of unclean foods, never sufficiently washed in his person or his garments, a British islander. I will no longer bear it. The veil of your hypocrisy is rent by your own mouths: I should dishonor my country and my race by remaining here where both have been insulted. Until now I have supported the connexion between India and England because I knew that in the course of nature and by the justice of Brahma it must end in India ruling England just as I, by my wealth and my brains, govern this roomful of needy imbeciles. But I now cast you off. I return to India to detach it wholly from England, and leave you to perish in your ignorance, your vain conceit, and your abominable manners. Good morning, gentlemen. To hell with the lot of you. [*He goes out and slams the door*].

SIR ARTHUR. That one word nigger will cost us India. How could Dexy be such a fool as to let it slip!

SIR BEMROSE [*very serious—rising solemnly*] Arthur: I feel I cannot overlook a speech like that. After all, we are white men.

SIR ARTHUR. You are not, Rosy, I assure you. You are walnut color, with a touch of claret on the nose. Glenmorison is the color of his native oatmeal: not a touch of white on him. The fairest man present is the Duke. He's as yellow as a Malayan headhunter. The Chinese call us Pinks. They flatter us.

SIR BEMROSE. I must tell you, Arthur, that frivolity on a vital point like this is in very bad taste. And you know very well that the country cannot do without Dexy. Dexy was at school with me before I went to Dartmouth. To desert him would be for me not only an act of political bad faith but of personal bad feeling. I must go and see him at once. [*He goes very sadly to the door*].

SIR ARTHUR. Make my apologies to Sir Jafna if you overtake him. How are we to hold the empire together if we insult a man who represents nearly seventy per cent of its population?

SIR BEMROSE. I dont agree with you, Arthur. It is for Pandy to apologize. Dexy really shares the premiership with you; and if a Conservative Prime Minister of England may not take down a heathen native when he forgets himself there is an end of British supremacy.

SIR ARTHUR. For Heaven's sake dont call him a native. You are a native.

SIR BEMROSE [*very solemnly*] Of Kent, Arthur: of Kent. Not of Ceylon. [*He goes out*].

GLENMORISON. I think I'd better clear out too. I can make allowances for Sir Dexter: he is an Englishman, and has not been trained to use his mind like us in Scotland. But that is just what gives him such a hold on the Country. We must face it: he's indispensable. I'll just go and assure him that we have no intention of breaking with him. Ta ta. Good morning, Duke. [*He goes out*].

SIR ARTHUR [*rising and strolling round to the other side of the table like a cleaned-out gambler*] That finishes me, I'm afraid.

He throws himself into the middle chair. Basham rises moodily and goes to the window to contemplate the street. The Duke comes sympathetically to Sir Arthur and sits down beside him.

THE DUKE. Oh Arthur, my dear Arthur, why didnt you play golf on your holiday instead of thinking? Didnt you know that English politics wont bear thinking about? Didnt you know that as a nation we have lost the trick of thinking? Hadnt you noticed that though in our great British Constitution there is a department for everything else in the world almost—for agriculture and health and fisheries, for home affairs and foreign affairs and education, for the exchequer and the Treasury and even the Chiltern Hundreds and the Duchy of Lancaster—we have no department for thinking? The Russians have a special Cabinet for it; and it has knocked the whole place to pieces. Where should you and I be in Russia today? [*He resumes his seat with a hopeless shrug*].

SIR ARTHUR. In our proper place, the dustbin. Yet they got their ideas from us. Karl Marx thought it all out in Bloomsbury. Lenin learnt his lesson in Holford Square, Islington. Why can we never think out anything, nor learn any lessons? I see what has to be done now; but I dont feel that I am the man to do it.

THE DUKE. Of course not. Not a gentleman's job.

SIR ARTHUR. It might be a duke's job, though. Why not have a try at it?

THE DUKE. For three reasons, Arthur. First, I'm not built that way. Second, I'm so accustomed as a duke to be treated with the utmost deference that I simply dont know how to assert myself and bully people. Third, I'm so horribly hard up for pocket money without knowing how to do without it that Ive lost all my self-respect. This job needs a man with nothing to lose, plenty of hard driving courage, and a complete incapacity for seeing any side of a question but his own. A mere hereditary duke would be no use. When Domesday Towers is sold to an American I shall have no family seat left, and must fall back on my political seat, which is at present on the fence. From that eminence I shall encourage the dictator when he arrives as far as I can without committing myself dangerously. Sorry I can be of no use to you, my dear Arthur.

SIR ARTHUR. What about you, Basham? You are a man of action.

BASHAM. I have a jolly good mind to go to the King and make him take the bit between his teeth and arrest the lot of you.

SIR ARTHUR. Do, Basham, do. You couldnt make a worse hash of things than we have.

THE DUKE. Theres nothing to prevent you. Look at Kemal Pasha! Look at Mussolini! Look at Hitler! Look at De Valera! Look at Franklin Roosevelt!

BASHAM. If only I had ambition enough I'd think very seriously over it. As it is, I'll go back quietly to Scotland Yard. [*He is going out when he is confronted in the doorway by Hipney*]. Hallo! What the devil are you doing here?

SIR ARTHUR. I am afraid you are late, Mr Hipney. The deputation has been here. They have all gone.

HIPNEY [*seating himself beside Sir Arthur with his usual calm*] I came with them, Srarthur. I been listening on the quiet as you might say. I just came in to tell you not to mind that parliamentary lot. Theyre all the same, west end or east end, parkside or riverside. Theyll never do anything. They dont want to do anything.

BASHAM [*sitting down again in Hilda's chair*] Hipney: I may as well tell you that I have had my eye on you for some time. Take care I have no objection to your calling yourself a revolutionary Socialist: they all do that. But I suspect you of really meaning business.

HIPNEY. I do, Sir Broadfoot: I do. And if Srarthur means business, then let him come out of Parliament and keep out. It will take the life out of him and leave him a walking talking shell of a man with nothing inside. The only man that ever had a proper understanding of Parliament was old Guy Fawkes.

SIR ARTHUR. But even if he had blown that Parliament up, they would just have elected another.

HIPNEY. Yes; but it was a sort of gesture as you might say. Symbolic, I call it. Mark my words: some day there will be a statue to old Guy in Westminster on the site of the present House of Commons.

THE DUKE. Democracy, Arthur, democracy. This is what it ends in.

SIR ARTHUR [*introducing*] His Grace the Duke of Domesday, Mr Hipney.

HIPNEY. Bless you, I know his Grace. About town, as you might say, though weve never been introduced.

THE DUKE. Very much honored, Mr Hipney.

HIPNEY. No great honor, your Grace. But old Hipney can tell you something about Democracy at first hand. Democracy was a great thing when I was young and we had no votes. We talked about public opinion and what the British people would stand and what they wouldnt stand. And it had weight, I tell you, sir: it held Governments in check: it frightened the stoutest of the tyrants and the bosses and the police: it brought a real reverence into the voices of great orators like Bright and Gladstone. But that was when it was a dream and a vision, a hope and faith and a promise. It lasted until they dragged it down to earth, as you might say, and made it a reality by giving everybody votes. The moment they gave the working men votes they found that theyd stand anything. They gave votes to the women and found they were worse than the men; for men would vote for men—the wrong men, but men all the same—but the women wouldnt even vote for women. Since then politics have been a laughing stock. Parliamentary leaders say one thing on Monday and just the opposite on Wednesday; and nobody notices any difference. They put down the people in Egypt, in Ireland, and in India with fire and sword, with floggings and hangings, burning the houses over their heads and bombing their little stores for the winter out of existence; and at the next election theyd be sent back to Parliament by working class constituencies as if they were plaster saints, while men and women like me, that had spent their lives in the service of the people, were booted out at the polls like convicted criminals. It wasnt that the poor silly sheep did it on purpose. They didnt notice: they didnt remember: they couldnt understand: they were taken in by any nonsense they heard at the meetings or read in the morning paper. You could stampede them by crying out that the Russians were coming, or rally them by promising them to hang the Kaiser, or Lord knows what silliness that shouldnt have imposed on a child of four. That was the end of democracy for me; though there was no man alive that had hoped as much from it, nor spoke deeper from his heart about all the good things that would happen when the people came to their own and had votes like the gentry. Adult suffrage: that was what was to save us all. My God! It delivered us into the hands of our spoilers and oppressors, bound hand and foot by our own folly and ignorance. It took the heart out of old Hipney; and now I'm for any Napoleon or Mussolini or Lenin or Chavender that has the stuff in him to take both the people and the spoilers and oppressors by the scruffs of their silly necks and just sling them into the way they should go with as many kicks as may be needful to make a thorough job of it.

BASHAM. A dictator: eh? Thats what you want.

HIPNEY. Better one dictator standing up responsible before the world for the good and evil he does than a dirty little dictator in every street responsible to nobody, to turn you out of your house if you dont pay him for the right to exist on the earth, or to fire you out of your job if you stand up to him as a man and an equal. You cant frighten me with a word like dictator. Me and my like has been dictated to all our lives by swine that have nothing but a snout for money, and think the world is coming to an end if anybody but themselves is given the power to do anything.

SIR ARTHUR. Steady, Mr Hipney, steady! Dont empty the baby out with the bath. If the people are to have no voice in the government and no choice of who is to govern them, it will be bad for the people.

HIPNEY. Let em have a voice. Let em have a choice. Theyve neither at present. But let it be a voice to squeal with when theyre hurt, and not to pretend they know more than God Almighty does. Give em a choice between qualified men: theres always more than one pebble on the beach; but let them be qualified men and not windbags and movie stars and soldiers and rich swankers and lawyers on the make. How are they to tell the difference between any cheap Jack and Solomon or Moses? The Jews didnt elect Moses: he just told them what to do and they did it. Look at the way they went wrong the minute his back was turned! If you want to be a leader of the people, Srarthur, youve got to elect yourself by giving us a lead. Old Hipney will follow anyone that will give him a good lead; and to blazes with your elections and your Constitution and your Democracy and all the rest of it!

THE DUKE. The police wont let him, Mr Hipney.

BASHAM [*rising and planting himself between Hipney and Sir Arthur*] Ha ha ha! Dont be too sure of that. I might come down on your side, Arthur, if I spotted you as a winner. Meanwhile, Hipney, I have my eye on you as a dangerous character.

SIR ARTHUR. And on me?

BASHAM. You dont matter: he does. If the proletariat

comes to the top things will be more comfortable for Hipney; but they wont be more comfortable for you. His heart is in the revolution: you have only your head in it. Your wife wouldnt like it: his would, if he has one.

HIPNEY. Not me. I'm under no woman's thumb. She's dead; and the children are grown up and off my hands. I'm free at last to put my neck in a noose if I like.

BASHAM. I wonder should I find any bombs in your house if I searched it.

HIPNEY. You would if you put them there first, Sir Broadfoot. What good would a police chief be if he couldnt find anything he wanted to find?

BASHAM. Thats a suggestion, Hipney, certainly. Isnt it rather rash of you to put it into my head?

HIPNEY. There's plenty to put it into your head if I didnt. You could do it if you liked; and you know it, Sir Broadfoot. But perhaps your conscience wouldnt let you.

BASHAM. Perhaps.

HIPNEY [rising with a chuckle] Aha! [Impressively] You take it from me, you three gentlemen: all this country or any country has to stand between it and blue hell is the consciences of them that are capable of governing it.

THE DUKE [rising] Mr Hipney: I find myself in complete agreement with you. Will you lunch with me at the Carlton?

HIPNEY. No: them big clubs is too promiscuous for the like of you and me. You come and lunch with me: I know a nice little place where the cooking's good and the company really select. You wont regret it: come along. Morning, Srarthur. Morning, Boss. [He goes out, greatly pleased].

SIR ARTHUR AND BASHAM [*simultaneously*] Morning. Morning.

THE DUKE. You would never have got rid of him, Arthur, if I hadn't made that move. Goodbye. Goodbye, Sir Broadfoot. [*He goes to the door*].

BASHAM. Goodbye. I wish you joy of your host.

THE DUKE. You dont appreciate him. He is absolutely unique.

BASHAM. In what way, pray?

THE DUKE. He is the only politician I ever met who learnt anything from experience [*he goes out*].

BASHAM [*making for the door*] Well, I must be off to the Yard. The unemployed are going to have a general election to amuse them. I suppose youll be off to your constituency right away.

SIR ARTHUR [*rising*] No. I am not going to stand.

BASHAM [*returning to him in amazement*] Not stand! What do you mean? You cant chalk up a program like that and then run away.

SIR ARTHUR. I am through with parliament. It has wasted enough of my life.

BASHAM. Dont tell me you are going to take your politics into the street. You will only get your head broken.

SIR ARTHUR. Never fear: your fellows wont break my head: they have too much respect for an ex-Prime Minister. But I am not going into the streets. I am not a man of action, only a talker. Until the men of action clear out the talkers we who have social consciences are at the mercy of those who have none; and that, as old Hipney says, is blue hell. Can you find a better name for it?

BASHAM. Blackguardocracy, I should call it.

SIR ARTHUR. Do you believe in it? I dont.

BASHAM. It works all right up to a point. Dont run your head against it until the men of action get you past that point. Bye bye.

SIR ARTHUR. Bye bye. I wont.

Basham goes out through the main door. Sir Arthur drops into his chair again and looks rather sick, with his elbows on his knees and his temples on his fists. Barking and Miss Brollikins break into the room simultaneously by the private door, struggling for precedence, Sir Arthur straightens up wearily.

BARKING. I was here first. You get out and wait for your turn.

ALOYSIA. Ladies first, if you please. Sir Arthur—

BARKING [*barring her way with an arm of iron*] Ladies be damned! youre no lady. [*He comes past the table to Sir Arthur's right*]. Sir Arthur: I have proposed for the hand of your daughter Flavia; and all I can get out of her is that she is not a gold digger, and wouldnt be seen at a wedding with a lousy viscount. She wants to marry a poor man. I said I'd go over her head straight to you. You cant let her miss so good a match. Exert your authority. Make her marry me.

SIR ARTHUR. Certainly. I'll order her to marry you if you think that will get you any further. Go and tell her so, like a good boy. I'm busy.

BARKING. Righto! [*he dashes out through the masked door*].

SIR ARTHUR. Sit down, Miss Brollikins. [*She comes round to Hipney's chair; and Sir Arthur takes the Duke's chair*]. Have you consulted David?

ALOYSIA [*sitting down rather forlornly*] Of course I have. But he's obstinate. He wont look at it the right way.

SIR ARTHUR. Did he object? He should have jumped at it.

ALOYSIA. It's very nice of you to say so if you really mean it, Sir Arthur. But he has no sense. He objects to my name. He says it's ridiculous.

SIR ARTHUR. But your marriage will change it.

ALOYSIA. Yes; but he says it would be in The Times in the births marriages and deaths: Chavender and Brollikins. My name's not good enough for him. You should have heard what he said about it.

SIR ARTHUR. I hope he did not use the adjective his sister applied to poor young Barking's title.

ALOYSIA. Yes he did. The language you West End people use! I'm sure I dont know where you pick it up.

SIR ARTHUR. It doesnt mean anything, Miss Brollikins. You mustnt mind.

ALOYSIA. Would you mind calling me Aloysia, Sir Arthur? You can call me Brolly if you like; but I prefer Aloysia.

SIR ARTHUR. Certainly, Aloysia.

ALOYSIA. Thank you. I wish I could get rid of Brollikins. I'd never stoop to be ashamed of my name; but I cant deny there's something funny about it. I'm not to blame for that, am I?

SIR ARTHUR. But you can get rid of it quite easily. You can take a new name: any name you like, by deed poll. It costs only ten pounds; and David would have to pay it if it was on his account you changed. What about Bolingbroke [*he pronounces it Bullingbrook*]? Bolingbroke would be rather a nice name for The Times; and you wouldnt have to change your initials. No bother about your clothes at the laundry, for instance.

ALOYSIA. Thank you, Sir Arthur: thats a practical sug-

gestion. At any rate it will shut David up if he talks about my name again.

SIR ARTHUR. Well, now you can run off and marry him.

ALOYSIA. But thats not all, Sir Arthur. He's such a queer boy. He says he's never loved anyone but his sister, and that he hates his mother.

SIR ARTHUR. He had no right to tell you that he hates his mother, because as a matter of fact he doesn't. Young people nowadays read books about psycho-analysis and get their heads filled with nonsense.

ALOYSIA. Of course I know all about psycho-analysis. I explained to him that he was in love with his mother and was jealous of you. The Edipus complex, you know.

SIR ARTHUR. And what did he say to that?

ALOYSIA. He told me to go to Jericho. But I shall teach him manners.

SIR ARTHUR. Do, Aloysia. Did he make any further objection?

ALOYSIA. Well, he says his people couldnt stand my relatives.

SIR ARTHUR. Tut! the young snob! Still, snobbery is a very real thing: he made a point there, Aloysia. How did you meet it?

ALOYSIA. I said my people couldnt stand his relatives; and no more they could. I said I wasnt asking him to marry my relatives; nor was I proposing to marry his.

SIR ARTHUR. And what did he say to that?

ALOYSIA. He told me to go to hell. He's like that, you know.

SIR ARTHUR. Yes, a hasty boy.

ALOYSIA. He is, just that. But I shall cure him of it.

SIR ARTHUR [*gravely*] Take care, Aloysia. All young

women begin by believing they can change and reform the men they marry. They cant. If you marry David he will remain David and nobody else til death do you part. If he tells you to go to hell today instead of trying to argue with you, he will do the same on the morning of your silver wedding.

ALOYSIA [*grimly*] We shall see.

SIR ARTHUR. May I ask whether this match is your idea or David's? So far I do not gather that he has expressed any strong feeling of—of—shall I say devotion?—to you.

ALOYSIA. We have discussed all that.

SIR ARTHUR. Satisfactorily?

ALOYSIA. I suppose so. You see, Sir Arthur, I am not like David. I am a reading thinking modern woman; and I know how to look at these things objectively and scientifically. You know the way you meet thousands of people and they mean nothing to you sexually: you wouldnt touch one of them with a barge pole. Then all of a sudden you pick out one, and feel sexy all over. If he's not nice you feel ashamed of yourself and run away. But if he is nice you say "Thats the man for me." You have had that experience yourself, havnt you?

SIR ARTHUR. Quite. The moment I saw Lady Chavender I said "Thats the woman for me."

ALOYSIA. Well, the moment I laid eyes on David I went all over like that. You cant deny that he is a nice boy in spite of his awful language. So I said—

SIR ARTHUR. "David's the man for me"?

ALOYSIA. No. I said "Evolution is telling me to marry this youth." That feeling is the only guide I have to the evolutionary appetite.

SIR ARTHUR. The what??

ALOYSIA. The evolutionary appetite. The thing that wants to develop the race. If I marry David we shall develop the race. And thats the great thing in marriage, isnt it?

SIR ARTHUR. My dear Aloysia, the evolutionary appetite may be a guide to developing the race; but it doesnt care a rap for domestic happiness. I have known the most remarkable children come of the most dreadfully unsuitable and unhappy marriages.

ALOYSIA. We have to take our chance of that, Sir Arthur. Marriage is a lottery. I think I can make David as happy as anybody ever is in this—

SIR ARTHUR. In this wicked world. Ah yes. Well, I wont press that.

ALOYSIA. I was about to say "in the capitalist phase of social development." I dont talk like your grandmother, if you will excuse me saying so.

SIR ARTHUR. I beg your pardon. I suppose I do. Have you explained this evolutionary view of the situation to David?

ALOYSIA. Of course I have. I don't treat him as a child.

SIR ARTHUR. And what did he say?

ALOYSIA. He told me to go and— Oh, I really cannot repeat what he told me to go and do. But you see how familiar we are together. I couldnt bear his being distant with me. He talks just as if we were married already.

SIR ARTHUR. Quite. But does he feel about you as you feel about him? Has he picked you out from among the thousand ladies to whom he is indifferent? To use your own expression, does he come all over like that in your presence?

ALOYSIA. He does when I get hold of him. He needs educating in these matters. I have to awaken David. But he's coming along nicely.

SIR ARTHUR. Well, if it must be it must be. I shall not withhold my blessing. That is all I can say. [*He rises: she does the same and prepares to go*]. You see, Aloysia, the effete society in which I move is based on the understanding that we shall all speak and behave in the manner in which we are expected to behave. We are helpless when this understanding is violated. We dont know what to say or what to do. Well, you have violated it recklessly. What you have said has been unexpected to the last possible degree—

ALOYSIA. It has been true.

SIR ARTHUR. That is the climax of unexpectedness in polite society. Therefore I am at a loss. Apparently my son was not at a loss. He knows how to deal with you: I do not. I must really refer you back to him for further consideration and report.

They are about to shake hands when Lady Chavender comes in through the masked door.

LADY CHAVENDER. Still here, Miss Brollikins! I thought you had gone. [*She comes past the table to Sir Arthur's right*].

SIR ARTHUR. She wants to marry David, my dear.

LADY CHAVENDER [*calmly*] Very naturally. I think if I were in Miss Brollikins' position I should want to marry David.

ALOYSIA. I know your class point of view, Lady Chavender. You think it would be a big catch for me and a come-down for him.

LADY CHAVENDER. We both know that point of view, Miss Brollikins; but it is you, not I, that have mentioned it. Wont you sit down? [*She sits down herself in the nearest chair*].

ALOYSIA [*murmurs*] I was just going. [*She resumes her seat*].

Sir Arthur also sits.

LADY CHAVENDER. I daresay a match with you might be a very good thing for David. You seem to have all the qualities in which he is deficient. And he has been declaring for some months past that if he ever marries he will marry a factory girl.

ALOYSIA. Well, I have been a factory girl. I started as a school teacher; but when they cut my salary I went into the factory. I organized the girls there, and became a trade union secretary. Wherever I went I rose because I couldnt keep down. But I am proletarian, bone and blood, if thats what David wants.

LADY CHAVENDER. Nobody is that in England, Miss Brollikins. We have never had a noble caste: our younger sons have always been commoners.

SIR ARTHUR. Yes, Aloysia: all British blood is blue.

ALOYSIA. Well, call it what you like. All I say is that I belong to the common working people and am proud of it; and that is what David wants, isnt it?

LADY CHAVENDER. What I said was that he wants to marry a factory girl. But I do not know what his attitude will be when a factory girl wants to marry him. Have you proposed to him?

SIR ARTHUR. Yes. He told her to go to hell.

LADY CHAVENDER. David has rather a habit of telling people to go to hell when he is too lazy to think of anything better to say. Miss Brollikins is a resolute and successful young woman. David is an irresolute and unsuccessful young man. If she has made up her mind to marry him she will probably succeed. She will have to support him; but I daresay she can do that as easily as she can support herself.

ALOYSIA. I shall expect him to work for his living.

LADY CHAVENDER. Marriage seldom fulfils all our expectations. You dont know David yet.

ALOYSIA. I will find him a job and see that he does it. I will interest him in it.

SIR ARTHUR. Splendid!

ALOYSIA [*puzzled*] But I cant make out you two. You havnt flared up as I thought you might; but are you for me or against me?

LADY CHAVENDER. Miss Brollikins: I am sorry; but there are two things that I cannot bring myself to take the smallest interest in: parliamentary affairs and love affairs. They both bore me to distraction.

ALOYSIA [*to Sir Arthur*] Well, dont you take an interest in David?

SIR ARTHUR. David is at the age at which young men have to break loose from their fathers. They are very sensitive about being interfered with at that age. He would regard my taking an interest in him as parental tyranny. Therefore I am particularly careful not to take any interest in him.

ALOYSIA [*rising*] Well, you preach at me because my conversation is unexpected; but you two are the most unexpected lot I have ever been up against. What am I to understand? Will you play fair and let David take his own way?

SIR ARTHUR [*rising*] We will even let him take your way if he wishes, Aloysia.

LADY CHAVENDER [*rising*] You may leave me out of the question, Miss Brollikins. It is not my business, but my son's. I am neither his enemy nor yours.

ALOYSIA [*perplexed*] But do you think I ought to

marry him?

LADY CHAVENDER. Nobody ought to marry anybody, Aloysia. But they do.

ALOYSIA. Well, thank you for calling me Aloysia, anyhow. It's about all the satisfaction I have got here.

She is about to go when David breaks in obstreperously through the masked door, and strides between the table and the window to Aloysia's left.

DAVID. Look here, Aloysia. What are you up to here? If you think you can get round me by getting round my parents, youre very much mistaken. My parents dont care a damn what I do as long as I take myself off their hands. And I wont be interfered with. Do you hear? I wont be interfered with.

ALOYSIA. Your parents are too good for you, you uncivilized lout. Youve put me right off it by talking that way in front of your mother. If I was your mother I'd smack some manners into you.

DAVID [*appalled and imploring*] Aloysia! [*He tries to take her in his arms*].

ALOYSIA. Take your dirty hands off me [*she flings him off*]. It's off, I tell you, off. Goodbye all. [*She storms out through the main door*].

DAVID [*in loud lament to his mother*] Youve ruined my whole life. [*He goes in pursuit, crying*] Aloysia, Aloysia, wait a moment. [*With anguished intensity*] Aloysia. [*His cries recede in the distance*].

LADY CHAVENDER ⎱ *simultane-* ⎰ He might do worse.
SIR ARTHUR   ⎰   *ously*   ⎱ He might do worse.

LADY CHAVENDER. I beg your pardon. What did you say?

SIR ARTHUR. I said he might do worse.

LADY CHAVENDER. That is what I said. David is overbred: he is so fine-drawn that he is good for nothing; and he is not strong enough physically. Our breed needs to be crossed with the gutter or the soil once in every three or four generations. Uncle Theodore married his cook on principle; and his wife was my favorite aunt. Brollikins may give me goose flesh occasionally; but she wont bore me as a lady daughter-in-law would. I shall be always wondering what she will say or do next. If she were a lady I'd always know. I am so tired of well-bred people, and party politics, and the London season, and all the rest of it.

SIR ARTHUR. I sometimes think you are the only really revolutionary revolutionist I have ever met.

LADY CHAVENDER. Oh, lots of us are like that. We were born into good society; and we are through with it: we have no illusions about it, even if we are fit for nothing better. I dont mind Brollikins one bit.

SIR ARTHUR. What about Barking?

LADY CHAVENDER. I—

Barking enters through the masked door, jubilant. He comes between the pair as they rise, and claps them both on the shoulders right and left simultaneously. They flinch violently, and stare at him in outraged amazement.

BARKING. Good news, old dears! It's all right about Flavia. We may put up the banns. Hooray! [*He rubs hands gleefully*].

SIR ARTHUR. May I ask how you have got over her craze for marrying a poor man?

BARKING. Oh, that was a girlish illusion. You see, she had a glimpse today, at the unemployed meeting, of what poor men are really like. They were awfully nice to her. That did the trick. You see, what she craved for before was their rough manners, their violence, their brutality and filthy language, their savage treatment of their women folk. That was her ideal of a delightful husband. She found today that the working man doesnt realize it. I do. I am a real he-man. I called her the foulest names until she gave in. She's a dear. We shall be perfectly happy. Good old mother-in-law. [*He kisses Lady Chavender, who is too astounded to resist or speak*]. Tootle loo, Chavender. [*He slaps him on the shoulder*]. I am off to buy her a lot of presents. [*He dashes out through the main door*].

SIR ARTHUR. So thats that.

LADY CHAVENDER. The brute! How dare he kiss me? [*She rubs the place with her handkerchief*].

SIR ARTHUR. Do you realize that we two are free at last? Free, dearest: think of that! No more children. Free to give up living in a big house and to spend the remainder of our lives as we please. A cottage near a good golf links seems to be indicated. What would you like?

LADY CHAVENDER. But your political career? Are you really going to give up that?

SIR ARTHUR. It has given me up, dearest. Arnt you glad?

LADY CHAVENDER. Arthur: I cant bear this.

SIR ARTHUR. Cant bear what?

LADY CHAVENDER. To see you discouraged. You have never been discouraged before: you have always been so buoyant. If this new departure is to do nothing for you but take away your courage and high spirits and self-confidence, then in Heaven's name go back to your old way of life. I will put up with anything rather than see you unhappy. That sort of unhappiness kills; and if you die I'll die too. [*She throws herself into a chair and hides her face on the table*].

SIR ARTHUR. Dont fuss, dearest: I'm not unhappy. I am enjoying the enormous freedom of having found myself out and got myself off my mind. That looks like despair; but it is really the beginning of hope, and the end of hypocrisy. Do you think I didnt know, in the days of my great speeches and my roaring popularity, that I was only whitewashing the slums? I did it very well—I dont care who hears me say so—and there is always a sort of artistic satisfaction in doing a thing very well, whether it's getting a big Bill through the House, or carrying a big meeting off its feet, or winning a golf championship. It was all very jolly; and I'm still a little proud of it. But even if I had not had you here to remind me that it was all hot air, I couldnt help knowing as well as any of those damned Socialists that though the West End of London was chockful of money and nice people all calling one another by their Christian names, the lives of the millions of people whose labor was keeping the whole show going were not worth living. I knew it quite well; but I was able to put it out of my mind because I thought it couldnt be helped and I was doing the best that could be done. I know better now: I know that it can be helped, and how it can be helped. And rather than go back to the old whitewashing job, I'd seize you tight round the waist and make a hole in the river with you.

LADY CHAVENDER [*rising*] Then why, dearest love, dont you—

SIR ARTHUR. Why dont I lead the revolt against it all? Because I'm not the man for the job, darling; and nobody knows that better than you. And I shall hate the man who will carry it through for his cruelty and the desolation he will bring on us and our like.

Shouting, as of an excited mob suddenly surging into the street; and a sound of breaking glass and police whistling.

LADY CHAVENDER. What on earth is that?

Hilda comes from her office and runs to the window.

LADY CHAVENDER [*joining her*] What is going on, Hilda?

HILDA. The unemployed have broken into Downing Street; and theyre breaking the windows of the Colonial Office. They think this side is only private houses.

SIR ARTHUR [*going to see*] Yes: they always break the wrong windows, poor devils!

HILDA. Oh! here come the mounted police.

SIR ARTHUR. Theyve splendid horses, those fellows.

HILDA. The people are all running away. And they cant get out: theyre in a cul-de-sac. Oh, why dont they make a stand, the cowards?

LADY CHAVENDER. Indeed I hope they wont. What are you thinking of, Hilda?

SIR ARTHUR. Men are like that, Hilda. They always run away when they have no discipline and no leader.

HILDA. Well, but cant the police let them run away without breaking their heads? Oh look: that policeman has just clubbed a quite old man.

SIR ARTHUR. Come away: it's not a nice sight. [*He draws her away, placing himself between her and the window*].

HILDA. It's all right when you only read about it in the papers; but when you actually see it you want to throw stones at the police.

Defiant singing through the tumult.

LADY CHAVENDER [*looking out*] Someone has opened the side gate and let them through into the Horse Guards Parade. They are trying to sing.

SIR ARTHUR. What are they singing? The Red Flag?

LADY CHAVENDER. No. I dont know the tune. I caught the first two words, "England, arise."

HILDA [*suddenly hysterical*] Oh, my God! I will go out and join them [*she rushes out through the main door*].

LADY CHAVENDER. Hilda! Hilda!

SIR ARTHUR. Never mind, dear: the police all know her: she'll come to no harm. She'll be back for tea. But what she felt just now other girls and boys may feel tomorrow. And just suppose—!

LADY CHAVENDER. What?

SIR ARTHUR. Suppose England really did arise!

Unemployed England, however, can do nothing but continue to sing, as best it can to a percussion accompaniment of baton thwacks, Edward Carpenter's verses